The Complete Herbalist

Also available

- Ayurvedic Materia Medica For Domestic Use (**In 2 Volumes**)
  Thomas J. Graham
- Ayurvedic System of Medicine (The) (**In 2 Volumes**)
  Kaviraj Nagendra Nath Sengupta
- Complete Herbal and English Physician Enlarged (The)
  Nicholas Culpeper
- Family Herbal : Comprising a Description, and The Medical Virtues/ **Matthew Robinson**
- Herbal Simples Approved for Modern Uses of Cure (**In 2 Volumes**)/ **W.T. Fernie**

The Complete Herbalist

Volume One

Prof. O. Phelps Brown

LOGOS PRESS
New Delhi-110 002

ISBN-13: 978-81-7268-190-6 (Set)
ISBN-10: 81-7268-190-9 (Set)

ISBN-13: 978-81-7268-191-3 (Vol. I)
ISBN-13: 978-81-7268-192-0 (Vol. II)
ISBN-10: 81-7268-191-7 (Vol. I)
ISBN-10: 81-7268-192-5 (Vol. II)

2009

Printed and Published by

LOGOS PRESS

Building No. 4788-90, Street No. 23, Ansari Road,
Darya Ganj, **New Delhi**-110 002 (India)

Phone : 23272187

Email : mail@logospressindia.com
Website : www.logospressindia.com

CONTENTS

Volume One

- A Brief History of Medicine 3-8
- The Herbal World 8-22
- Epitome of Botany 23
  - Anatomy of a Plant 23
    - The Root 23-24
    - The Stem 24
    - The Leaf 24-25
    - The Flower 25-26
    - The Fruit 26-27
    - The Seed 27
- Medicinal Properties and Preparations 27-30
- Weights and Measures 30-31

PART–I

Herbal Materia Medica

- Acacia Vera 32
- Adder's Tongue (*Erythronum Americanum*) 33
- Agrimony (*Agrimonia Eupatoria*) 33-34
- Alder (*Prinos Verticillatus*) 34
- Ale Hoof (*Nepeta Glechoma*) 34-35
- All-Heal (*Prunella Vulgaris*) 35
- Almonds (*Amygdalus Communis*) 35-36
- Alnus Rubra (*Tag Alder*) 36
- Amaranth (*Amaranthus Hypochondriasis*) 37
- Anemone (*Anemone Nemorosa*) 37
- Angelica (*Angelica Atropurpurea*) 38
- Anise (*Pimpinella Anisum*) 38
- Aloes (*Aloe Spicata*) 38-39
- Asarabacca (*Asarum Europæum*) 39
- Aya-Pana (*Aya-Pana Eupatorium*) 39-41

- Balm (*Melissa Officinalis*) 41
- Balmony (*Chelone Glabra*) 41-42
- Barberry (*Berberis Vulgaris*) 42
- Bayberry (*Myrica Cerifera*) 42-43
- Bearberry (*Arctostaphylos Uva-Ursi*) 43-44
- Bears Bed (*Polytrichicum Juniperum*) 44-45
- Bead Tree (*Melia Azedarach*) 45
- Belladonna (*Atropa Belladonna*) 45-46
- Beth-Root (*Trillium Pendulum*) 46-47
- Birds' Nest (*Monotropa Uniflora*) 47
- Bitter Root (*Apocynum Androsæmifolium*) 47-48
- Bitter-Sweet (*Amara Dulcis, Solanum Dulcamara*) 48-49
- Blue Flag (*Iris Versicolor*) 49
- Blue Vervain (*Verbena Hastata*) 49-51
- Black Cohosh (*Cimicifuga Racemosa*) 51-52
- Blazing Star (*Liatris Squarrosa*) 52
- Boneset (*Eupatorium Perfoliatum*) 52-53
- Black Root (*Leptandria Virginica*) 53-54
- Bloodroot (*Sanguinaria Canadensis*) 54-55
- Box (*Buxus Sempervirens*) 55-56
- Buchu (*Barosma Crenata*) 56-57
- Burning Bush (*Euonymus Atropurpureus*) 57
- Butter Weed (*Erigeron Canadense*) 57-58
- Cahinca (*Chiococca Racemosa*) 58
- Calico Bush (*Kalmia Latifolia*) 58-59
- Cancer Root (*Orobanche Virginiana*) 59
- Cannabis Indica 59-60
- Cassia Marilandica 60-61
- Catechu (*Acacia Catechu*) 61
- Cedron (*Simaba Cedron*) 61-62
- Celandine (*Chelidonium Majus*) 62-63
- Centaury (*Sabbatia Angularis*) 63-64
- Century Plant (*Agave Americana*) 64
- Chamomile (*Anthemis Nobilis*) 64-65
- Cherry Laurel (*Prunus Laurocerasus*) 65
- Chickweed (*Stellaria Media*) 66
- Chocolate Root, Geum Rivale (*Water Avens*), Geum Virgini Anum (*White Avens*) 66-67

- Cinchona 67-68
- Cinque-Foil (*Potentilla Canadensis*) 68-69
- Cleavers (*Galium Aparine*) 69-70
- Coca (*Erythroxylon Coca*) 70-71
- Colocynth (*Cucumis Colocynthis*) 71-72
- Colt's Foot (*Tussilago Farfara*) 72
- Columbo (*Cocculus Palmatus*) 72-73
- Comfrey (*Symphytum Officinale*) 73-74
- Cundurango (*Equatoria Garciana*) 74-75
- Copaiba (*Copaifera Officinalis*) 75-76
- Cranberry (High)—(*Viburnum Opulus*) 76-77
- Cranesbill (*Geranium Maculatum*) 77-78
- Crawley (*Corallorhiza Odontorhiza*) 78-79
- Crowfoot (*Ranunculus Bulbosus*) 79
- Cubebs (*Piper Cubeba*) 79-80
- Daisy (*Leucanthemum Vulgare*) 80
- Dandelion (*Leontodon Taraxacum*) 80-81
- Devil's Bit (*Helonias Diocia*) 81
- Dock (*Rumex Crispus*) 81-82
- Dogwood (*Cornus Florida*) 82-83
- Dragon Root (*Arum Triphyllum*) 83-84
- Elder (*Sambucus Canadensis*) 84-85
- Elecampane (*Inula Helenium*) 85
- Ergot (*Secale Cornutum*) 85-86
- Eryngo (*Eryngium Aquaticum*) 86
- Eye-Bright (*Euphrasia Officinalis*) 86-87
- Ferns (*Filices*) 87
- Female Fern (*Polypodium Vulgare*) 87-88
- Male Fern (*Aspidium Filix Mas*) 88-89
- Feverfew (*Pyrethrum Parthenium*) 89
- Figwort (*Scrophularia Nodosa*) 89-90
- Fireweed (*Erecthites Hieractifolius*) 90
- Frost-Weed (*Helianthemum Canadense*) 90-91
- Fumitory (*Fumaria Officinalis*) 91-92
- Gambir Plant (*Uncaria Gambir*) 92
- Gelsemin (*Gelseminum Sempervirens*) 93
- Gentian (*Gentiana Lutea*) 93-95
- Gillenia (*Gillenia Trifoliata*) 95

- ❖ Gossypium Herbaceum 95-96
- ❖ Globe Flower (*Cephalanthus Occidentalis*) 96
- ❖ Golden Seal (*Hydrastis Canadensis*) 96-97
- ❖ Gold Thread (*Coptis Trifolia*) 97-98
- ❖ Guaiac (*Guaiacum Officinale*) 98-99
- ❖ Hazel (Witch) (*Hamamelis Virginica*) 99
- ❖ Hellebore (American) (*Veratrum Viride*) 100-101
- ❖ Henbane (*Hyoscyamus Niger*) 101-102
- ❖ Hoarhound (*Marrubium Vulgare*) 102-103
- ❖ Hound's Tongue (*Cynoglossum Officinale*) 103-104
- ❖ Hops (*Humulus Lupulus*) 104-105
- ❖ House-Leek (*Sempervivum Tectorum*) 105
- ❖ Hyssop (*Hyssopus Officinalis*) 105
- ❖ Iberis Amara 106
- ❖ Iceland Moss (*Cetraria Islandica*) 106
- ❖ Iron Weed (*Vernonia Fasciculata*) 106-107
- ❖ Ivy (American) (*Ampelopsis Quinquefolia*) 107
- ❖ Jalap (*Ipomœa Jalapa*) 107-108
- ❖ Jamestown Weed (*Datura Stramonium*) 108-109
- ❖ Juniper (*Juniperus Communis*) 109
- ❖ Kino (*Pterocarpus Marsupium*) 109-10
- ❖ Kidney Liver-Leaf (*Hepatica Americana*) 110
- ❖ Kousso (*Brayera Anthelmintica*) 110-11
- ❖ Ladies' Slipper (*Cypripedium Pubescens*) 111-12
- ❖ Larch (*Abies Larix*) 112
- ❖ Large Flowering Spurge (*Euphorbia Corollata*) 112-13
- ❖ Larkspur (*Delphinum Consolida*) 113
- ❖ Lavender (*Lavandula Vera and Lavandula Spica*) 114
- ❖ Lever-Wood (*Astrya Virginica*) 114
- ❖ Life-Root (*Senecio Aureus*) 114-15
- ❖ Lily (Meadow) (*Lilium Candidum*) 115
- ❖ Lion's Foot (*Nabulus Albus*) 115-16
- ❖ Lobelia (*Lobelia Inflata*) 116-17
- ❖ Lousewort (*Gerardia Pedicularia*) 117
- ❖ Lungwort (*Pulmonaria Officinalis*) 117
- ❖ Madder (*Rubia Tinctorum*) 118
- ❖ Mad-Dog Weed (*Alisma Plantago*) 118
- ❖ Maidenhair (*Adiantum Pedatum*) 118-19

- Magnolia (*Magnolia Glauca*) 119
- Mallow (Common) (*Malva Sylvestris*) 119-20
- Mandrake (*Podophyllum Peltatum*) 120-21
- Matico (*Piper Angustifolium*) 122
- Mechameck (*Convolvulus Panduratus*) 122-23
- Meadow Saffron (*Colchicum Autumnale*) 123
- Monkshood (*Aconitum Napellus*) 123-24
- Moss (Corsican), (*Fucus Helminthicorton*) 124
- Motherwort (*Leonurus Cardiaca*) 124-25
- Mullein (*Verbascum Thapsus*) 125
- Myrrh (*Balsamodendron Myrrha*) 125-26
- Narrow Leaf Virginia Thyme (*Pycanthemum Virginicum*) 126
- Nettle (*Urtica Dioca*) 126-27
- Net Leaf Plantain (*Goodyera Pubescens*) 127-28
- Nightshade (Garden) (*Solanum Nigrum*) 128
- Norway Pine (*Abies Excelsa*) 128
- Nux Vomica (*Strychnos Nux Vomica*) 128-29
- Oak—White, Red and Black (*Quercus Alba, Rubra and Tinctoria*) 129-30
- Old Man's Beard (*Chionanthus Virginïca*) 130
- Old Field Balsam (*Gnaphalium Polycephalum*) 130-31
- Opium (*Papaver Somniferum*) 131
- Papoose Root (*Caulophyllum Thalictroides*) 132
- Pareira Brava (*Cissampelos Pareira*) 132
- Parsley (*Petroselinum Sativum*) 132-33
- Partridge Berry (*Mitchella Repens*) 133-34
- Pennyroyal (*Hedeoma Pulegioides*) 134
- Peony (*Pœonia Officinalis*) 134-135
- Peruvian Balsam (*Myrospermum Peruiferum*) 135
- Pinkroot (*Spigelia Marilandica*) 135-36
- Pipsissewa (*Chimaphila Umbellata*) 136
- Pleurisy Root (*Asclepias Tuberosa*) 136-37
- Poke (*Phytolacca Decandra*) 137-38
- Pomegranate (*Punica Granatum*) 138
- Prickly Ash (*Xanthoxylum Fraxineum*) 138-39
- Privet (*Ligustrum Vulgare*) 139-40
- Quassia (*Picrœnia Excelsa*) 140
- Queen of the Meadow (*Eupatorium Purpureum*) 140-41

- ❖ Ragged Cup (*Silphium Perfoliatum*) 141
- ❖ Rattle Bush (*Baptisia Tinctoria*) 141-42
- ❖ Red Raspberry (*Rubus Strigosus*) 142-43
- ❖ Red Root (*Ceanothus Americanus*) 143
- ❖ Rhatany (*Krameria Triandria*) 143-44
- ❖ Rheumatism Root (*Jeffersonia Diphylla*) 144
- ❖ Rhubarb (*Rheum Palmatum*) 144-45
- ❖ Rosemary (*Rosmarinus Officinalis*) 145
- ❖ Pyrola (Round-Leaved) (*Pyrola Rotundifolia*) 146
- ❖ Saffron (Dyers) (*Carthamus Tinctorius*) 146-47
- ❖ Sage (*Salvia Officinalis*) 147
- ❖ St. Ignatius' Bean (*Ignatius Amara*) 147-48
- ❖ St. John's Wort (*Hypericum Perforatum*) 148
- ❖ Sanicle (*Sanicula Marilandica*) 148-49
- ❖ Sarsaparilla (*Smilax Officinalis*) 149
- ❖ Sassafras (*Laurus Sassafras*) 150
- ❖ Savory (Summer) (*Satureja Hortensis*) 150
- ❖ Scull-Cap (*Scutellaria Lateriflora*) 150-51
- ❖ Seneka (*Polygala Senega*) 151
- ❖ Skunk Cabbage (*Symplocarpus Fœtidus*) 152
- ❖ Soap-Wort (*Saponaria Officinalis*) 152-53
- ❖ Solomon's Seal (*Convallaria Multiflora*) 153
- ❖ Sorrel (Wood) (*Oxalis Acetosella*) 153-54
- ❖ Squirting Cucumber (*Momordica Elaterium*) 154
- ❖ Star-Grass (*Aletris Farinosa*) 155
- ❖ Stillingia (*Stillingia Sylvatica*) 155-56
- ❖ Stoneroot (*Collinsonia Canadensis*) 156
- ❖ Sumach (*Rhus Glabrum*) 156-57
- ❖ Swamp Beggars' Tick (*Bidens Connata*) 157-58
- ❖ Sweet Gum (*Liquidambar Styraciflua*) 158
- ❖ Tacamahac (*Populus Balsamifera*) 158-59
- ❖ Tansy (*Tanacetum Vulgare*) 159
- ❖ Thyme (*Thymus Vulgaris*) 159-60
- ❖ Tolu (*Myrospermum Toluiferum*) 160
- ❖ Turkey Corn (*Corydalis Formosa*) 160-61
- ❖ Valerian (*Valeriana Officinalis*) 161
- ❖ Vanilla (*Vanilla Aromatica*) 161-62
- ❖ Wafer-Ash (*Ptelea Trifoliata*) 162

❖ Walnut (White), (*Juglans Cinerea*) 162-63
❖ Water Pepper (*Polygonum Punctatum*) 163-64
❖ Wormseed (*Chenopodium Anthelminticum*) 164
❖ Wormwood (*Artemisia Absinthium*) 164-65
❖ Yam (Wild), (*Dioscorea Villosa*) 165-66
❖ Yarrow (*Achillea Millefolium*) 166
❖ Yellow Parilla (*Menispermum Canadense*) 167
❖ Yellow Root (*Xanthorrhiza Aphfolia*) 168

Plants

❖ Their Collection and Preservation 169-70

Essays on Hygiene, etc.

❖ Food and Drinks 171-81
❖ Clothing 181-84
❖ Sleep 184-86
❖ Bathing 186
❖ Exercise—Physical and Mental Development 186-90
❖ Air and Sunshine 190-93
❖ Old Age, or Longevity 193-96
❖ Life, Health, and Disease 197-99
❖ Regulating the Passions 199-201
❖ Things for the Sick-Room 201-07

How to Assist the Doctor

❖ The Sick-Room 207-09
❖ Nurses and Nursing 209-13

Volume Two

PART–II

- ❖ Diseases 214-15
- ❖ Miasmatic Fevers 215-16
- ❖ Intermittent Fever 216-17
- ❖ Remittent Fever 217-19
- ❖ Yellow-Fever 219-20
- ❖ Typhus Fever 220-22
- ❖ Eruptive or Exanthematous Fevers 222
- ❖ Typhoid Fever 222-23
- ❖ Diphtheria 223-24
- ❖ Small-Pox (*Variola*) 224-25
- ❖ Chicken Pox (*Varicella*) 225
- ❖ Measles (*Rubeola*) 225-26
- ❖ Scarlet Fever (*Scarlatina*) 226
- ❖ Nettle Rash 227
- ❖ Erysipelas 227-28
- ❖ Rose Rash (*Roseola*) 228
- ❖ Erythema 228
- ❖ Glanders 228-29
- ❖ Dandy Fever (*Dengue*) 229
- ❖ Purpura 229-30
- ❖ Anatomy of the Organs of Digestion 230-33
- ❖ Diseases of the Digestive Organs 233
  - ✱ Stomatitis 233
  - ✱ Glossitis 233-34
  - ✱ Quinsy (*Tonsillitis*) 234
  - ✱ Pharyngitis 234-35
  - ✱ Parotitis (*Mumps*) 235
  - ✱ Œsophagitis 235-36
  - ✱ Inflammation of the Stomach (*Gastritis*) 236
  - ✱ Cancer of the Stomach 236-37
  - ✱ Heart-Burn (*Gastralgia*) 237
  - ✱ Gastralgia, or Gastrodynia 237

* ✳ Spasm of the Stomach 237-38
* ✳ Water-Brash (*Pyrosis*) 238
* ✳ Dyspepsia, or Indigestion 238-40

❖ Anotomy of the Liver 240-41

❖ Diseases of the Liver 241
* ✳ Hepatitis 241
* ✳ Chronic Hepatitis 241-42
* ✳ Cirrhosis 242-43
* ✳ Gall-Stones 243
* ✳ Jaundice (*Icterus*) 244

❖ Anatomy of the Spleen 245
* ✳ Splenitis 245-46

❖ Diseases of the Pancreas 246

❖ Diseases of the Bowels 247

❖ Dysentery (*Colitis*) 247-48

❖ Diarrhœa 248

❖ Constipation 249-50

❖ Intestinal Worms 250-53

❖ Peritonitis 253

❖ Summer Complaint (*Cholera Infantum*) 253-54

❖ Cholera Morbus 254

❖ Asiatic Cholera 254-55

❖ Prolapsus of the Rectum 255-56

❖ Anal Fistula 256

❖ Piles (*Hemorrhoids*) 256-57

❖ Diseases of the Absorbent System 257
* ✳ Scrofula 257-59
* ✳ Tabes Mesenterica 259

❖ Anatomy of the Respiratory Organs
* ✳ Larynx 259-60
* ✳ Trachea 260
* ✳ The Lungs 260-61

❖ Diseases of the Respiratory and Circulatory System
* ✳ Coryza 261-62
* ✳ Ozœna 262
* ✳ Catarrh 262-65
* ✳ Laryngitis 265-66
* ✳ Bronchitis 266-67

- ✳ Croup 267
- ✳ Pneumonia 267-68
- ✳ Asthma 268-69
- ✳ Pleurisy 269-70
- ✳ Apnœa, or Asphyxia 270
  - ◆ Asphyxia by Extreme Cold 270-71
  - ◆ Asphyxia by Inhalation of Gases 271
  - ◆ Asphyxia by Submersion, Drowning 271-72
  - ◆ Consumption (Phthisis) 272-76

❖ Anatomy of the Heart 276-79

❖ Diseases of the Heart and Circulatory System 279

- ✳ Palpitation 279-80
- ✳ Angina Pectoris 280
- ✳ Pericarditis 280-81
- ✳ Endocarditis 281
- ✳ Chronic Valvular Disease of the Heart 281-82
- ✳ Atrophy of the Heart 282-83
- ✳ Hypertrophy and Dilatation of the Heart 283
- ✳ Cyanosis, or Blue Disease 283-84
- ✳ Diseases of the Blood-Vessels
  - ◆ Arteritis 284
  - ◆ Aneurism 284-85
  - ◆ Phlebitis and Varicose Veins 285-86
  - ◆ Milk Leg (*Phlegmasia Dolens*) 286-87
  - ◆ Diseases of the Blood 287
    - Scurvy (*Scorbutus*) 287-88
- ✳ Hemorrhages 288
  - ◆ Bleeding from the Nose (*Epistaxis*) 288-89
  - ◆ Hæmoptysis 289
  - ◆ Hæmatemesis 289-90
  - ◆ Hæmaturia 290
  - ◆ Dropsies 290-91
- ✳ Bright's Disease of the Kidney 291-92
  - ◆ Ascites 292-93
  - ◆ Hydrothorax 293
  - ◆ Dropsy of the Heart 293
  - ◆ Dropsy of the Ovaries 293-94
  - ◆ Dropsy of the Scrotum (*Hydrocele*) 294

❖ Anatomy of the Urinary Organs 294
  ✻ Kidneys 294-95
  ✻ Bladder 295-96
❖ Diseases of the Urinary Organs
  ✻ Nephritis 296
  ✻ Diuresis 296
  ✻ Diabetes Mellitus 297
  ✻ Gravel (*Lithiasis*) 297-98
  ✻ Ischuria, or Suppression of Urine 298
  ✻ Incontinence of Urine (*Enuresis*) 298
  ✻ Cystitis 298-99
❖ Anatomy of the Nervous System 299
  ✻ Spinal Marrow 299
  ✻ The Brain 299-300
  ✻ Cranial Nerves 300-01
❖ Diseases of the Nervous System 301
  ✻ Inflammation of the Brain (*Cerebritis*) 301
  ✻ Apoplexy 301-02
  ✻ Congestion of the Brain 303
  ✻ Sunstroke 303
  ✻ Insanity 303-05
  ✻ Delirium Tremens 305-06
  ✻ Headache (*Cephalalgia*) 306-07
  ✻ Hypochondria 307-08
  ✻ Neuralgia 308-09
  ✻ Bilious Colic 309
  ✻ Hiccough 309
  ✻ Whooping Cough (*Pertussis*) 310
  ✻ Spasm of the Glottis 310
  ✻ Epilepsy 310-13
  ✻ Hysterics 313-14
  ✻ Catalepsy 314
  ✻ St. Vitus's Dance (*Chorea*) 314-15
  ✻ Locked-Jaw (*Tetanus*) 315
  ✻ Paralysis (*Palsy*) 315-16
  ✻ Hydrophobia 316-17
❖ Diseases of the Skin 317
  ✻ Humid Tetter (*Eczema*) 317-18
  ✻ Tetter, Shingles (*Herpes*) 318

* ✱ Itch (*Scabies*) 318-19
* ✱ Watery Blebs (*Pemphigus*) 319-20
* ✱ Rupia 320
* ✱ Crusted Terrer (*Impetigo*) 320
* ✱ Papulous Scale (*Ecthyma*) 320-21
* ✱ Leprosy 321
* ✱ Dry Tetter (*Psoriasis*) 321-22
* ✱ Pityriasis 322
* ✱ Lupus 322
* ✱ Elephantiasis 322-23
* ✱ Acne 323
* ✱ Warts and Corns 323-24
* ✱ Pruritis 324
* ✱ Maculæ, or Spots 324
* ✱ Scalled Head (*Tinea Favosa*) 324-25
* ✱ Tinea Sycosis 325
* ✱ Baldness (*Alopecia*) 325-26
* ✱ Entozoa 326-27
* ✱ Trichiniasis 327

❖ The Proper Care of Children 328-30
* ✱ Teething 330

❖ General Diseases 330
* ✱ Gout 330-31
* ✱ Rheumatism 331-32
* ✱ Hip Disease (*Morbus Coxarius*) 332
* ✱ White Swelling (*Hydrarthrus*) 332-33
* ✱ Hectic Fever 333-34
* ✱ Curvature of the Spine 334
* ✱ Imperfections of the Human Form 335-36
* ✱ Abscess 336-37
* ✱ Felon (*Paronychia*) 337
* ✱ Ulcers 337-38
* ✱ Boils (*Furunculus*) 338
* ✱ Carbuncle (*Anthrax*) 339
* ✱ Chilblain's (*Pernio*) 339
* ✱ Burns and Scalds 339-40
* ✱ Goitre (*Bronchocele*) 340
* ✱ Rupture (*Hernia*) 340-42

❖ Diseases of the Eye and Ear 342
* Conjunctivitis 342-43
* Catarrhal Ophthalmia 343
* Purulent Ophthalmia 343
* Scrofulous Ophthalmia 344
* Stye (*Hordeolum*) 344
* Amaurosis 344
* Foreign Bodies in the Eyes 344-45
* Foreign Substances in the Ear 345
* Ear Ache (*Otalgia*) 345
❖ Malignant and Venereal Diseases
* Cancer (*Carcinoma*) 345-46
* Syphilis 347-48
* Gonorrhœa 348-49
* Gleet 349
* Debility or Loss of Vitality 350-53
* Satyriasis 353
* Stricture of the Urethra 353-54
* Prostatitis 354
* Orchitis 354-55
* Varicocele 355
* Diseases of the Female Sexual Organs 355-56
* Vulvitis 356
* Clitoritis 356
* Imperforate Hymen 357
* Vaginitis 357
* Menstruation 357-59
* Amenorrhœa 359
* Dysmenorrhœa 359-60
* Menorrhagia 360
* Vicarious Menstruation 360
* Chlorosis 360-61
* Cessation of the Menses 361
* Leucorrhœa 361-62
* Ulceration of the Womb 362
* Falling of the Womb (*Prolapsus Uteri*) 362-63
* Uterine Dropsy (*Hydrometra*) 363
* Anteversion and Retroversion 363
* Hydatids 363-64

❖ Pregnancy and Its Accidents 364
* Pregnancy 364-67
* Puerperal Fever 367-68
* Inversion of the Uterus 368
* Miscarriage 368-69
* Inflammation and Abscess of the Breasts 369
* Sore Nipples 369
* Relaxation of the Abdominal Muscles 370
* The Conduct of A Case of Labor 371
* How Do You Know That The Patient is in Labor? 371
* What Will You Do Next? 371-72
* What Next? 372-73
* Your Work is not Done Yet 373
* Lochia 374

❖ The Treatment in Accidents 374
* Wounds 374-75
* Fractures 375
* Head 376
* Collar Bone 376
* Broken Ribs 376
* Fracture of the Humerus 376
* Fracture of the Bones of the Forearm 377
* Fracture of the Bones in the Hand, Foot, or Ankle 377
* Fracture at the Hip-Joint 377
* Fracture of the Thigh-Bone 377-78
* Fracture of the Cap of the Knee or Patella 378
* Fracture of the Leg 378

❖ Dislocations 378
* Broken Neck, or Back 378-79
* Dislocation of the Jaw 379
* Dislocation at the Shoulder 379
* Dislocations at the Elbow 379-80
* Dislocations at the Wrist 380
* Dislocation of the Bones of the Hand 380
* Dislocation of the Ribs 380
* Dislocation at the Hip 381
* Dislocation of the Knee-Cap 381
* Dislocation at the Ankle 381

- ❖ Prevention of Epidemic Diseases 382-84
- ❖ Auscultation 385-87
- ❖ Urinary Deposits 387-88
- ❖ Analysis of Healthy Urine 389

TREATMENT OF CHRONIC DISEASES

The Author's Speciality

- ❖ Important to the Suffering Sick, Male or Female 390-95
- ❖ Questions for Reference 395-98

PART–III

- ❖ The Philosophy of the Sexes 399
  - ✳ Anatomy of the Male Generative Organs 399-400
  - ✳ Anatomy of the Female Generative Organs 400
  - ✳ Social Status of the Procreative Organs....................... 400-02
  - ✳ Preservation of the Health of those Organs 402-04
  - ✳ Marriage 404-06
  - ✳ Polygamy 406-08
  - ✳ Monogamy.. 409-10
  - ✳ Marriage Customs 410
  - ✳ The Basis of a Happy Marriage 410-16
  - ✳ Married Life 416-33
  - ✳ Advice to the Childless 433-38
  - ✳ Sterility and Special Weakness of the Male 439-41
  - ✳ The Philosophy of Generation.................................... 441-46
  - ✳ Divorce 446-49
- ❖ Bridal Tours 449-52
- ❖ Poisons and Their Antidotes 452-53
  - ✳ Arsenic 453
  - ✳ Acids 453
  - ✳ Antimony 453-54
  - ✳ Bismuth 454
  - ✳ Copper 454
  - ✳ Gold 454
  - ✳ Iodine 454
  - ✳ Iron 454

- ✱ Lead 455
- ✱ Mercury 455
- ✱ Phosphorus 455
- ✱ Silver 455
- ✱ Tin 455-56
- ✱ Zinc 456
- ✱ Volatile Oils 456
- ✱ Alkalies 456
- ✱ Prussic Acid 456

❖ Vegetable Poisons
- ✱ Opium 457
- ✱ Strychnine 457
- ✱ Other Poisonous Plants, or Seeds 457-58
- ✱ Animal Poisons 458-59

RECIPES

- ❖ Golden Tincture 460
- ❖ Pulmonary Remedy 460
- ❖ Liver Cordial 460
- ❖ Anti-Bilious Pill 460
- ❖ An Expectorant 461
- ❖ For Producing Sleep 461
- ❖ For Sick and Nervous Headache 461
- ❖ Tonic Tincture 461
- ❖ Sarsaparilla Syrup 461
- ❖ Rheumatic Tincture 461
- ❖ For Bronchitis 461
- ❖ Compound Spirits of Lavender 461
- ❖ Nerve Tonic 461
- ❖ Stomachic Bitters 461
- ❖ Fever and Ague 462
- ❖ Strengthening Plaster 462
- ❖ Acetic Blood-Root Syrup 462
- ❖ A Good Emetic 462
- ❖ Nerve Tonic and Antispasmodic 462

- Dysentery Syrup 462
- Cough Preparation 462
- Pulmonary Syrup 462
- Chronic Diseases of the Mucous Surfaces 462
- Liniment for Chilblains 463
- Liniment for Neuralgia etc. 463
- Sleeplessness 463
- Chronic Rheumatism 463
- Remedy for Bowel Complaint 463
- Worm Mixture 463
- Painful Menstruation 463
- Stomach Pill 463
- Bronchial Troches (*For Temporary Relief*) 463
- Diarrhœa 464
- Neuralgia 464
- Pile Ointment 464
- Stomachic Pill 464
- Aromatic Bitters (*Stimulant*) 464
- Tonic Tea (*Debility*) 464
- Spiced Bitters (*For weak patients*) 464
- Tonic (*For chlorosis, or Green Sickness*) 464
- Whooping Cough Mixture 464
- Tincture for Fever and Ague, etc. 464
- Anti-Spasmodics 465
- Tonic and Cathartic 465
- Discutient Ointment (*For scrofulous and glandular tumors*) . 465
- For Suppression of Urine in Children 465
- Gargles 465
- Honey Balsam 465
- Anti-Dysentery Cordial 465
- For Gravel, Dropsy, etc. 465
- Cough Syrup 465
- For Dysmenorrhœa 466
- For Diarrhœa 466
- Injection 466
- For the Blues, or Low Spirits 466

❖ Skin Diseases with Much Irritation 466
❖ Chilblain Ointment 466
❖ Acidity of the Stomach 466
❖ Hemorrhoids Piles 466
❖ Sore Throat 466
❖ Injection for Costiveness 466
❖ To Produce Perspiration 466
❖ Poultice for a Fester 466
❖ Cataplasms, or Poultices 466
❖ Toothache 467
❖ A Fragrant Breath 467
❖ Foot Bath 467
❖ To Improve the Voice 467
❖ Headache, Neuralgic Pains 467
❖ Stings 467
❖ A Stomachic 467
❖ For Fevers and Other Acute Diseases 467
❖ Offensive Breath 467
❖ Antidote for Rattlesnake Poison 467
❖ For Cancer 468
❖ For Hip Disease 468
❖ For Bruises 468
❖ For Diphtheria 468
❖ Gargle for the Elongation of the Uvula 468
❖ For Bilious Colic 468
❖ To Remove Warts and Corns 468
❖ For the Teeth 468
❖ A Good Medicated Wine 468
❖ Injection for Asiatic Cholera 468
❖ Bleeding at the Nose 468
❖ For Old Ulcers 468

NATURE'S HERBAL REMEDIES

❖ The Restorative Assimilant 469-70
❖ The Acacian Balsam 470-71
❖ The Blood Purifier 471

❖ The Male Fern Vermifuge 471-72
❖ The Herbal Ointment 472-73
❖ The Renovating Pill 473
❖ The Woodland Balm 473-74
❖ Liver Invigorator 474
❖ Frederick W. Hale's 475
  ✳ Standard Fluid Extracts 475-76
  ✳ Fluid Extracts 476-79

Glossary 480-88
Index 489-504

The
Complete Herbalist

THE COMPLETE HERBALIST.

A BRIEF HISTORY OF MEDICINE.

In presenting this work on Crude Organic Remedies—the Constituents of Plants, and their Officinal Preparations—I do not propose to "run a tilt" against any of the systems of Medical Practice, however much some of them may be opposed to common sense and reason, and to the Divine ordinances of Nature; nor shall I treat with contempt the teachings and practices of great and wonderful names, or oppose the pride, interest, expectation, and conscientious convictions of a learned, honorable, and influential profession; my object is simply to present many new and curious, if not startling facts, not only well worthy of the earnest consideration of the more intelligent portion of the community, who demand reasons the most profound to lead them to conviction of a TRUTH, but of the great mass of humbler people, who desire, amid all the great *Reforms* in human society, above all things to secure a "*sound mind in a sound body*," and to feel something of that exalted state of happiness which alone can arise from the possession of the most robust and rubicund physical and moral HEALTH.

It must be palpable to every thinking mind that Therapeutical and Pharmaceutical science is the very foundation of the "HEALING ART DIVINE." In the language of Holy Writ, "*The Lord has created medicines out of the earth, and he that is wise will not abhor them.*"*

> Yea, happy he that can the knowledge gain,
> To know the Eternal God made naught in vain."

The use of medicine is no doubt coincident with the History of the Human Race; but writers generally agree that medicine first became a profession among the Egyptians. The priests of the earlier nations

* Ecclesiasticus xxxviii, 4.

were the practitioners of the Healing Art, but it does not seem that women were excluded from the right of administering medicine for the purpose of healing the sick, since mention is made of a certain Queen ISIS, who became greatly celebrated among them, and was worshipped as a "GODDESS OF HEALTH." Although the practitioners among the Egyptians, Assyrians, and Jews were in the habit of employing incantations, which, of course, produced their good and bad impressions through the medium of the imagination, yet their efficiency in curing diseases was mainly due to their knowledge of the medicinal virtues of many of the vegetable products of Nature. They seemed to look up as high as the *stars* to know the reason of the operation of the Herbs in the various affections of the human race.

Among the Greeks, HIPPOCRATES first caused medicine to be regarded as a *science*, while ÆSCULAPIUS was the first who made medicine an exclusive study and practice. His sons, MACHAON and PODALIRIUS, are celebrated in Homer's "Iliad" for their medical skill as surgeons in the Greek armies or during the Trojan war. Two daughters also of Æsculapius, PANAKEIA and HYGEIA, were no less distinguished than their renowned brothers; the latter being the inventor of many valuable herbal preparations, whose success in curing diseases won for her, as in the case of Queen Isis of Egypt, the proud honor and deification of the Greeks as an especial "GODDESS OF HEALTH." We have no knowledge that Æsculapius or his immediate followers, the Asclepiadæ, ever conceived the idea of curing disease by drug or mineral preparations. Ablutions, bandages, fomentations, ointments, etc., were administered externally, and preparations of aromatic herbs, roots, flowers, balms, gums, etc., constituted their whole materia medica for all *internal* ailments. Next the Pythagorean school became famous, and these were the first to visit the sick at their homes.

The next most prominent medical practitioner after these was HIPPOCRATES, the "Coan Sage," who, being one of the most sagacious, observing, and industrious men that ever lived, was entitled the "*Father of Medicine.*" He traveled much in foreign countries, devoting himself with untiring energy to the study and practice of medicine. His writings were numerous, and even to this day his doctrines are extensively recognized. His practice was consistently founded on the phenomena of Nature as exhibited in human beings during health and disease. His materia medica was derived almost wholly from the vegetable kingdom. His internal remedies were purgatives, sudorifics, diuretics, and injections, while his external were ointments, plasters, liniments, etc. The great principle which directed all his operations was the supposed operations of Nature in superintending and regulating all the actions of the system. This mode of practice had the good effect of enabling the practitioner to make himself well acquainted with all the phenomena of disease, and thus to diagnosticate correctly, and to meet the varied indications by the administration of some *herbal* remedy, which would induce the crisis requisite to the removal of disease and restoration to sound or vigorous health.

About three hundred years before the Christian era, the Ptolemies founded a medical school in Alexandria, Egypt. The most famous of the professors were ERASISTRATUS and HEROPHILUS, who dissected the bodies of criminals obtained from government. They oppoed bleeding and violent remedies, trusting more to nature than to art. Herophilus paid particular attention to the action of the heart, and was the first to give anything like an accurate description of the various kinds of *pulse*, though Praxagoras of Cos, the last of the Asclepiadæ, had before observed the relation which exists between the pulse and the general condition of the system. From that time to the present the pulse has been, as it were, the guide for determining the character, extent, and probable cause of the disease afflicting the patient, and the description of treatment required to produce a change for the better. I, however, derive great assistance from the temperament, age, sex, etc.

We pass over the days of the Dogmatics and Empirics, the Pneumatics, and other sects of medical practitioners (who, though they employed *herbal* remedies as a general rule, were strangely given to the promulgations of theories and doctrines utterly at variance with the most ordinary ratiocinations of Philosophy and Reason), until we come to the period when GALEN first made his appearance, at the request of the Emperor AURELIUS. Galen was a native of Pergamos, born A.D. 130, having traveled much and written largely on subjects directly or indirectly connected with medicine before settling himself at Rome. He was entirely independent in his opinions, paid very little respect to authority, and so great was his learning and wisdom, and rare skill in medicine, that he came to be regarded by many as an "Oracle." Thoroughly educated in all the schools of philosophy, he selected from them all except the Epicurean, which he totally rejected. His treatment of disease was principally by Herbal remedies. From Galen have sprung the sect that is now generally known as Eclectics, who do not confine remedies exclusively to the herbal practice, but employ many of the mineral substances upon which the Allopathic and Homœopathic systems of medicine of the present day are based.

About the middle of the seventeenth century, on the death of PAULUS, the Greek school of medicine terminated, the Arabians having conquered a large portion of the semi-civilized world, and destroyed an immense Alexandrian library. The Arabian physicians soon adopted the opinions of Galen, but, owing to the invention of chemistry, it was speedily made subservient to medicine. They produced medical works, some of which have enjoyed great celebrity, without having really added anything substantial to medical science as previously understood. With AVERROES terminated the Arabic or Saracenic School of medicine, the great reputation of which is mainly owing to the circumstance, that from the eighth to the twelfth centuries, when all Europe was sunk in deep barbarism, the principal remains of a taste for literature and science existed among the Moors and Arabs. Their physicians added many vegetable products and a few metallic oxides in the catalogue of remedies. From the employment of chemical and mineral remedies by the Arabian physicians may be dated the disastrous consequences of medical science that were subsequently inaugurated by that Prince of Quacks—PARACELSUS.

After the Arabians, from the twelfth to the fifteenth century, the practice of medicine was chiefly confined to the hands of the priests, who, being men of great learning and followers of Æsculapius, Hippocrates, and Galen, became the principal physicians, and a little medicine was taught in the monasteries; for a long time the Benedictine monks of Monte Casino enjoyed in this respect great reputation. The Jews also became celebrated physicians; and though not allowed to administer medicines to Christians, yet obtained access to the courts, and even to the palace of the Roman pontiffs.

The European feudal system was at length greatly shaken by the Crusades. MAHOMET the second, about the middle of the fifteenth century, captured Constantinople, and soon after the ruin of the Byzantine empire the *Reformation* occurred, and about the same time the art of printing was invented. These events gave a powerful impulse to the world of mind, and reawakened investigation into all the departments of science, literature, and the arts; but, although many works were written, very few facts were gleaned concerning the physiological, anatomical, and pathological phenomena incident to the Structure, Health, and Disease of the human being.

The alchemic art, however, was at length transferred from Arabia into European countries, and medical chairs were established in various Universities on the continent during the thirteenth century, and finally LINACRE, who had been educated at Oxford, and having traveled in Italy, and spent some time at the court of Florence, returned to England, and succeeded in founding medical professorships at Oxford and Cambridge, from which circumstance was laid the foundation of the London College of Physicians. Thus chemistry, after having been employed in various pharmaceutical processes, was applied to physiology, pathology, and therapeutics. The chemical doctors were very wild and extravagant in advancing unnatural theories; but they had an ever-present champion in the name of Galen, who was well entitled to be called the "Prince of Medical Philosophers." He *was* a philosopher—a *natural* philosopher; for he studied Nature closely, deeply, profoundly, and de-duced his indications of cure from an accurate observation of her laws His system, however, was destined to be utterly overthrown by an adventurous vagrant, whose quackery never had its equal on earth. This impudent and unprincipled charlatan was none other than Paracelsus, to whom the medical world is more indebted for the *mineral* drugging system than to all other physicians who have ever lived. He introduced the *mercurial* and *antimonial* practice, which still constitutes the great strength of the popular materia medica of the day, and which also continues to exhibit its terribly devastating power on all human constitutions that come under its sway or influence. In the fulness of his pride, pomp, and arrogance, Paracelsus burned, with great solemnity, the works of Galen and Avicenna, declaring that he had found the philosopher's stone, and that mankind had no further use for the medical works of others. He lived a disappointed vagabond, and died prematurely at the age of forty-eight, his famous *elixir vitæ* having failed to save him from a most horrible fate. Still his abominable doctrines prevailed, and his infatuated followers have added several hundred other chemical or mineral preparations to the materia medica of the great Quicksilver Quack. At the present day, among a certain class of physicians, there is hardly a disease in the catalogue of human ailments in which the employment of mercury, antimony, arsenic, and other deadly drugs is not employed.

During the seventeenth century the doctrines of Hippocrates again rose to some consideration in medical philosophy. Anatomy made progress. HARVEY discovered the circulation of the blood; others traced out the absorbent system, and explained the functions and structure of the lungs; while BOYLE disengaged chemistry from the mystery by which it was surrounded, and explained its *true province* to be, "not the manufacture of solid gold, nor liquid nostrums, nor gaseous theories, but an investigation into the change of properties which bodies experience in their action upon each other."

From this time to the beginning of the eighteenth century, notwithstanding many facts had accumulated in chemistry, anatomy, and physiology, physicians, as a body, held no more natural views of the *true nature* of disease than were advanced by Hippocrates, three thousand years before. Indeed, it is positively certain that none of the most eminent *new* schools or sects of the present day had been more successful in curing diseases than were Hippocrates, Galen, and Sydenham. Meantime, however, there have arisen physicians, who, while they readily received all new facts in respect to the structure of the human organism, still adhered to the instinctive inductions of Nature, and treated diseases with most abundant success by means of Herbal preparations alone. We have at this day as bright a galaxy of names—scholars, philosophers, philanthropists, and humanitarians—as ever adorned any age of the world, devoting themselves with a zeal and industry worthy of all praise to the study and practice of medicine, but, failing to perceive the *grand results* anticipated in their laborious researches after truth, do not hesitate to admit that our actual information does not increase in any degree in proportion to our experience. All their array of learning, and their multitudinous writings, have only served to make confusion worse confounded, and all from the very simple fact that they have neglected to follow the requirements of Nature and common sense, in maintaining the Herbal Practice as the only true and philosophical foundation of the Healing Art. Amidst all the jarrings, conflicts, and dogmas of the medical world, is it any wonder that the great masses are rapidly losing all confidence in Medical Science, and crying for a more natural system of medication—even one founded in the principles of irrefragable Nature? With this view I have devoted many years of my life, and having traveled in numerous lands, I feel that I am now qualified, from a long medical experience and deep research into the physiology of Plants, to present to the world of suffering humanity all those curative elements best calculated to ensure perfect health, and the utmost length of life, to all who may feel disposed to be guided by the doctrines and system of medication which it is the object of this volume to make known.

THE HERBAL WORLD.

IN the foregoing pages we have seen, that from the earliest period in the history of the human race to the present time, the administration of the juices and essences of Herbs and Plants, in all forms of disease, has ever been considered by judicious and philosophical minds as the most rational and natural means of relieving the economy of all abnormal obstructions and derangements, and restoring all the functions to their original or primitive vigor and healthful working. Notwithstanding the innovations of the *mineral* practice, I have ever held most rigidly to the *Herbal* System of medication; but having failed to meet with the uccess reasonably anticipated by pursuing the ordinary routine of Therapeutics, I was finally led to reject the many changes in medical doctrines and practice, and start forth on a path of investigation of my own into the mysteries of the mineral and vegetable Kingdoms, especially as they might bear upon the health and happiness of the human being; accordingly, early in my professional career I attempted, by proper chemical analyses and practical experiment, to determine the best *specific* means for the healing of the maladies of mankind. The results of these researches, since confirmed by many years' successful medical experience based upon them, have but the more strongly strengthened my opposition to the use of all the mineral preparations of the modern schools of medicine, and to establish my faith all the more firmly in the employment of HERBAL elements exclusively—whether in the materia of roots, barks, seeds, or flowers—as the surest and safest means for the thorough eradication of every form of disease.

In saying all this, however, I do not deny the fact that many mineral substances enter into the composition of the human being, and are necessary for his full health and perfection—as chalk or lime is requisite to form bone, iron to enrich or strengthen the blood, and other mineral substances for the formation of the tissues, as phosphorus for the tissues of the brain and nerves, etc.—but I stoutly contend that all such inorganic substances are taken up by plants and distributed to the various tissues and elements of the human being, either in the way of food or medicine, in exactly the precise quantity requisite for man's perfect health, if rightly used, neither in excess or diminution, agreeably to the laws of Nature; and their virtues are thus prepared and eliminated in a way far superior to any chemical manipulation ever conceived or known to man, with all the elements of chemical science at his command. That this is the case is demonstrated by chemical analyses of plants Coca contains phosphorus; twinleaf, the salts of potassa, lime, iron, magnesia, silica, etc.; the houseleek, super-malate of lime; Matico, the salts of lime, iron, sulphur, etc. *Spongia usta*, carbon, silica, sodium, lime, magnesium, iron, and phosphorus, either in combination or free; coffee, chlorogenate of potassa; in fact, all the chemical elements composing the organism of man are also found in plants. The reader will find these chemical elements given in the history of plants. I also refer him to page 390, where, in the article "Treatment of Chronic Diseases," he will find that this chemical nature of plants forms the basis of all therapeutical science.

The herbal physician has, moreover, decided advantages over the mineral physician, with reference to the administration of mineral substances. He gives them in natural combinations—in such chemical association which, for exactness and propriety, can only occur in the great laboratory of Nature; while the dispenser of mineral drugs gives them wholly as isolated elementary principles, as furnished by the inorganic chemist, who, like all humans, is liable to err. Let us illustrate this advantage by iodine. The algæ, such as the *fuci* and *laminariæ* (deep-sea-water plants, growing at the depth of three hundred fathoms), furnish this principle in abundance. The mineral physician, not content to administer the alterative in the best possible combination, as it exists in the sea-weed, subjects the plants to chemical operations, releases the iodine, and then either exhibits it by itself or in association with sodium.

potassium, mercury, etc. The true herbal physician acts more wisely in this respect: he administers the plant in substance, tincture, extract, etc., and has the consciousness that the iodine which Nature furnishes him is pure, and not the inferior adulterated article of commerce. In plants where its chemical nature may be concentred into one compound principle, and the residue but inert matter, it is judicious to separate it from the plant, but radically wrong to release but one simple elementary mineral quality of the plant.

The advocate of mineral medication may retort by asking the use of administering the whole plant, when the iodine alone constitutes its therapeutical value. Why give the refuse matter with the iodine? To this sophistical argument and foolish inquiry I will reply, Why eat the whole peach, when its flavor only makes it pleasant as an edible? Why not release the flavor and fatten on that delectable principle?

The best argument, however, in favor of herbal medication, and one which establishes it as the correct philosophy, is the comparison of results from both systems; and with these the author became fully acquainted by practical experiment, and which led him, and not prejudice, to adopt exclusively the herbal system of medication. I may justly claim this system of practice, in its most important relations, as solely my own, and for which I have been the recipient of all encouragement of scientific men and societies; but the homage that I value most, and which afforded the motive and stimulated my ambition, is the gratitude of almost numberless invalids whom I have thus been enabled to cure of diseases which were pronounced, and in fact are, incurable by physicians who rely upon minerals for their agents of cure.

The true theory of *disease* and its *cure* is embodied in two chemical forces, which, like the currents of electricity, are *positive* and *negative*. Thus, if the positive force of disease is manifested upon any organ, it disturbs the harmony and functional action of that organ, and the disorganization will continue as long as the negative force of cure is not placed in antagonism with it, to neutralize the activity of the positive force. When this is done the autonomy of the organ is re-established, and its function becomes again natural and healthful.

Again, if upon discovery any organ or tissue becomes deficient in its chemical elements, it must be supplied by such plants as contain them; or if any organ or tissue becomes surcharged with its chemical constituents, negative chemical elements must be exhibited to reduce them to their normal quantities. See article on "The Treatment of Chronic Diseases," page 390.

These forces in various ways control the whole organic world. Increase the centrifugal force, and the earth flies into space: remove the centripetal, and it rushes headlong to the sun. If they are, as they exist, co-equal, the earth rolls on in its orbit in grand precision and admirable harmony.

Having thus philosophized, and finally realized that the entire universe was composed of *contrary* elements—of *negative* and *positive* principles—yet that the whole worked, or acted, in the most perfect harmony, agreeably to the wisdom of a Great First Cause, when such elements were not disarranged or disturbed by any *violation* of the laws of pristine *Nature*, I was soon led to a *logical deduction* of the general laws which govern the virtues or medicinal properties of all the varieties of plants, with a view to employ them as remedial agents in the cure of disease. In a word, I found in the being, MAN, an epitome of all creation—found in his organism all the elements of universal nature—and necessarily discerned that, as there are summer and winter, night and day, in regular and systematic succession, such alternations of nature could not but have the most important influences in respect to the health and diseases of the human being—Heaven's last, most perfect work. I realized that in accordance with the various operations of nature, man remained in health, or became afflicted with disease. Hence it became necessary for me to fully understand or comprehend the *cause* of any departure from the normal or natural condition of man, and to provide the cure, or the remedy best adapted for the restoration of the equilibrium of the functions of his entire organism.

I ascertained by experiment what was before a preconceived idea, that plants afforded the best agents to antagonize the force of disease, and to re-establish the integrity of any organ or tissue assailed. The discovery was made apparent, however, that indiscriminate selection of medicinal plants was injudicious, and that the curative property of a plant was developed only in proportion as certain essential conditions were provided. These conditions proved to be those necessary to the full health of man, viz., proper climate, air, and food.

The first great essential of a plant which is to be selected for its medical qualities is its nativity. If indigenous to the locality or country wherein found, it is a proper one to select. Plants that are introduced from other countries are lessened or deprived of their virtues unless they meet in their new home all the essential conditions possessed in their native place.

The *geographical* distribution of plants is affected by climatic influences, constituents of soil, heat, moisture, altitude of situation, etc. The flowers, shrubs, and trees which adorn the plains of India and South America, are not the same with those which clothe the valleys of England and North America Nor are their *medicinal* properties the same, however those herbal products may resemble each other. The plants which flourish on the sea-shore of Great Britain are not the same as those on the coast of Africa, nor are these, again, allied to the maritime vegetation of Chili, South America. Nearly all the beautiful plants which adorn our green-houses are natives of a limited space near the Cape of Good Hope, as are also many of our most beautiful bulbs; but the *medicinal* properties of all become *weakened and changed* by transplantation. The curious stafelias, that smell so offensively, are found wild only in South Africa. They are there used for *medical* purposes by the Aborigines. The trees that bear balsam grow principally in Arabia and on the banks of the Red Sea. The umbelliferous and cinciferous plants spread across Europe and Asia. The *Cacti* are found only in tropical America, while the lobiatæ and cariophyllacea are seldom discovered but in Europe. The peculiar ranges and centres of vegetation, as they are termed, are all owing to chemical, climatic, and electrical influences, and yield their *medicinal* properties in exact *ratio of quality*, in accordance with the latitudes or places in which they are *indigenous*.

From the many facts existing, we must believe that there is not a single disease in man that may not have its remedy or cure, in some herb or other, if we but knew *which* plant, and *where* to find it, in this, or that, or any clime or portion of the world—agreeably to the providence of Nature.

This fact or law is proven in the lower animal kingdom. Who has not often seen not only our familiar domestic animals, but many of the untamed creatures of the forests, fields, and air, seek out some one or peculiar herb, when laboring under sickness or derangement of the functions of its organism?

Truly, Nature has wisely implanted a *definite* instinct in every organ ic creature, in order to serve for its health, or for its restoration to health from disease. In man, however, such instinct is not so plainly marked, but to him has been given reason and judgment, and (in some *few* of the race) a disposition to investigate the laws and mysteries of creation, in order to secure his own highest health and perfection, and to find the means for the healing of his kind, when they have become diseased through ignorance, perversion, and violation of the immutable ordinances of Creation.

As the proverb says, "There are sermons in stones, and books in running brooks;" so do we behold volumes of wisdom in all the herbal kingdom—in every emerald and variegated leaf, in every tinted blossom—in *all*, there is a voiceless language, eternally singing significant psalms in praise of "HIM who doeth all things well."

Thus we find that *adaptation* is the *law* of the universe—and nowhere is it more vividly portrayed than in the growth and development of the *Herbal* world.

It will thus be seen that it is only by carefully studying the physiology or functions, or nature of plants, we can derive instruction for the proper regulation or government of our own organisms. The causes which influence the growth and development of plants, are conditions necessary to be understood, in order to preserve the health or integrity of our systems.

Dependent upon the causes I have already named, the plants, also, may lose their medicinal virtues; while much will be owing to the season of the year when they are gathered, in order to adapt them to medico-chemical purposes.

For instance, in the Spring of the year the common *Nettle* plant may afford a palatable food for man; but if selected at a later period, instead of serving as a savory vegetable, or purifier of morbid elements from the blood and system of man, might be converted into or *act* as a virulent or dangerous poison upon his organism.

In China the *Ginseng* (so called from the two Chinese words *gen sing*, "first of plants") plant or root is regarded—weight for weight—as silver, for medicinal purposes; whereas the same herb grown in America, or other countries, does not possess a tithe of the value of the Chinese production for healing purposes.

The American chamomile, though in all respects the same as the European, is positively inert in its medicinal qualities.

There must be, therefore, I repeat, a combination of influences to insure the full development of perfection of any plant. There must be not only internal but external stimuli, to develop the virtues of the herb. The external, as we have seen, consist of certain nutritious matters contained in the soil, water, atmospheric gases, electricity, light, and heat, besides the elements of oxygen, both in its combined or simple form, nitrogen, etc.

If we take a stem cut from a pine tree, in the forests of North Carolina, and place it in contact with the trunk of a healthy growing pine, the former would destroy the latter in the course of the season. The worms generated in the severed or decayed stem will pass to the living tree, and rapidly cause its destruction.

Any farmer knows that if the lordly oak be felled in June it will pass into a state of decay in the course of from four to eight weeks; but if it be cut down at a proper season (which is in Fall and early Spring, when the tree is nearly destitute of sap), it affords the best timber for the building of ships. It may be of interest, also, to state that at such times the transplantation of trees should be made. The tree should be removed at night, and set out in the same relative position to the sun as in its former aspect. If these rules are followed, no tree will rarely ever die, unless its most vital parts are too extensively injured.

We all know that a plant stripped of its leaves will soon perish. Among the reasons for this is, that the absorption by the roots is insufficient to supply all the materials for its nourishment. Let us look a little more closely into these phenomena of nature. There must be a certain number of stages for all herbal growths. First, the ascending sap dissolves the nutritive deposits of the root and stem, and conveys them to assist in the development of leaves and flowers. Hence it is evident that if the root, bark, or stem be gathered at this season, it will prove deficient in medicinal virtues, or be altogether inert. The leaves also will be found worthless for remedial purposes. On the other hand, if we wait a little longer, or until the plant is fully developed, we will find that either the bark or root, the leaves or flowers, are full of rare medicinal virtues.

The *precise* moment when all the assimilative processes of the plant have been perfected—whether it be Summer or Winter, Spring or Autumn—*is the time to gather it* for a remedial agent in disease, inasmuch as we know that the laws of chemical decomposition and recombination know no rest; hence, as in the case of the nettle, while it may be a good food in its earlier stages of development, it would prove a poison in a more advanced stage of its growth.

The peculiar properties of herbs as medicines will often depend upon the greenness or ripeness of the plant, and other circumstances attendant upon its cutting, and the length of time it is kept after being gathered.

For instance, the concrete juice of the Manna ash (*Fraxinus Ornus*)—the manna of commerce—increases in purgative qualities by age. The Oak-bark, for tanning hides, improves in value for a period of four or five years after it has been stripped from the trunk; in the same manner, its medicinal properties are either diminished or improved, according to the season when the bark is gathered, or the manner in which it is converted into tannic acid for medical or scientific purposes.

It must be apparent to all, that herbs are liable to suffer from the vicissitudes of soil, climate, season, etc., and, as a matter of course, from these causes will vary the medicinal principles attributed to them.

Repeated analysis demonstrates the fact, that specimens of the same plant, grown in different localities, will vary infinitely in the proportions of the medicinal principles yielded. Take, for example, the Butterfly-weed, or Pleurisy-root (*Asclepias Tuberosa*), which grows in the barren and sandy soil of New Jersey, and it will be found to yield from one to two hundred per cent. of its medicinal virtues more than the same plant grown in the rich alluvial soils of the West. Hence, when given as medicine, the quantity must correspond accordingly—be either increased or diminished, in order to secure its proper curative effects upon the system. Thus it is seen that a medicine, prepared from plants culled at an improper season, will prove entirely inert or useless, while the same herb, gathered at a proper time in a proper climate, especially and properly prepared, would secure the restoration of a patient from disease to health.

There is likewise a wide difference between the virtues of a plant growing in a wild or *natural* condition from that of the same herb when artificially cultivated. The transference of plants from their native locations, to soils prepared by the hands of man, induces many changes in their individual elements. Many plants formerly used for medicines are now cultivated for the table alone. The small acid root of the *Brassica Rupa* has become the large and nutritious article of diet known as the *turnip*. The dandelion, when grown in natural localities, possesses well-defined medical properties, all of which are lost when the plant is artificially cultivated. In the cultivated plant the proportions of starch, grape-sugar, and other non-medical principles are largely increased, while that which is gathered in its wild or native state is known to possess rare virtues in affections of the liver, kidneys, and respiratory organs. In the cultivated rose the stamens are converted into petals. The castor-oil plant in Africa is a woody tree—in our gardens it is an annual. The mignonette, in Europe, is an annual plant, but becomes perennial in the sandy deserts of Egypt.

I repeat, from what has been seen it is evident that all herbs, perhaps, possess some property suitable for medical purposes. These virtues may be found in the root of one plant, in the bark of another, in the leaves of another, in the blossoms of another, in the seeds of another, or in the whole combined. Even the *color* of the flower has much to do with the therapeutic properties of the plant--as, for instance, the *Blue Vervain*, as used in my Fits and Dyspepsia remedy, is the only kind that is used for medical purposes—all the other species being entirely useless, or else more or less dangerous.

In fact, it is evident to the comprehension of the simplest mind that climatic influences have much to do with the full development of plants. This may be illustrated in the *Tobacco* raised in Cuba and that grown in Connecticut—the one being grown in a Southern and the other in a Northern climate. The poison *nicotine* is derived from the tobacco plant; the exhilarating *caffeine* and *theine* are obtained from the coffee berry and tea plant. Thus it is possible that some therapeutic agent or other may be derived from every plant grown on the surface of the globe.

The Red Men of the American forests are never at a loss to know which plant is best, nor the time it should be gathered, to cure them of disease. They know how to treat their complaints in physic, surgery, and midwifery with a skill that far surpasses that of many a learned doctor of the big medical schools, with all their science, and the medical teachings of physicians for upwards of four thousand years. What other guide have the poor Indians—those untutored savages of the woods—but their reason and their instinct, and their practical experience in the use of herbs?

This is the same in the East Indies, South America, South Sea

Islands, Patagonia, Africa, and other lands. The negroes in the interior parts of Africa possess a knowledge of the medicinal properties of plants which is really surprising, and, by consequence, are rarely afflicted with disease. The art of healing in Sumatra consists in the application of plants, in whose medicinal virtues they are surprisingly skilled. In fact, the Sumatrans have a degree of botanical knowledge that surprises the European or American. They become acquainted at an early age not only with the names, but the qualities and properties of every shrub and herb among that exuberant variety with which their country abounds.

In gathering herbs for medical purposes, we should not only know the season when they should be culled, out we should be qualified to comprehend the principles of which the plant is composed—whether they be resins, alkaloids, or neutrals—and be able also to separate the one ingredient or element from the other, as a *distinct* medicinal property, or combine the whole for the purpose of a *compound* medical agent.

Plants by their appearance often invite the invalid to cull them for his restoration, and assume such shapes as to suggest their curative properties. For instance, herbs that simulate the shape of the *Lungs*, as Lungwort (*see figure adjoining*), Sage, Hounds-tongue, and Comfrey, are all good for pulmonary complaints.

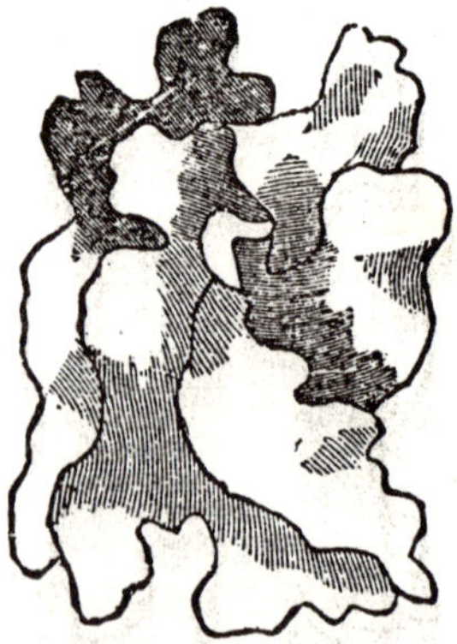
Lungwort.

Plants which bear in leaves and roots a *heart*-like form, as Citron Apple, Fuller's Thistle, Spikenard, Balm, Mint, White-beet, Parsley, and Motherwort, will yield medicinal properties congenial to that organ. Vegetable productions like in figure to the *ears*, as the leaves of the Coltfoot or Wild Spikenard, rightly prepared as a conserve and eaten, improve the hearing and memory; while *oil* extracted from the shells of sea-snails, which have the turnings and curvings of the ears, tends wonderfully to the cure of deafness. A decoction of Maiden Hair and the moss of Quinces, which plants resemble the *hairs of the head*, is good for baldness. Plants resembling the human *nose*, as the leaves of the Wild Water Mint, are beneficial in restoring the *sense of smell*. Plants having a semblance of the *Womb*, as Birthwort, Heart Wort, Ladies' Seal or Briony, conduce much to a safe *accouchement*. Shrubs and Herbs resembling the bladder and gall, as Nightshade and Alkekengi, will relieve the gravel and stone. Liver-shaped plants, as *Liverwort* (*see the following figure*), Trinity, Agaric, Fumitory, Figs, etc., all are efficacious in *bilious* diseases. Walnuts, Indian nuts,

Leeks, and the root of Ragwort, because of their form, when duly prepared will further generation and prevent sterility. Herbs and seeds in shape like the teeth, as Toothwort, Pine-kernel, etc., preserve the dental organization. Plants of knobbed form, like knuckles or joints, as Galingale, and the knotty odoriferous rush, *Calamus*, are good for diseases of the spine and reins, foot, gout, knee swellings, and all joint pains whatsoever. Oily vegetable products, as the Filbert, Walnut, Almond, etc., tend to fatness of the body.

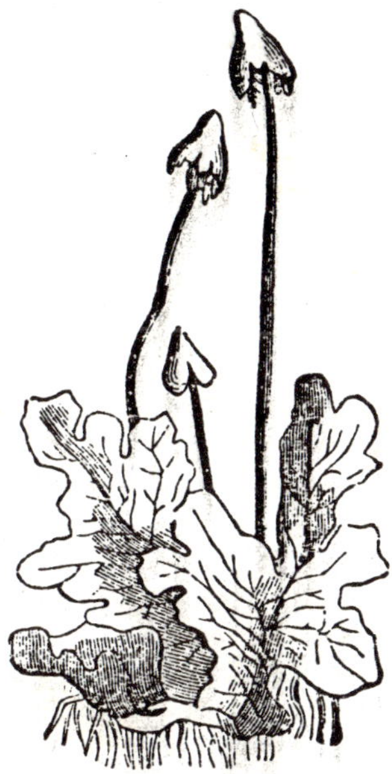

Liverwort.

Plants naturally *lean*, as Sarsaparilla or long-leaved *Rosa Solie* emaciate those who use them.

Fleshy plants, such as Onions, Leeks, and Colewort, make flesh for the eaters. Certain plants, as the Sensitive plant, Nettles, the roots of Mallows, and the herb *Neurus*, when used as *outward* applications, fortify and brace the *nerves*. Milky herbs, as Lettuce and the fruit of the Almond and Fig trees, propagate *milk*. Plants of a *serous* nature, as Spurge and Scammony, purge the noxious humors between the flesh and the skin. Herbs whose acidity turns milk to curd, such as Galium and the seeds of Spurge, will lead to procreation. Rue mixed with Cummin will relieve a sore breast, if a poultice of them be applied, when the milk is knotted therein ; while plants that are *hollow*, as the stalks of Grain, Reeds, Leeks, and Garlic, are good to purge. open, and soothe the hollow parts of the body. Many more instances of such adaptation of herbs and plants to diseases of the body might be cited if deemed necessary.

The *vitality* of plants may be destroyed by giving them deleterious or poisonous substances, such as arsenic, mercury, etc. In fact, *mineral* poisons act on plants and herbs in nearly the same way they do upon human beings or other animals.

The *color* of plants is generally under the influence of *solar* light, hence, plants grown in darkness become etiolated or blanched. The *green* of leaves is due to *nitrogen*, while in proportion as the *oxygen* of the air predominates, the leaves put on varied tints, as the beautiful red and crimson assumed by some leaves in Autumn.

The *color of flowers*, as a general rule, is influenced by *solar* light though the *magnetic* condition of the soil has much to do with the color. For instance, the petals of the common butter-cup are of as brilliant a yellow in town gardens enveloped in the smoke of London as on any country hill, while the tints of the rose remain, when languishing for lack of a clear atmosphere. The flowers of the common hydrangea, which are naturally *pink*, may be made *blue* by planting the shrub in soil impregnated with iron. So will certain medical preparations of iron turn *blue* the human flesh. The color of the flower of the tulips can be turned into white, yellow, brown, purple, and a beautiful tint of rose, by transplanting the plants from a poor soil to a rich one, and *vice versa*.

The *fragrances* of flowers and plants have their physiological or medical uses. The use of the fragrance in leaves, bark, and wood, is apparently to preserve them from the attacks of insects; as the smell of the red and Bermuda cedars (of which pencils are made) and of Camphor, also a *vegetable* product, is to keep moths and other vermin from attacking substances with which they are in contact.

Plants sometimes distil or secrete medicinal or nutritive fluids, which are contained in convenient receptacles. Such plants invariably grow far from the haunts of men, away from the course of streams or vicinity of ponds. Whose ordination is it that such plants have such a habitude? It is that Providence who, in his bountiful beneficence, places them where the traveler may not die of thirst or disease on his way of discovery. This is most beautifully illustrated in the *Nepenthes distillatoria* (see cut), in which the leaves terminate in a most singular manner, forming a sort of urn or vase, surmounted by a cover, which opens and shuts as occasion requires. This vessel is suspended at the extremity of a thread-like appendage to a winged petiole, which would seem to be altogether unfit to support it. An officer of marines writes as follows: "Three days after my arrival at Madagascar I lost myself during a short excursion into the interior, and was overtaken with an excessive lassitude, accompanied with a devouring thirst. After a long walk I was on the point of yielding to despair, when I perceived close to me, suspended to leaves, some small vases, somewhat like those used to preserve fresh water. I began to think I was under one of those hallucinations by which the sick are often visited

Nepenthes distillatoria.

in fever, when the refreshing draught seems to fly from their parched lips. I approached it, however, with some hesitation, threw a rapid glance at the pitchers: judge of my happiness when I found them filled with a pure and transparent liquid. The draught I partook gave me the best idea I have realized of the nectar served at the table of the gods." Plants of such description become extinct if civilization approaches their domain.

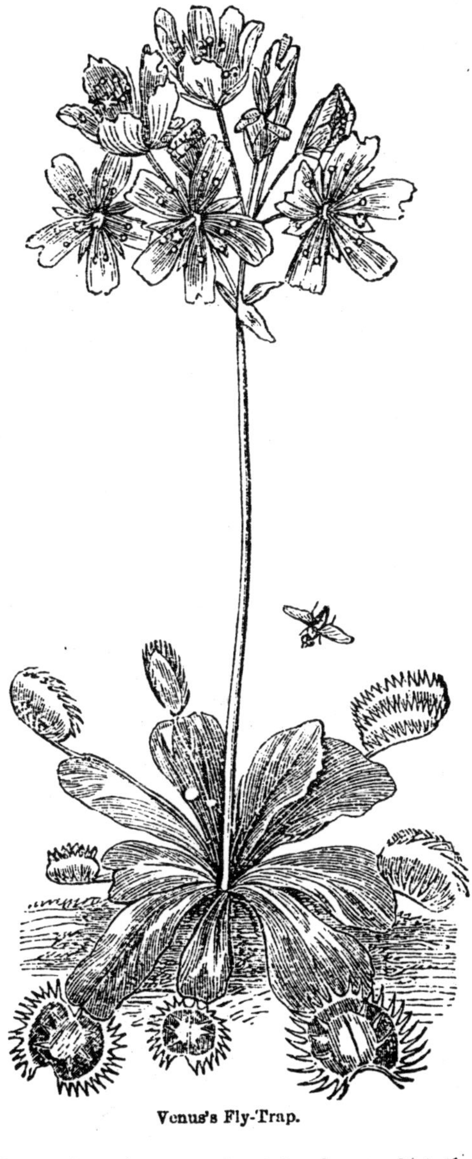

Venus's Fly-Trap.

Plants have attributes other than medical which are of interest to the general reader besides the botanist.

In many instances there seems to be a striking affinity between the herbal and animal kingdom, and other instances of the repelling character. For instance, a most remarkable instance of irritability by contact is that exhibited by the "Venus's Fly-Trap," *Dionœa muscipula*, a native of Canada, and nearly allied to the common "Sun-Dew" of the British commons. Its flowers have nothing remarkable about them, except that their petals roll up when they are about to decay; but the leaves are very curiously constructed. They have broad leaf-like petioles, at whose extremity there are two fleshy tubes, which form the real leaf, and which are armed with strong, sharp spines, three on the blade of each lobe, and a fringe of larger spines round the margin.

When an insect touches the base of the central spines the leaf collapses, and the poor insect is caught, been either impaled by the central spines or entrapped by the others. The leaf then remains closed, the fringe of long spines being firmly interlaced and locked together till the body of the insect has wasted away. This apparatus being the nearest approach to a stomach which has yet being observed in plants, an experiment was tried some years ago of feeding a *dionœa* (Venus's Fly-Trap, with very small particles of raw meat, when it was found that the leaves closed in the same way as they would have done over an insect, and did not open again until the meat was consumed. The leaves of this plant possess medicinal properties, which, when properly prepared in tincture or decoction, have been found of exceeding efficacy in many diseases of the digestive organs of the human being.

Sarracenia, or Side-Saddle flower, the leaves of which are pitcher-shaped, resembling an old-fashioned side-saddle, six of which generally belong to each plant. Each of these pitchers will hold nearly a wine-glassful, and are generally filled with water and aquatics, which undergo decomposition, or a sort of *digestion*, and serve as a nutriment to the plant.

This animal characteristic is also illustrated in the *sensitive plant* (Mimosa Sensitiva), which the slightest touch suffices to make it close its folioles. If we cut with scissors the extreme end of one foliole the others immediately approach in succession. This irritation is not local, but communicates from circle to circle, and propagates itself from leaf to leaf. Up to a certain point it gets accustomed to outside interference. Touching it again and again will habituate it to the movement and fail to respond, as if it were owing in the first instance to fright.

Sensitive Plant.

The sleep of plants vaguely recalls to us the sleep of animals. Their period of sleep is mostly at night, and any interested person may observe this habit in a variety of plants, as many of them when asleep are difficult to recognize in their bearing. The leaves are rolled up, or become reversed, as in the genus *Sida* and the *Lupinus*. The Vetch, the Sweet-pea, the Broad Bean, in their sleep rest their leaves during the night one against the other.

Parental solicitude is displayed in the orach-root (*Atriplex hortensis*). The leaves of this plant fall back upon the young shoots, and enclose them whenever the effects of the atmosphere would injure them. This is also seen in the chickweed at night.

The folding of some flowers in the absence of the sun, and the opening of others as soon as that luminary has withdrawn his beams, are ascribable to various causes. The white marigold closes its flowers on the approach of rain, and the dwarf *Colendrina* folds up its bright crimson corolla about four o'clock every afternoon; while, on the contrary, the plant commonly called *Four o'clock*, whose flower remains closed all day, opens precisely at the hour of four. The evening primrose will not open its large yellow flower till the sun has sunk below the horizon. On the other hand, the Sun-flower is always seen bending its face (*vis-à-vis*) in the direction of the sun, and follows its course during the entire diurnal round, from its rise in the Orient, or East, in the morning, to its decline in the Hesperian region, or west, in the evening. The *Silphium laciniatum*, or compass-weed, always points its leaves towards the north star. The Night-blowing Cereus only expands its flowers about midnight. Indeed, some flowers are so regular in their opening or shutting, that the great botanist, LINNÆUS, formed what he called "*Flora's Timepiece*," in which each hour was represented by the flower which opened or closed at that particular time. An arrangement of this kind may be seen in the following

FLORAL CLOCK:

Between 3 and 4 A.M	Bind-weed of the hedgerows.
At 5 A.M..................	Naked stalked Poppy and most of the Chichoraceæ.
Between 5 and 6 A.M......	Nipplewort and the Day Lily.
At 6 A.M..................	Many of the Solanaceæ (Night-shade) family.
Between 6 and 7 A.M......	Sow Thistle and Spurrey.
At 7 A.M..................	Water Lilies, Lettuces.
At 7 to 8 A.M.............	Venus' Looking-Glass.
At 8 A.M..................	Wild Pimpernel.
At 9 A.M..................	Wild Marigold.
At 9 to 10 A.M............	Ice Plant.
At 11 A.M.................	Purslain, Star of Bethlehem.
At 12.....................	Most of the Ficoid, or Mesembryanthemum family.
At 2 P.M..................	Scilla Pomeridiana.
Between 5 and 6 P.M......	Silene Noctiflora.
Between 6 and 7 P.M......	Marvel of Peru.
Between 7 and 8 P.M.	Cereus Grandiflorus, Tree Primrose.
At 10 P.M.................	Purple Convolvulus.

In addition to the above, I would remark that certain equinoctial flowers open and close at a fixed time in the same day; on the morrow, and for several following days, they again open and shut at the same regular hours. The Star of Bethlehem opens several days in succession at eleven in the morning, and closes at three. The *Ficoides Noctiflora* blows several days in succession at seven in the evening, and closes about six or seven in the morning.

Besides the cases in which flowers open and shut their corollas by the influence of light, instances are known in which merely the petals roll up by day, and resume their natural shape after sunset. A remarkable circumstance respecting the effect of atmospheric influence is, that the same causes do not affect all plants, and yet no peculiarity of construction has been discovered in those so affected to distinguish them from those that are not.

Every student of nature can witness much more that is of general interest regarding the habits, so to speak, and characteristics of plants. They have been a favorite theme in all ages. Lovers have dwelt on them and given them a language. Nearly every one delights in the flowering plants. Who would refuse a bouquet of choice flowers? This attachment to flowers was pathetically illustrated in the Highland emigrants in Canada, who wept when they found that the heather would not grow in their newly-adopted soil. And well they might, for it is the flower of their native mountains, and associated with all their brightest and tenderest recollections. In the age of chivalry the daisy was renowned; and St. Louis, of France, took it and a lily for a device in his ring, as emblematical of his wife and country. The thistle, like the famous geese of Rome, saved Scotland, and for this reason it is the national emblem of that country. During the Danish invasion, one of their soldiers placed his naked foot on the spiny leaves of a thistle, and instinctively uttered a cry which awoke the slumbering Scots, who turned upon their foes, defeated, and drove them from their land.

The poetry attached to plants, however, is not of immediate concern in this volume. It is their medicinal properties which engages our study and demands our labors. Yet I could not so well establish their superior fitness as curative agents above the mineral drug unless I gave that which is of general interest. One fact will be apparent to the reader, that plants have life, and hence are eminently suitable to give life to the suffering patient. The lifeless inorganic mineral has none, and can give no vital element.

EPITOME OF BOTANY.

THAT the reader may more intelligently understand the description of the medicinal plants in this book, the author has deemed it prudent to preface the part of this work dedicated to Herbal Materia Medica with a brief analysis of the plant, as made by the botanist. This becomes particularly necessary, inasmuch as a plant cannot be accurately described unless scientific language be employed; but, nevertheless, throughout this whole work it has been the aim of the author to use the plainest language, and not to weary the reader by as pedantic employment of technical terms and scientific language.

Nothing more will be given than the anatomy of the plant, as nothing of systematic botany need be known to the reader to recognize the plant, or to acquaint himself with the medicinal properties thereof. If he has not a common acquaintance with a medicinal plant, but desires it for domestic medication, it is important that he should know that he employs the proper herb, and not use one which simulates it. It has therefore been the aim of the author to give accurate descriptions of the herbs, so that the gatherer may not err in his selection of the plant which his case may need.

All parts of the plant are used in medicine—sometimes the seed only; in others the flower, the leaves, root, rhizome; in others two or more of these parts, and, again, in others the whole plant.

ANATOMY OF A PLANT.

THE ROOT.

The root of a plant is that portion which is usually found in the earth, the stem and leaves being in the air. The point of union is called the collar or neck of the plant.

A fibrous root is one composed of many spreading branches, as that of barley.

A conical root is one where it tapers regularly from the crown to the apex, as that of the carrot.

A fusiform root is one when it tapers up as well as down, as that of the radish.

A napiform root is one when much swollen at the base, so as to become broader than long, as that of the turnip.

A fasciculated root is one when some of the fibres or branches are thickened.

A tuberiferous root is one when some of the branches assume the form of rounded knobs, as that of the potato.

A palmate root is one when these knobs are branched.

Aerial roots are those emitted from the stem into the open air, as that of Indian corn.

A rhizoma, or root stock, is a prostrate stem either subterranean or resting on the surface, as that of calamus, or blood-root.

A tuber is an enlargement of the apex of a subterranean branch of the root, as that of the common potato or artichoke.

A cormus is a fleshy subterranean stem of a round or oval figure, as in the Indian turnip.

A bulb is an extremely abbreviated stem clothed with scales, as that of the lily.

THE STEM.

The stem is that portion of the plant which grows in an opposite direction from the root, seeking the light, and exposing itself to the air. All flowering plants possess stems. In those which are said to be stemless, it is either very short, or concealed beneath the ground.

An herb is one in which the stem does not become woody, but dies down to the ground at least after flowering.

A shrub is a woody plant, branched near the ground, and less than five times the height of man.

A tree attains a greater height, with a stem unbranched near the ground.

The stem of a tree is usually called the trunk; in grasses it has been termed the culm.

Those stems which are too weak to stand erect are said to be decumbent, procumbent, and prostrate.

A stolon is a form of a branch which curves or falls down to the ground, where they often strike root.

A sucker is a branch of subterraneous origin, which, after running horizontally and emitting roots in its course, at length rises out of the ground and forms an erect stem, which soon becomes an independent plant, as illustrated by the rose, raspberry, etc.

A runner is a prostrate, slender branch sent off from the base of the parent stem.

An offset is a similar but shorter branch, with a tuft of leaves at the end, as in the houseleek.

A spine is a short and imperfectly developed branch of a woody plant, as exhibited in the honey-locust.

A tendril is commonly a slender leafless branch, capable of coiling spirally, as in the grape vine.

THE LEAF.

The leaf is commonly raised on an unexpanded part or stalk which is called the petiole, while the expanded portion is termed the lamina limb, or blade. When the vessels or fibres of the leaves expand immediately on leaving the stem, the leaf is said to be **sessile**. In such cases the petiole is absent. When the blade consists of a single piece the leaf is **simple**; when composed of two or three more with a branched petiole, the leaf is **compound**.

The distribution of the veins or framework of the leaf in the blade is termed **venation**.

A **lanceolate** leaf has the form of a lance.

An **ovate** leaf has the shape of ellipsis.

A **cuneiform** leaf has the shape of a wedge.

A **cordate** leaf has the shape of a heart.

A **reniform** leaf has the shape of a kidney.

A **sagittate** leaf is arrow-shaped.

A **hastate** leaf has the shape of an ancient halberd.

A **peltate** leaf is shaped like a shield.

A **serrate** leaf is one in which the margin is beset with sharp teeth, which point forward towards the apex.

A **dentate** leaf is one when these teeth are not directed towards the apex.

A **crenate** leaf has rounded teeth.

A **sinuate** leaf has alternate concavities and convexities.

A **pinnate** leaf has the shape of a feather.

A **pectinate** leaf is one having very close and narrow divisions, like the teeth of a comb.

A **lyrate** leaf has the shape of a lyre.

A **runcinate** leaf is a lyrate leaf with sharp lobes pointing towards the base, as in the dandelion.

A **palmate** leaf is one bearing considerable resemblance to the hand.

A **pedate** leaf is one bearing resemblance to a bird's foot.

An **obovate** leaf is one having the veins more developed beyond the middle of the blade.

When a leaf at its outer edge has no dentations it is said to be **entire**. When the leaf terminates in an acute angle it is **acute**, when in an obtuse angle it is **obtuse**. An obtuse leaf with the apex slightly depressed is **retuse**, or if more strongly notched, **emarginate**. An obovate leaf with a wider or more conspicuous notch at the apex become **obcordate**, being a cordate leaf inverted. When the apex is cut off by a straight transverse line the leaf is **truncate**; when abruptly terminated by a small projecting point it is **mucronate**; and when an acute leaf has a narrowed apex it is **acuminate**. In ferns the leaves are called **fronds**.

THE FLOWER.

The flower assumes an endless variety of forms, and we shall assume in the dissection merely the typical form of it.

The organs of a flower are of two sorts, viz.: 1st. Its leaves or envelopes; and 2d, those peculiar organs having no resemblance to the envelopes. The envelopes are of two kinds, or occupy two rows, one above or within the other. The lower or outer row is termed the **Calyx,** and commonly exhibits the green color of the leaves. The inner row, which is usually of more delicate texture and forms the most showy part of the flower, is termed the **Corolla.** The several parts of the leaves of the Corolla are called **Petals,** and the leaves of the Calyx have received the analogous name of **Sepals.** The floral envelopes are collectively called the **Perianth.**

The essential organs enclosed within a floral envelope are also of two kinds and occupy two rows one within the other. The first of these, those next within the petals, are the **Stamens.** A stamen consists of a stalk called the **Filament,** which bears on its summit a rounded body termed the **Anther,** filled with a substance called the **Pollen.**

The seed-bearing organs occupy the centre or summit of a flower, and are called **Pistils.** A pistil is distinguished into three parts, viz.: 1st., the **Ovary,** containing the **Ovales;** 2d, the **Style,** or columnar prolongation of the ovary; and 3d, the **Stigma,** or termination of the style.

All the organs of the flower are situated on, or grown out of, the apex of the flower-stalk, into which they are inserted, and which is called the **Torus** or **Receptacle.**

A plant is said to be **monœcious,** where the stamens and pistils are in separate flowers on the same individual, **diœcious,** where they occupy separate flowers on different individuals, and **polygamous** where the stamens and pistils are separate in some flowers and united in others, either on the same or two or three different plants.

THE FRUIT.

The principal kinds may be briefly stated as follows :—

A follicle is the name given to such fruit as borne by the larkspur or milkweed.

A legume or pod is the name extended to such fruit as the pea or bean.

A drupe is a stone fruit, as the plum, apricot, etc.

An achenium is the name of the fruit as borne by the butter-cup, &c.

A cremocarp is the fruit of the Poison Hemlock and similar plants.

A caryopsis is such fruit as borne by the wheat tribe.

A nut is exemplified by the fruit of the oak, chestnut, &c.

A samara is the name applied to the fruit of the maple, birch, and elm.

A berry is a fruit fleshy and pulpy throughout, as the grape, goose berry, &c.

A pome is such as the apple, pear, &c

A pepo is the name applied to the fruit of the pumpkin, cucumber, &c.

A capsule is a general term for all dry fruits, such as lobelia, &c.

A silique is such fruit as exhibited in Shepherd's purse, &c.

A cone or strobile is a collective fruit of the fir tribe, magnolia, &c.

THE SEED.

The seed, like the ovule of which it is the fertilized and matured state, consists of a nucleus, usually enclosed within two integuments, The outer integument or proper seed coat is variously termed the episperm, spermoderm, or testa.

An annual plant is one which springs from the seed, flowers and dies the same year

A biennial plant, such as the radish, carrot, beet, &c., does not flower the first season.

A perennial plant is one not absolutely depending upon the stock of the previous season, but annually produces new roots and new accumulations.

MEDICINAL PROPERTIES AND PREPARATIONS.

EVERY herb employed in the cure of diseases, whether in its natural state or after having undergone various preparations, belongs to the Herbal Materia Medica, in the extended acceptation of the term. It shall, however, be our purpose only to describe each separate herb in its living state, or the medicinal part thereof, and not dwell much upon the forms usually prepared by the apothecary or physician. In this portion of our work we propose to give an account of all the most important medicinal herbs necessary for the cure of diseases. No herb, however, is to be despised or regarded as worthless because of its not finding mention in this work; but, as previously stated, that each and every plant has its virtues, though to describe all recognized as medicinal would make the work too voluminous, and in price far exceed the reach of the million. The various properties of medicinal agents have been designated as follows:—

ABSORBENTS or ANTACIDS are such medicines that counteract acidity of the stomach and bowels.

ALTERATIVES are medicines which, in certain doses, work a gradual cure by restoring the healthy functions of different organs.

ANODYNES are medicines which relieve pain.

ANTHELMINTICS are medicines which have the power of destroying or expelling worms from the intestinal canal.

ANTISCORBUTICS are medicines which prevent or cure the scurvy.

ANTISPASMODICS are medicines given to relieve spasm, or irregular and painful action of muscles or muscular fibres, as in Epilepsy, St. Vitus' Dance, etc.

AROMATICS are medicines which have a grateful smell and an agreeable pungent taste.

ASTRINGENTS are those remedies which, when applied to the body, render the solids dense and firmer.

CARMINATIVES are those medicines which dispel flatulency of the stomach and bowels.

CATHARTICS are medicines which accelerate the action of the bowels, or increase the discharge by stool.

DEMULCENTS are medicines suited to prevent the action of acrid and stimulating matters upon the mucous membranes of the throat, lungs, etc.

DIAPHORETICS are medicines that promote or cause perspirable discharge by the skin.

DIURETICS are medicines which increase the flow of urine by their action upon the kidneys.

EMETICS are those medicines which produce vomiting.

EMMENAGOGUES are medicines which promote the menstrual discharge.

EMOLLIENTS are those remedies which, when applied to the solids of the body, render them soft and flexible.

ERRHINES are substances which, when applied to the lining membrane of the nostrils, occasion a discharge of mucous fluid.

EPISPASTICS are those which cause blisters when applied to the surface.

ESCHAROTICS are substances used to destroy a portion of the surface of the body, forming sloughs.

EXPECTORANTS are medicines capable of facilitating the excretion of mucus from the chest.

NARCOTICS are those substances having the property of diminishing the action of the nervous and vascular systems, and of inducing sleep.

RUBEFACIENTS are remedies which excite the vessels of the skin and increase its heat and redness.

SEDATIVES are medicines which have the power of allaying the actions of the systems generally, or of lessening the exercise of some particular function.

SIALAGOGUES are medicines which increase the flow of the saliva.

STIMULANTS are medicines capable of exciting the vital energy whether as exerted in sensation or motion.

TONICS are those medicines which increase the tone or healthy action, or strength of the living system.

PHARMACEUTIC PREPARATIONS.

ACETA or VINEGARS are medicinal preparations where vinegar is used as the dissolving agent.

ÆTHEREA or ETHERS are ethereal tinctures.

AQUÆ or WATERS consist of water impregnated with some medicinal substance, as a volatile oil.

CATAPLASMS are external applications or poultices.

CERATES are agents intended for external application, and are composed of wax, spermaceti, combined with fatty matter, and in which resins and powders, etc., are frequently amalgamated.

CONFECTIONS are medicines in the form of a conserve.

DECOCTIONS are solutions procured from the various parts of herbs by boiling them in water.

DRAGEES are sugar-coated pills.

ENEMAS or INJECTIONS. These consist of medicinal agents in the form of infusion, decoction, or mixture, and designed to be passed into the rectum and other passages.

EXTRACTS. When an infusion, decoction, or tincture is reduced to a soft solid mass, by evaporation, it is termed an extract.

FLUID-EXTRACTS. These are concentrated medicinal principles, not reduced to a solid or nearly semi-fluid consistence, the evaporation not being carried so far as in ordinary extracts. (See page 475)

INFUSIONS are solutions of vegetable principles in water, effected without boiling.

LINIMENTS. These preparations are designed for external application, and should always be of such a consistence as will render them capable of easy application to the skin with the naked hand or flannel.

LOTIONS. These comprise all compounds used as external washes in which vegetable substances are dissolved.

MIXTURES are either liquid or solid compounds, and which are suspended in aqueous fluids by the intervention of some viscid matter, as mucilage, albumen, etc.

OILS are the products of various herbs by distillation with water.

PILLS are medicinal properties formed into a mass and rolled into globular forms. A *bolus* is a large pill.

PLASTERS are designed for external application; the medicinal agent is usually spread on cloth or chamois leather.

POWDERS are medicinal herbs in a pulverized state.

SATURATES are similar to fluid-extracts, being, however, prepared without the employment of heat.

SYRUPS are liquid medicines of a viscid consistence, produced by concentrated solutions of sugar alone or mixed with honey.

TINCTURES. These are preparations obtained by subjecting medicinal herbs to the action of alcohol.

TROCHEES OR LOZENGES are medicinal substances in powder, which are formed into solid cakes by the aid of sugar and gum.

UNGUENTA OR OINTMENTS are fatty matters, in which are incorporated certain medicines, and are designed for external use.

WINES. These are tinctures of medicinal agents which are insoluble in water, or which do not require as stimulant a solvent as alcohol, but which are capable of yielding their virtues to wine.

WEIGHTS AND MEASURES.

THAT no error may occur, I will here append the weights and measures employed in pharmacy, together with the symbols designating each quantity. It is necessary to understand but two measures, as the author has conformed all the solid or liquid quantities to these measures. These are:—

1ST.—APOTHECARIES' WEIGHT.

20 grains (gr.)	1 scruple.
3 scruples (℈)	1 drachm.
8 drachms (ʒ)	1 ounce.
12 ounces (℥)	1 pound (℔).

The doses of powders, extracts, and all such that are not fluid are intended to correspond with this weight.

2D.—APOTHECARIES' MEASURE.

60 minims (♏)	1 fluid drachm.
8 fluid drachms (f ʒ)	1 fluid ounce.
16 fluid ounces (f ℥)	1 pint.
8 pints (O)	1 gallon (cong).

The quantities of all fluids mentioned in this book agree with this measure, though the word fluid or the symbol (f) is omitted in most instances.

It is not to be supposed, however, that in all families measuring graduates are to be found; hence a comparison of these measures with tea, dessert, and table spoons, etc., becomes necessary to simplify the fluid measure The weight of any quantity I should always advise to be correctly ascertained by scales :—*

Comparison.

A *drop*	corresponds with a	minim.
A teaspoonful	" " "	fluid drachm.
A dessertspoonful	" " "	three fluid drachms.
A tablespoonful	" " "	one-half fluid ounce.
A wineglassful	" " "	two fluid ounces.
A teacupful	" " "	gill (4 f ℥).

In the body of this work the quantity has been stated, with but few exceptions, in which each medicine must ordinarily be given to produce its peculiar effects upon the adult patient. But there are circumstances which modify the dose, and demand attention, the most important of which is the age; hence the following table, exhibiting the dose proportioned to the age, should receive careful reference in domestic practice :—

Table.

The dose for a person of age being	1 or	1 drachm.
That of a person from 14 to 21 years will be	$\frac{2}{3}$ or	2 scruples.
7 to 14 " " "	$\frac{1}{2}$ or	$\frac{1}{2}$ drachm.
4 to 7 " " "	$\frac{1}{3}$ or	1 scruple.
of 4 " " "	$\frac{1}{4}$ or	15 grains.
3 " " "	$\frac{1}{6}$ or	10 grains.
2 " " "	$\frac{1}{8}$ or	8 grains.
1 " " "	$\frac{1}{12}$ or	5 grains.
½ " " "	$\frac{1}{15}$ or	4 grains.

The following rule, however, is a little more simple :—

For children under 12 years the dose of most medicines must be diminished in the proportion of the age to the age increased by 12: thus, at two years the dose will be $\frac{1}{7}$ of that for adults, viz. :—

$$\frac{2}{2+12}=\frac{2}{14} \text{ or } \frac{1}{7}\text{; at 4, it will be } \frac{4}{4+12}=\frac{4}{16} \text{ or } \frac{1}{4}.$$

* The weights used in the British Pharmacopœia are the Imperial or avoirdupois pound, ounce, and grain, and the terms *drachm* and *scruple*, as designating specific weights, are discontinued. The ounce contains 437½ grains, and the pound 7,000 grains. The Imperial Measure contains 8 fluid drachms to the ounce, 20 fluid ounces to the pint, and 8 pints to the gallon.

PART I.

HERBAL MATERIA MEDICA.

ACACIA VERA.

COMMON NAMES. *Gum Arabic, Egyptian Thorn.*

MEDICINAL PART. *The concrete juice or gum.*

Description.—Acacia Vera is a small tree or shrub, but sometimes attains the height of forty feet. The leaves are bipinnate and smooth, leaflets eight or ten pairs. Spines sharp and in pairs. Flowers in globose heads, and the fruit a legume.

Acacia Vera.

History.—The tree inhabits the southern portion of Asia and the upper portion of Africa. The gum flows naturally from the bark of the trees, in the form of a thick and rather frothy liquid, and speedily concretes into tears; sometimes the discharge is promoted by wounding the trunk and branches. The more ruptured the tree, the more gum it yields. The best quality of Gum Arabic is colorless, or very pale yellow-white, shining, transparent in small fragments, hard but pulverable, inodorous, and of a sweet and viscous taste. It invariably forms a white powder. Cold or hot water dissolves its own weight, forming a thick mucilaginous solution.

Properties and Uses.—The gum is nutritive and demulcent, and exerts a remarkably soothing influence upon irritated or inflamed mucous surfaces, by shielding them from the influence of deleterious agents, atmospheric air, etc. It is useful, in diarrhœa and dysentery, to remove griping and painful stools, in catarrh, cough, hoarseness, consumption, gonorrhœa, and all inflammatory conditions of the mucous surfaces. For lung diseases it is especially an indispensable vehicle in which to carry the necessary curative and powerful corrective agents, while at the same time its nutritive qualities also exert a good influence, often supplying the place of food where the stomach is too weak to partake of anything else. It may be given almost *ad libitum* in powder, lozenge, or solution, alone or combined with syrups, decoctions, etc. It constitutes the menstruum of my well-known Acacian Balsam, see page 470.

ADDER'S TONGUE (Erythronum Americanum).

Common Names. *Dog-Tooth Violet, Serpent's Tongue, etc.*

Medicinal Parts. *The bulb and leaves.*

Description.—This is a perennial plant, springing from a bulb at some distance below the surface. The bulb is white internally and fawn-colored externally. The leaves are two, lanceolate, pale green, with purplish or brownish spots, and one nearly twice as wide as the other. It bears a single drooping yellow flower, which partially closes at night and on cloudy days. Fruit a capsule.

History.—This beautiful little plant is among the earliest of our spring flowers, and is found in rich open grounds, or in thin woods throughout the United States, flowering in April or May. The leaves are more active than the roots; both impart their virtues to water.

Properties and Uses.—It is emetic, emollient, and antiscorbutic when fresh; nutritive when dried. The fresh root simmered in milk, or the fresh leaves bruised and often applied as a poultice to scrofulous tumors or ulcers, together with a free internal use of an infusion of them, is highly useful as a remedy for scrofula. The expressed juice of the plant, infused in cider, is very beneficial in dropsy, and for relieving hiccough, vomiting, and hematemesis, and bleeding from the lower bowels.

AGRIMONY (Agrimonia Eupatoria).

Common Names. *Cockleburr or Sticklewort.*

Medicinal Parts. *The root and leaves.*

Description.—Agrimony has a reddish, tapering, not creeping root, with brown stems covered with soft silky hairs; two or three feet high; leaves alternate, sessile, interruptedly pinnate. The stipule of the upper leaves large, rounded, dentate, or palmate. The flowers grow at the top of the stem, are yellow, small, and very numerous, one above another in long spikes, after which come rough heads hanging downwards, which will stick to garments or anything that rubs against them.

History.—This perennial plant is found in Asia, Europe, Canada, and the United States, along roadsides, and in fields and woods, flowering in July or August. Both the flowers and roots are fragrant but harsh and astringent to the taste, and yield their properties to water or alcohol.

Agrimony.

Properties and Uses.—It is a mild tonic, alterative, and astringent. Useful in bowel complaints, chronic mucous diseases, chronic affections of the digestive organs, leucorrhœa, certain cutaneous diseases, etc. A strong decoction, sweetened with honey, is an invaluable cure for scrofula, if persisted in for a length of time. It is exceedingly useful in gravel, asthma, coughs, and obstructed menstruation. As a gargle for sore throat and mouth, it is very serviceable.

Dose.—Powder, one teaspoonful; decoction, a wineglassful.

ALDER (PRINOS VERTICILLATUS).

COMMON NAME. *Winterberry.*

MEDICINAL PARTS. *The bark and berries.*

Description.—This is an indigenous shrub of irregular growth, with a stem six or eight feet in height; bark grayish and alternate branches. The leaves are ovate, acute at the base, olive green in color, smooth above and downy beneath. Flowers small and white; calyx small and six-cleft; corolla divided into six obtuse segments. Fruit a berry.

History.—Black Alder is common throughout the United States and England, growing in moist woods, swamps, etc., flowering from May to July, and maturing its fruit in the latter part of autumn. It yields its virtues to water by decoction or infusion. The bark has a bitterish, sub astringent taste, and the berries have a sweetish taste.

Properties and Uses.—It is tonic, alterative, and astringent. It is very beneficial in jaundice, diarrhœa, gangrene, dropsy, and all diseases attended with great weakness. Two drachms of the powdered bark and one drachm of powdered golden seal infused in a pint of boiling water, and, when cold, taken in the course of the day, in doses of a wineglassful, and repeated daily, has proved very efficacious in dyspepsia. Externally the decoction forms an excellent local application in gangrene, indolent ulcers, and some affections of the skin. The berries are cathartic and vermifuge, and form, with cedar apples, a pleasant and effectual worm medicine for children.

Dose.—Powdered bark, half a drachm to a drachm; decoction, a teaspoonful three or four times a day.

ALE HOOF (NEPETA GLECHOMA).

COMMON NAMES. *Gill-go-by-the-ground, Ground Ivy, Cat's-Foot, Turnhoof, &c.*

MEDICINAL PART. *The leaves.*

Description.—This plant is a perennial gray, hairy herb, with a procumbent creeping stem, varying in length from a few inches to one or two feet. The leaves have petioles, cordate, and hairy on both sides. The flowers are bluish purple. The corolla is about three times as long as the calyx.

History.—This plant is common to the United States and Europe, where it is found in shady places, waste grounds, dry ditches, &c. It flowers in May or August. The leaves impart their virtues to boiling water by infusion. They have an unpleasant odor, and a harsh, bitterish, slightly aromatic taste.

Properties and Uses.—It is stimulant, tonic, and pectoral, and is useful in diseases of the lungs and kidneys, asthma, jaundice, hypochondria, and monomania. An infusion of the leaves is very beneficial in lead-colic, and painters who make use of it are seldom, if ever, troubled with that affection. The fresh juice snuffed up the nose often cures the most inveterate headache.

Dose.—Powder, half a drachm to a drachm; infusion, one or two fluid ounces.

ALL-HEAL (PRUNELLA VULGARIS).

COMMON NAMES. *Hercules Wound Wort, Panay, etc.*

MEDICINAL PART. *The root.*

Description.—This shrub sometimes attains the height of five feet, but is usually much smaller. The stem is strong and round, with many joints, with some leaves thereat. The leaves consist of five or six pair of wings, and when chewed have a bitterish taste. The root is thick and long, the juice of which is hot and biting. The flower is a small and yellow one, and the seeds whitish yellow, short and flat.

History.—This plant is found in England and other parts of Europe. In England it flowers usually until the end of summer, but in other parts of Europe it flowers from May to December.

Properties and Uses.—All-heal is a pungent and bitter tonic and anti-spasmodic. It has also vermifuge properties, and is slightly diuretic. It is excellent for cramps, fits, falling sickness, convulsions, etc. (inferior, however, to Blue Vervain). In obstructions of the liver it serves a good purpose. It sometimes cures the toothache by inserting cotton saturated with the juice into the decayed places of the teeth.

ALMONDS (AMYGDALUS COMMUNIS).

AMYGDALA AMARA, *Bitter Almonds;* AMYGDALA DULCIS, *Sweet Almonds.*

MEDICINAL PART. *The kernels.*

Description.—The almond tree is from ten to eighteen feet high, with a pale-brown rugged bark, and dividing into many branches. The leaves are of a bright light green, two to four inches long, and about three-fourths of an inch wide. Flowers are moderately large, pink or white, sessile, in pairs, and appearing before the leaves. Calyx reddish. petals variable in size. The fruit is a hoary drupe; stone oblong or ovate, hard in various degrees, always rugged and pitted with irregular holes. Both the bitter and sweet almonds come from this tree.

History.—The almond tree is indigenous to most of the southern parts of Asia and Barbary, but is cultivated in Southern Europe. The best of the sweet kind comes from Malaga. The sweet kernel is without odor, and of a pleasant flavor; that of the bitter is also inodorous, unless rubbed with water, when it exhales a smell similar to Prussic acid. Its taste is similar to that of peach-meats. Both varieties contain oil—the sweet a fixed oil, the bitter both a fixed and an essential oil, impregnated with Prussic acid. The oil of bitter almonds has a golden color, an agreeable odor, an acid bitter taste, combustible, and is a poison acting in the same manner as Prussic acid. One drachm of this oil, dissolved in three drachms of alcohol, forms the "essence of almonds" much used by confectioners, perfumers, etc. The oil is also much used by soap-makers.

Properties and Uses.—Triturated with water, sweet almonds produce a white mixture called *emulsion*, or *milk of almonds*, bearing a remarkable analogy with animal milk. It is used as a demulcent and vehicle for other medicines. The oil is demulcent in small quantity, in larger doses laxative. It is frequently employed in cough, diseases dependent upon intestinal irritation, and for mitigating acrimonious urine in calculous affections.

Dose.—Of the oil, a teaspoonful.

ALNUS RUBRA (TAG ALDER).

COMMON NAMES. *Common Alder, Smooth Alder.*

MEDICINAL PART. *The bark.*

Description.—This is a well-known shrub, growing in clumps, and forming thickets on the borders of ponds and rivers, and in swamps. The stems are numerous, and from six to fifteen feet high. The leaves are obovate, acuminate, smooth, and green, from two to four inches long.

History.—The Alnus Rubra is indigenous to Europe and America, and blossoms in March and April. The bark is the part used medicinally.

Properties and Uses.—The bark is universally acknowledged to be alterative and emetic, and is especially recommended for scrofula, secondary syphilis (inferior, however, to Rock Rose or Stillingia), and cutaneous diseases, of which there are many varieties, some of which have and some of which have not been classified. The active principle of *Alnus Rubra*, as prepared for practitioners, is called *Alnuin*, and is most excellent in cases of dyspepsia produced by inactivity of the gastric glands.

AMARANTH (AMARANTHUS HYPOCHONDRIASIS).

COMMON NAMES. *Prince's Feather, Red Cock's Comb, etc.*

MEDICINAL PART. *The leaves.*

Description.—This is an annual herb, with a stout upright stem, from from three to four feet high. The leaves are oblong, lanceolate, mucronate, green, with a red purplish spot, clustered flowers, five stamens.

History.—This plant is a native of the Middle States, where it is cultivated in gardens as an ornamental plant, but contains more medicinal virtues in its wild state. It flowers in August. The leaves impart their virtues to water.

Properties and Uses.—Amaranth is astringent. The decoction drank freely is a valuable domestic remedy for menorrhagia, diarrhœa, dysentery, and hemorrhage from the bowels. It is useful as a local application to ulcers of the mouth and throat, as an injection for leucorrhœa, and as a wash to foul, indolent ulcers.

Amaranth.

ANEMONE (ANEMONE NEMOROSA).

COMMON NAME. *Wind Flower.*

MEDICINAL PARTS. *Root, herb, and seed.*

Description.—This is a delicate and pretty plant, with a creeping root, simple erect stem, six to nine inches high, bearing but a single flower; leaves ternate; sepals, four to six; stamens and ovaries numerous.

History.—This plant is common to Europe and the United States, bearing purplish and white flowers in April and May. The *Meadow Anemone* of Europe is the most active in its medicinal qualities. Its active principle is called *Anemonine.* This plant affords the *Pulsatilla* of the *Homœopaths.*

Properties and Uses.—Anemone in solution has been applied externally to scald head, ulcers, syphilitic nodes, paralysis, cataract, and opacity of the cornea, with benefit. A decoction is sometimes used as an emmenagogue for secondary syphilis, whooping-cough, etc. The leaves, fresh and bruised, act as a rubefacient. Care should be taken in its internal administration, as it is acrid and poisonous.

A plant of the same family, *Anemone Cylindrica*, is used by the Indians for the cure of the rattle-snake bite. They chew some of the tops of the plant, swallowing but little of the saliva, then apply it to the bite; in a few minutes the bite is rendered harmless.

Dose.—Decoction, a tablespoonful; anemonine, one grain.

ANGELICA (Angelica Atropurpurea).

Common Name. *Masterwort.*

Medicinal Part. *Root, herb, and seed.*

Description.--This plant is five or six feet high. The root has a purple color; leaves ternate, with large petioles; calyx five-toothed, with equal petals, and the fruit a nut.

History.—The plant is perennial, and grows in fields and damp places, developing greenish-white flowers from May to August. The plant has a powerful, peculiar, but not unpleasant odor, a sweet taste, afterwards pungent; but in drying it loses much of these qualities.

Properties and Uses.—It is aromatic, stimulant, carminative, diaphoretic, expectorant, diuretic, and emmenagogue. It is used in flatulent colic and heart-burn. It is serviceable in diseases of the urinary organs The *A. Archangelica*, or *Archangel*, may be substituted for this.

Dose.—Decoction, two to four ounces; powder, thirty to sixty grains.

ANISE (Pimpinella Anisum).

Common Name. *Aniseed.*

Medicinal Part. *The fruit.*

Description. —Anise has a perennial, spindle-shaped, woody root, and a smooth, erect, branched stem, about ten or twelve inches in height. The leaves are petiolated, roundish, cordate, serrate; flowers small and white, disposed on long stalks. *Calyx* wanting, or minute. The fruit is ovate, about an eighth of an inch long, dull brown, and slightly downy.

History.—It is a native of Egypt, but now cultivated in many of the warm countries of Europe. The Spanish Aniseed is commonly used for medicinal purposes. The odor of anise is penetrating and fragrant, the taste aromatic and sweetish. It imparts its virtues wholly to alcohol, only partially to water. That used in cordials is the *Star Anise*, which is procured from the *Illicium Anisatum*, a plant of Eastern Asia. Its volatile oil is often fraudulently substituted for the European oil of anise.

Properties and Uses.—Stimulant and carminative; used in cases of flatulency, colic of infants, and to remove nausea. Sometimes added to other medicines to improve their flavor or to correct disagreeable effects.

Dose.—Of the seed, twenty to forty grains; essence, thirty drops to a teaspoonful.

ALOES (Aloe Spicata).

Medicinal Part. *The inspissated juice of the leaves.*

Description.—The spiked aloe is an inhabitant of the southern parts of Africa, growing in sandy soil. The stem is woody, round, and about four feet high, and from three to five inches in diameter. The leaves are thick and fleshy, with a few white spots. Spike a foot long; flowers scarlet, and filled with purplish honey. This tree furnishes the *Cape Aloes* of commerce. There are other varieties, the *A. Socotrina* and the *A. vulgaris.* The Socotrine aloes is an inhabitant of Socotra, and the Aloe Vulgaris is generally found in the East Indies and Barbary

History.—Aloes is of a deep brown or olive color; odor unpleasant, taste peculiar and bitter, powder a bright yellow. These properties change somewhat in the different varieties. It is almost completely dissolved in water.

Properties and Uses.—Aloes is tonic, purgative, emmenagogue, and anthelmintic. As a laxative its applications are limitless. It acts chiefly upon the rectum, causing heat and irritation about the anus; it is therefore improper, unless associated with other medicines, to give it to patients suffering with piles. It promotes the menstrual flow, but when used for this purpose it had better be combined with myrrh. Its chief use is as a purgative, and it should never be given in inflammatory affections, in gastritis or enteritis, or to females liable to sudden uterine evacuation, or during pregnancy.

Dose.—Two to ten grains in pill.

ASARABACCA (ASARUM EUROPÆUM).

COMMON NAMES. *Hazlewort, or Wild Nard.*

MEDICINAL PARTS. *Root and leaves.*

Description.—The stem of this plant is very short, simple round and herbaceous, bearing dark-green reniform leaves; also one drooping flower of purple color, without corolla. The fruit is a capsule.

History.—This is a European plant, growing in moist hilly woods, and flowers from May to August. The root, when dried, has a pepper-like odor, spicy taste, and yields an ash-colored powder; the leaves give a green powder, and have the same medicinal properties as of the root. They impart their virtues to water or alcohol.

Properties and Uses.—Emetic, cathartic, and errhine. Used principally as an errhine in certain affections of the brain, eyes, face, and throat, toothache, and paralysis of the mouth and tongue. It is used by drunkards in France to promote vomiting.

Dose.—Powder, 10 or 12 grains; as an emetic, from one-half to one drachm.

AYA-PANA (AYA-PANA EUPATORIUM).

MEDICINAL PARTS. *The whole plant.*

Description.—While traveling in Paraguay, South America, some years ago, I became acquainted with a species of *Eupatorium* or *Lungwort* called *Aya-pana*, possessed of most extraordinary virtues in consumption and other diseases of the chest. In Paraguay, which is a very paradise on earth, numerous medicinal herbs of exceeding great value grow to the greatest perfection. The *Aya-pana* belongs to the class of *Eupatorium Perfoliatum*, though quite unlike the *Lungwort* and *Thorough-wort*, indigenous to North America. The *Aya-pana* is only found on the eastern slope of the Andes, on the mountain sides, along the sunny banks of streams, and beautifully luxuriant on all the tributaries to the Amazon, and La Plata especially. It is a perennial plant, with numerous erect, round, hairy stems, five to ten feet high, the stalk plain below, but branching out in numerous stems near the top. The leaves grow on the opposite sides of the stalk in pairs, each pair being joined at the base. The direction of each pair of leaves is at right angles with that of the pair either above or beneath. The leaves are long and narrow, broadest at the base where they coalesce, gradually tapering to a serrated point, wrinkled, palish green on the under surface, and beset with white silken hairs, which add much effect to their greenish-gray color. The flowers are snow-white, slightly tinged with a purplish hue at the end, very numerous, supported on hairy peduncles. The calyx is cylindrical, and composed of imbricated, lanceolate, hairy scales, inclosing from twelve to fifteen tubular florets, having their border divided into five spreading segments. There are five black anthers united in a tube, through which a bifid filiform style projects above the flower, rendering the whole a beautiful and picturesque plant.

Aya-pana.

History.—It flowers constantly during the dry or sunny season, the blossoms and leaves being only used for medicinal purposes. The flowers are better than the leaves, have an aromatic odor, resembling slightly chamomile, and possess a strong bitter taste, somewhat like horehound or quassia, which virtue is imparted either to water or alcohol. Resin, gum, balsam, and mucilage are among the principal constituents of the flowers. The flowers are gathered in the morning on sunny days, carefully dried in the sun or by artificial heat, when they are put up in bags or cedar boxes, and become ready for medicinal use. Prepared in this way, the flowers and leaves retain their properties for years, improving in their virtues by age, adding to their rich honey-like yellow coloring matter when distilled for medical purposes.

Properties and Uses.– This plant may rightly be regarded as a specific in all forms of pulmonary and bronchial affections. It has also great influence over the valvular action of the heart, in its healthful invigoration of the arterial and venous systems, and its wonderful power in expelling carbonic acid from the air-cells and pulmonary vessels, prior to the elimination of rich vermilion blood through the great aorta of the human economy.

It is one of the ingredients of my "Acacian Balsam" (see page 470), which, with various other remarkable medicinal agents, forms one of the most wonderful remedies for coughs, colds, and consumption ever compounded. The plant is not much known in this country, and only imported by myself, and can consequently not be had in apothecaries'.

BALM (MELISSA OFFICINALIS).

MEDICINAL PART. *The herb.*

Description.—Balm is a perennial herb, with upright, branching, four-sided stems, from ten to twenty inches high. The leaves are broadly ovate, acute, and more or less hairy. The flowers are pale yellow, with ascending stamens.

History.—Balm is a native of France, but naturalized in England and the United States. It grows in fields, along road-sides, and is well known as a garden plant, flowering from May to August. The whole plant is officinal or medicinal, and should be collected previous to flowering. In a fresh state it has a lemon-like odor, which is nearly lost by drying. Its taste is aromatic, faintly astringent, with a degree of persistent bitterness. Boiling water extracts its virtues. Balm contains a bitter extractive substance, a little tannin, gum, and a peculiar volatile oil. A pound of the plant yields about four grains of the oil, which is of a yellowish or reddish-yellow color, very liquid, and possessing the fragrance of the plant in a high degree. The *Nepeta Citriodora*, a powerful emmenagogue, is sometimes cultivated and employed by mistake for Balm. It has the same odor, but may be distinguished by having both surfaces of the leaves hairy.

Properties and Uses.—It is moderately stimulant, diaphoretic, and antispasmodic. A warm infusion, drank freely, is very serviceable to produce sweating, or as a diaphoretic in fevers. It is also very useful in painful menstruation, and also to assist the courses of females. When given in fevers, it may be rendered more agreeable by the addition of lemon-juice. The infusion may be taken at pleasure.

BALMONY (CHELONE GLABRA).

COMMON NAMES. *Snake head, Turtle bloom, Salt rheum weed.*

MEDICINAL PART. *The leaves.*

Description.—This is a perennial, smooth, herbaceous plant, with a simple erect stem about two or three feet high. The leaves are opposite, sessile, oblong-lanceolate, acuminate, serrate, and of a dark shining green color. The fruit is a capsule.

History.—This valuable medical plant is found in the United States, in damp soils, flowering in August and September. The flowers are ornamental, and vary in color according to the variety of the plant. The leaves are exceedingly bitter, but inodorous, and impart their virtues to water and alcohol.

Properties and Uses.—It is tonic, cathartic, and anthelmintic; very valuable in jaundice, liver diseases, and for the removal of worms. In small doses it is a good tonic in dyspepsia, debility of the digestive organs, and during convalescence from febrile and inflammatory diseases. An ointment made from the fresh leaves is valuable for piles, inflamed breasts, tumors, and painful ulcers.

Dose.—Of the powdered leaves, one drachm; of the tincture, one or two teaspoonsful; of the active principle, *Chelonin*, one or two grains.

BARBERRY (Berberis Vulgaris).

Medicinal Part. *Bark and berries.*

Description.—Barberry is an erect, deciduous shrub, from three to eight feet high, with leaves of an obovate-oval form, terminated by soft bristles, about two inches long, and one-third as wide. The flowers are small and yellow, in clusters, and the fruit bright-red oblong berries, in branches, and very acid.

History.—This shrub is found in the New England States, on the mountains of Pennsylvania and Virginia, among rocks and hard gravelly soil. Occasionally it is found in the West on rich grounds. It flowers in April and May, and ripens its fruit in June. Its active principle is *Berberina.*

Properties and Uses.—It is tonic and laxative, indicated in jaundice, chronic diarrhœa, and dysentery. The berries form an agreeable acidulous draught, useful as a refrigerant in fevers; the bark is bitter and astringent, and used in the treatment of jaundice. The bark of the root is the most active; a teaspoonful of the powder will act as a purgative. A decoction of the bark or berries will be found of service as a wash or gargle in aphthous sore mouth and chronic ophthalmia.

BAYBERRY (Myrica Cerifera).

Common Name. *Wax Myrtle.*

Medicinal Part. *The bark of the root.*

Description.—This shrub is branching and partially evergreen, and varies in height from two to a dozen feet. The flowers appear in May, before the leaves are fully expanded. The fruits are small and globular, resembling berries, which are at first green, but become nearly white. They consist of a hard stone, inclosing a two-lobed and two-seeded kernel. On the outside of the stone are gunpowder-like grains, and over these is a crust of dry greenish-white wax.

Bayberry.

History.—Bayberry is found in woods and fields, from Canada to Florida. The bark of the root is the officinal part, but the wax is also used. Water must be employed to extract the astringent principles of the root-bark, alcohol to extract its stimulating virtues. The period at which the root should be collected is the latter part of fall. Cleanse it thoroughly, and while fresh separate the bark with a hammer or club. Dry the bark thoroughly and keep it in a dry place; then pulverize, and keep the powder in dark and sealed vessels. In order to obtain the wax, boil the berries in water; the wax will soon float on the surface, and may be removed when it becomes cold and hardened.

Properties and Uses.—The bark has been successfully used in scrofula, jaundice, diarrhœa, dysentery, and in other cases where astringent stimulants were indicated. Powdered, it has been employed as a snuff, with curative effect, in catarrh of the head and nasal polypus. It is sometimes applied, in poultice form, to old ulcers, sores, tumors, etc.; but is better for these when combined with Bloodroot. The wax possesses mild astringent with narcotic properties. The real properties of Bayberry bark are found in a preparation called *Myricin*, which is a stimulant and astringent, and can be employed to the best advantage in dysentery with typhoid symptoms, chronic diarrhœa, scrofula, and follicular stomatitis. Its greatest and most salutary influence is exerted over a diseased condition of the mucous surface. Myricin should be administered internally by the advice of a physician acquainted with its virtues. It may be applied externally to sores, ulcers, etc., by anybody; but its immediate effects must be neutralized by a poultice of slippery elm.

BEARBERRY (ARCTOSTAPHYLOS UVA-URSI).

COMMON NAME. *The Upland Cranberry.*

MEDICINAL PART. *The Leaves.*

Description.—Bearberry is a small, perennial shrub, having a long fibrous root. The stems are woody and trailing; bark smooth. The leaves are alternate, evergreen, obovate, acute, and have short petioles The fruit is a small, scarlet-colored drupaceous berry.

History.—This plant is a perennial evergreen, common in the northern part of Europe and America. It grows on dry, sterile, sandy soils, and gravelly ridges. The berries ripen in winter, although the flowers appear from June to September. The green leaves, picked from the stems in the fall and dried in a moderate heat, are the parts used. These leaves are odorless until reduced to powder, when the odor emitted is like that of dried grass. The powder is of a light brown color, tinged with a yellowish green. The taste is astringent and bitterish. The properties of the leaves are extracted by alcohol or water. A preparation called *Ursin* is made from them.

Properties and Uses.—Uva Ursi is especially astringent and tonic, depending upon these qualities for the most of its good effects. It is particularly useful in chronic diarrhœa, dysentery, profuse menstruation, piles, diabetes, and other similar complaints. It possesses rare curative principles when administered for diseases of the urinary organs, more especially in chronic affections of the kidneys, mucous discharges from the bladder, inflammation of the latter organ, and all derangements of the water-passages. It is also a valuable assistant in the cure of gonorrhœa of long standing, whites, ulceration of the *cervix uteri* (or neck of the womb), pain in the vesical region, etc. Many physicians now rely upon it as the basis of their remedy for gonorrhœa which is accompanied by mucous discharges, and for all kindred afflictions. Its tannic acid gives it great power in rectifying and extirpating the obstinate and disagreeable complaints we have mentioned.

Dose.—The dose of the powder is ten to forty grains; of the decoction, one to two fluid ounces—(to make this, boil a pint and a half of pure water, containing one ounce of uva ursi, down to a pint); of the extract, five to ten grains.

BEARS BED (POLYTRICHIUM JUNIPERUM).

COMMON NAMES. *Hair-cap Moss, Robin's Rye, Ground Moss.*

MEDICINAL PART. *The whole plant.*

Description.—This is an indigenous plant, having a perennial stem, slender, of a reddish color, and from four to seven inches high; leaves lanceolate, and somewhat spreading. The fruit a four-sided oblong capsule.

History.—This evergreen plant is found in high, dry places, along the margins of dry woods, mostly on poor sandy soil. It is of darker green color than the mosses in general. It yields its virtues to boiling water.

Properties and Uses.—This plant is not much known as a remedial agent, but is nevertheless a valuable remedy. It is a powerful diuretic, and very serviceable in dropsy. It is very useful in gravel and urinary obstructions. It causes no nausea or disagreeable sensations in the stomach, and may be used with the hydragogue cathartics with decided advantage in dropsical affections.

BEAD TREE (MELIA AZEDARACH).

COMMON NAME. *Pride of China.*

MEDICINAL PART. *The bark of the root.*

Description.—This is an elegant tree, which attains the height of thirty or forty feet, with a trunk about a foot and a half in diameter. The bark is rough; leaves bipinnate; flowers lilac color; calyx five-parted; corolla has five petals; stamens deep violet; anthers yellow. The fruit is a five-celled bony nut.

History.—It is a native of China, but cultivated in the warm climates of Europe and America. It does not grow to any extent north of Virginia, and flowers early in the spring. Its name of *Bead Tree* is derived from the use to which its hard nuts are put in Roman Catholic countries, viz., for making rosaries. The recent bark of the root is the most active part for medicinal purposes. It has a disagreeably bitter taste and a very unpleasant odor, and imparts its properties to boiling water.

Properties and Uses.—The bark is anthelmintic, and in large doses narcotic and emetic. It is useful in worm fevers and in infantile remittents, in which, although worms are absent, yet the symptoms are similar to those accompanying the presence of worms.

The fruit is somewhat saccharine, and is an excellent remedy to expel worms. Its pulp is used as an ointment for destroying lice and other ectozoa, as well as in treatment of scald head and other diseases of the skin. The oil of the nuts is useful as a local application in rheumatism, cramps, obstinate ulcers, etc.

Dose.—Of the powdered bark, twenty grains; of the decoction (which is the best form for administration—two ounces of the bark to a pint of water, and boiled down to a half a pint), a tablespoonful every one, two, or three hours, till the desired effect is obtained. A purgative should follow its employment.—See "*Renovating Pill*," page 473.

BELLADONNA (ATROPA BELLADONNA).

COMMON NAMES. *Deadly Night-shade, Dwale, Black Cherry, etc.*

MEDICINAL PART. *The leaves.*

Description.—This perennial herb has a thick, fleshy, creeping root, and an annual erect leafy stem about three feet high. Leaves ovate, acute, entire, on short petioles, and of a dull green color. The flowers are dark purple, and fruit a many-seeded berry.

History.—This plant is common to Europe, growing among ruins and waste places, blossoming from May to August, and maturing its fruit in September. The leaves should be gathered while the plant is in flower. They yield their virtues to water and alcohol.

Belladonna.

Properties and Uses. — Belladonna is an energetic narcotic. It is anodyne, antispasmodic, calmative, and relaxant; exceedingly valuable in all convulsive diseases. It is much used as a preventive of scarlatina, and as a cure for whooping-cough. It dilates the pupil of the eyes very measurably, and they should always be watched whenever the plant is administered. In the hands of the educated herbal physician it is a very useful remedy; but I caution my readers not to use it in domestic practice.

BETH-ROOT (TRILLIUM PENDULUM).

COMMON NAMES. *Wake Robin, Indian Balm, Ground Lily, etc.*

MEDICINAL PART. *The root.*

Description.—This is an herbaceous, perennial plant, having an oblong tuberous root, from which arises a slender stem from ten to fifteen inches high. The leaves are three in number, acuminate, from three to five inches in diameter, with a very short petiole. The flowers are white, sepals green, petals ovate and acute, styles erect, and stigmas recurved.

History.—This plant is common in the Middle and Western States, growing in rich soils and shady woods, flowering in May and June. There are many varieties, all possessing analogous medicinal properties. These plants may be generally known by their three net-veined leaves, and their solitary terminal flower, which varies in color in the different species, being whitish-yellow and reddish-white. The roots have a faint turpentine odor, and a peculiar aromatic and sweetish taste. When chewed they impart an acid astringent impression to the mouth, causing a flow of saliva and a sensation of heat in the throat and fauces. *Trilline* is its active principle.

Properties and Uses.—It is astringent, tonic, and antiseptic, and is successfully employed in bleeding from the lungs, kidneys, and womb, excessive menstruation, and likewise in leucorrhœa or whites, and cough, asthma, and difficult breathing. Boiled in milk, it is of eminent benefit in diarrhœa and dysentery. The root made into a poultice is very useful in tumors, indolent and offensive ulcers, stings of insects, and to restrain gangrene; and the leaves boiled in lard are a good application to ulcers, tumors, etc. The red Beth-root will check ordinary epistaxis, or bleeding of the nose. The leaves boiled in lard is a good external application in ulcers and tumors. A strong infusion of powdered Beth-root, of from two to four tablespoonfuls, is the most pleasant form of administration of this valuable remedy.

Dose of the powdered root is one drachm, to be given in hot water; of the infusion, two to four ounces.

BIRDS' NEST (MONOTROPA UNIFLORA).

COMMON NAMES. *Ice Plant, Fit Plant, Ova-ova, Indian Pipe.*

MEDICINAL PART. *The root.*

Description.—This plant has a dark-colored, fibrous, perennial root, matted in masses like a chestnut vine, from which arise one or more short ivory-white stems, four to eight inches high, adorned with white, sessile, lanceolate leaves.

History.—This singular plant is found from Maine to Carolina, and westward to Missouri, growing in shady, solitary places, in rich moist soil, or soil composed of decayed wood and leaves. The whole plant is ivory-white, resembling frozen jelly, and when handled melts away like ice. It flowers from June to September. It is evidently a parasite of the roots at the base of trees.

Properties and Uses.—It is tonic, sedative, and antispasmodic. It is useful in fevers, and employed in instances of restlessness, pains, nervous irritability, etc., in place of opium. It cures remittent and intermittent fevers, and may be employed instead of quinine. Prompt success has followed its use in convulsive diseases. The juice of the plant mixed with rose-water forms an excellent application to sore eyes, or as an injection in gonorrhœa. It is very singular that people will use injurious drugs, or permit themselves to take them, when in this queer little herb that grows all around them, and which by its singular character invites attention to it, they can find a sovereign remedy for numberless ills.

Dose.—Of the powdered root, half a drachm to a drachm, two or three times a day.

BITTER ROOT (APOCYNUM ANDROSÆMIFOLIUM).

COMMON NAMES. *Dog's-bane, Milk-weed, etc.*

MEDICINAL PART. *The root.*

Description.—This is a smooth, elegant plant, five or six feet high, with a large perennial root. The leaves are dark-green above, pale beneath, ovate, and about two or three inches long and an inch wide. Corolla white, calyx five-cleft, and stamens five. Fruit a follicle. Every part of the plant is milky.

History.—This plant is indigenous to the United States, growing in dry, sandy soils, and in the borders of woods, from Maine to Florida.

flowering from May to August. When any part of the plant is wounded a milky juice exudes. The large, milky root is the part used for medicinal purposes. It possesses an unpleasant amarous taste. It yields its properties to alcohol, but especially to water. Age impairs its medicinal quality.

Properties and Uses.—Emetic, diaphoretic, tonic, and laxative. It is very valuable in all liver or chronic hepatic affections. In conjunction with *Menispermin*, it is excellent in dyspepsia and amenorrhœa. When it is required to promptly empty the stomach, without causing much nausea or a relaxed condition of the muscular system, the powdered root may be given in two or three scruple doses; but much prostration is apt to ensue. As a laxative it is useful in constipation. As a tonic, ten or twenty grains may be given to stimulate the digestive apparatus, and thus effect a corresponding impression on the general system. It is also useful as an alterative in rheumatism, scrofula, and syphilis.

BITTER-SWEET (AMARA DULCIS, SOLANUM DULCAMARA).

COMMON NAMES. *Mortal, Woody Nightshade, Felon Wort, etc.*

MEDICINAL PART. *Bark of root and twigs.*

Description.—Bitter-Sweet is a woody vine, with a shrubby stem several feet in length, having an ashy green bark. Leaves acute, and generally smooth, lower one cordate, upper ones hastate. The flowers are purple, and the fruit a scarlet, juicy and bitter berry, which, however, should not be eaten or used.

Bitter-Sweet.

History.—Bitter-Sweet is common to both Europe and America, growing in moist banks, around dwellings, and in low damp grounds, about hedges and thickets, and flowering in June and July. The berries ripen in autumn, and hang upon the vines for several months. After the foliage has fallen the twigs should be gathered. Boiling water and dilute alcohol extract their virtues.

Properties and Uses.—It is a mild narcotic, diuretic, alterative, diaphoretic, and discutient. It is serviceable in cutaneous diseases, syphilitic diseases, rheumatic and cachectic affections, ill-conditioned ulcers, scrofula, indurations, sores, glandular swellings, etc. In obstructed menstruation it serves a good purpose.

It is of incalculable benefit in leprosy, tetter, and all skin diseases. It excites the venereal functions, and is in fact capable of wide application and use. I regard this plant as important as any in the herbal kingdom, and too little justice is done to it by those under whose care the sick are entrusted. It receives but half the homage that is due to it.

The world knows the virtues of my "Herbal Ointment" (see page 472), and which is in great measure due to Bitter-Sweet, as it is one of the ingredients.

Dose.—Of the decoction, one or two fluid ounces; extract, two to five grains; powdered leaves, ten to thirty grains.

BLUE FLAG (IRIS VERSICOLOR).

MEDICINAL PART. *The rhizome.*

Description.—Blue Flag is an indigenous plant, with a fleshy, fibrous rhizome. The stem is two or three feet in height, round on one side, acute on the other, and frequently branched. The leaves are ensiform, about a foot long, half an inch to an inch wide. The fruit a three-celled capsule.

History.—Blue Flag is common throughout the United States, growing in moist places, and bearing blue or purple flowers from May to July. The root has a peculiar odor, augmented by rubbing or pulverizing, and a disagreeable taste. It imparts its virtues to boiling water, alcohol, or ether. The root should be sliced transversely, dried, and placed in dark vessels, well closed, and placed in a dark place; it will then preserve its virtues for a long time. The *oleo-resin* obtained from it is called Iridin, its active principle.

Properties and Uses.—This is one among our most valuable medicinal plants, capable of extensive use. It is alterative, cathartic, sialogogue, vermifuge, and diuretic. In scrofula and syphilis it acts as a powerful and efficient agent, and I employ it in my special treatment of chronic diseases extensively and successfully. It is useful in chronic hepatic, renal, and splenitic affections, but had best be combined with mandrake, poke, black cohosh, etc. It will sometimes salivate, but it need cause no apprehension; and when this effect is established, it may be distinguished from mercurial salivation by absence of stench, sponginess of the gums, and loosening of the teeth.

Dose.—Powdered root, five to ten grains; Iridin, one grain.

BLUE VERVAIN (VERBENA HASTATA).

COMMON NAMES. *Wild Hyssop, Simpler's Joy.*

MEDICINAL PART. *The root and herb.*

Description.—Vervain is an erect, tall, elegant, and perennial plant, with a four-angled stem three or four feet high, having opposite branches. The leaves are petiolate, serrate, acuminate, and hastate. The flower is a small purplish blue one, sessile, and arranged in long spikes. Seeds, four.

Blue Vervain.

History.— Vervain is indigenous to the United States, and grows along roadsides, and in dry, grassy fields, flowering from June to September. It is also found in England, growing among hedges, by the way-side, and other waste grounds, flowering in July, and the seeds ripening soon after.

Properties and Uses.— Vervain is tonic, expectorant, sudorific, and antispasmodic. It is serviceable in mismenstruation. It is an antidote to poke-poisoning. It expels worms, and is a capital agent for the cure of all diseases of the spleen and liver. If given in intermittent fever, in a warm infusion or powder, it never fails to effect a cure. In all cases of cold and obstinate menstruation it is a most complete and advantageous sudorific. When the circulation of the blood is weak and languid, it will increase it and restore it to its proper operation. The infusion, taken cold, forms a good tonic in cases of constitutional debility, and during convalescence from acute diseases. Its value has been found to be great in scrofula, visceral obstructions, and stone and gravel. It will correct diseases of the stomach, help coughs, wheezing, and shortness of breath, etc., but its virtues are more wonderful still in the effect they produce upon epilepsy, or falling sickness, and fits.

This great—very great—medicinal value of this plant was brought to my attention by an accidental knowledge of the good it had effected in a long-standing case of epilepsy. Its effects in that case were of the most remarkable character, and I was, therefore, led to study most carefully and minutely its medicinal peculiarities. I found, after close investigation and elaborate experiment, that, prepared in a certain way, and compounded with boneset, water-pepper, chamomile blossoms, and the best of whiskey, it has no equal for the cure of fits, or falling sickness, or anything like fits; also for indigestion, dyspepsia, and liver complaints of every grade. A more valuable plant is not found within the whole range of the herbal pharmacopœia. See "*Restorative Assimilant*," page 469.

The following application is singularly effective in promoting the absorption of the blood, effusion in bruises, and allaying the attendant pain: Take of Vervain, Senna, and White Pepper, of each equal parts make a cataplasm or plaster by mixing with white of eggs.

It is also most valuable as a cure for diarrhœa, stomachic and enteric pains, bowel complaints, and a superexcellent tonic.

I first brought the notice of physicians to this plant about twelve years ago, previous to which it was unknown as a remedy, but which is now used by very many physicians, whose reports of its virtues in various medical journals, published works, and to me by correspondence, are as flattering as my own.

Dose.—Of the powdered root, from one to two scruples; the dose of the infusion is from two to four wine-glassfuls three or four times a day, if an emetic is desired.

BLACK COHOSH (CIMICIFUGA RACEMOSA).

COMMON NAMES. *Rattleroot, Squaw Root, Black Snake Root.*

MEDICINAL PART. *The root.*

Description.—This plant is a tall, leafy perennial herb, with a large knotty root, having long slender fibres. The stem is simple, smooth, and furrowed, and from three to nine feet high. The flower is a small and fetid one.

Black Cohosh.

History.—It is a native of the United States, inhabiting upland woods and hillsides, and flowering from May to August. The root is the medicinal part. It contains a resin, to which the names of *Cimicifugin* or *Macrotin* have been given; likewise fatty substances, starch, gum, tannic acid, etc. The leaves of *Cimicifuga* are said to drive away bugs; hence its name from *cimex*, a bug, and *fugo*, to drive away.

Boiling water takes up the properties of the root but partially, alcohol wholly.

Properties and Uses.—It is a very active and useful remedy in many diseases. It is slightly narcotic, sedative, antispasmodic, and exerts a marked influence over the nervous system. It is successfully used in cholera, periodical convulsions, fits, epilepsy, nervous excitability, asthma, delirium tremens, and many spasmodic affections, and in consumption, cough, acute rheumatism, neuralgia, and scrofula. Also, very valuable in amenorrhœa, dysmenorrhœa, and other menstrual and uterine affections, leucorrhœa, etc. The saturated tincture of the root is a valuable embrocation in all cases of inflammation of the nerves, tic douloureux, *crick* in the back or sides, rheumatism, old ulcers, etc. It has an especial affinity for the uterus, and as it reduces very materially the arterial action, it is, hence, very useful in palpitation of the heart, and cardiac affections generally.

It exerts a tonic influence over mucous and serous tissues, and is a superior remedy in a variety of chronic diseases. In my special practice I use it largely, and its use, in conjunction with other indicated remedies, has afforded me flattering success in many chronic affections.

Dose.—Fluid extract, half a drachm to two drachms; solid extract, four to eight grains; of the tincture the dose is from one to three teaspoonsful; of *Cimicifugin* the dose is from one to six grains.

BLAZING STAR (LIATRIS SQUARROSA).

COMMON NAMES. *Gay Feather, Devil's Bit, etc.*

MEDICINAL PART. *The root.*

Description.—There are three varieties of this plant used in medicine. The above is the most common one. It has a tuberous root, and an erect annual stem from two to five feet high, linear leaves, and flowers sessile, and of bright purple color.

Liatris Spicata, or *Button Snake Root*, is very similar to the above.

Liatris Scariosa, or *Gay Feather*, has a perennial tuberous root, with a stout stem from four to five feet high. The leaves are numerous and lanceolate, lower one on long petioles.

History.—The two former are natives of the Middle and Southern States, and the latter is found from New England to Wisconsin. These splendid natives flower from August to September. The roots have a hot bitter taste and an agreeable turpentine odor. The virtues are extracted by alcohol.

Properties and Uses.—These plants are diuretic, tonic, stimulant, and emmenagogue. The decoction is very useful in gonorrhœa, gleet, and kidney diseases. It is also of service in uterine diseases. As a gargle in sore throat it is of great advantage. These plants are used for, and said to have antidotal powers over snake-bites.

BONESET (EUPATORIUM PERFOLIATUM).

COMMON NAME. *Thoroughwort.*

MEDICINAL PARTS. *The tops and leaves.*

Description.—Boneset is an indigenous perennial herb, with a horizontal crooked root; the stems being round, stout, rough and hairy, from one to five feet high, and the leaves veiny, serrate, rough, and tapering to a long point. The flowers are white and very numerous.

History.—Boneset grows in low grounds, on the borders of swamps and streams, throughout the United States, flowering in August and September. Alcohol or boiling water extracts the virtues of the parts used. It has a feeble odor, but a very bitter taste. It contains tannin and the extractive salts of potassa. It is called Boneset on account that it was formerly supposed to cause rapid union of broken bones.

Boneset.

Properties and Uses.—It is a very valuable medicinal agent. The cold infusion or extract is tonic and aperient, the warm infusion diaphoretic and emetic. As a tonic it is very useful in remittent, intermittent, and typhoid fevers, dyspepsia, and general debility. In intermittent fever a stong infusion, as hot as can be comfortably swallowed, is administered for the purpose of vomiting freely. This is also attended with profuse diaphoresis, and, sooner or later, by an evacuation of the bowels. During the intermission the cold infusion or extract is given every hour as a tonic and antiperiodic. In epidemic influenza the warm infusion is valuable as an emetic and diaphoretic, likewise in febrile diseases, catarrh, colds, and wherever such effects are indicated. The warm infusion is also administered to promote the operation of other emetics. *Externally*, used alone or in combination with hops or tansy, etc., a fomentation of the leaves applied to the bowels is very useful in inflammation, spasms, and painful affections.

Boneset is one of the ingredients of my "Restorative Assimilant," and is certainly an excellent adjuvant to the Blue Vervain. (See page 469.)

Dose.—Of the powder, from ten to twenty grains; of the extract, from two to four grains; of the infusion, from two to four wineglassfuls.

BLACK ROOT (LEPTANDRIA VIRGINICA).

COMMON NAMES. *Culver's Physic, Tall Speedwell.*

MEDICINAL PART. *The root.*

Description.—It is perennial, with a simple, straight, smooth, herbaceous stem, and grows from three to four or five feet in height. The leaves are short petioled, whorled in fours to sevens, lanceolate, acuminate, and finely serrated. The flowers are white, nearly sessile, and very numerous. Calyx four-parted, corolla small and nearly white; stamens, two. The fruit is a many-seeded capsule.

History.—This plant is indigenous to the United States, but is to be found in good condition only in limestone countries. It is often discovered in new soil, in moist woods, in swamps, etc., but its medicinal virtues are feeble, excepting when it is found where there is limestone. The root is the part used. It is perennial, irregular, horizontal, woody, and about as thick as the forefinger. It is gathered in the fall of the second year. The fresh root should never be used, as it is very violent and uncertain in its operations. The dried root, after having been properly prepared, is what may be relied upon for beneficial effects. *Leptandrin* is its active principle.

Properties and Uses.—The fresh root is too irritant to be used, although a decoction of it may, with care, be used in intermittent fever. The dried root is laxative, cholagogue, and tonic, and very much used in chronic hepatic diseases. It is an excellent laxative in febrile diseases, and peculiarly applicable in bilious and typhoid fevers. As a laxative and tonic it is very useful in dyspepsia, especially when associated with torpidity of the liver. In diarrhœa and dysentery, as a cathartic it frequently effects a cure in one active dose. This admirable remedy is one of the ingredients of my "Renovating Pill," see page 473.

Dose.—Powdered root, twenty to sixty grains; infusion, half an ounce; leptandrin, one-fourth grain to a grain.

BLOODROOT (SANGUINARIA CANADENSIS).

Bloodroot.

COMMON NAME. *Red Puccoon.*

MEDICINAL PART. *The root.*

Description.—Bloodroot is a smooth, herbaceous, perennial plant, with a fibrous root, which when cut or bruised emits an orange-colored juice. From each bud of the root stalk there springs a single leaf about six inches high, and which is cordate and reniform. The flower is white, stamens short, and anthers yellow. The fruit is a two-valved capsule.

History.—Bloodroot grows throughout the United States, in shaded woods and thickets, and rich soils generally, and flowers from March to June. Although the whole plant is medicinal, the root is the part chiefly used. The fresh root is fleshy, round, and from one to four inches in length, and as thick as the fingers. It presents a beautiful appearance when cut and placed under a microscope, seeming like an aggregation of minute precious stones. The dried root is dark brown outside, bright yellow inside; has a faint virose odor, and a bitter and acrid taste. It may be readily reduced to powder. Its active properties are taken up by boiling water or by alcohol. Age and moisture impair the qualities of the root, and it is of the utmost consequence to get that which has been properly gathered, and not kept too long. It yields several principles, among which are sanguinaria, puccine, chelidonic acid, a yellowish fixed oil, lignin, and gum.

Properties and Uses.—The actions of Bloodroot vary according to administration. In small doses it stimulates the digestive organs, acting as a stimulant and tonic. In large doses it is an arterial sedative. It is useful in bronchitis, laryngitis, whooping-cough, and other affections of the respiratory organs. It excites the energies of a torpid liver, and has proved beneficial in scrofula, amenorrhœa, and dysentery. Applied to fungous growths, ulcers, fleshy excrescences, cancerous affections, the powder acts as an escharotic, and the infusion is often applied with benefit to skin diseases.

Dose.—Of the powder as an emetic, ten to twenty grains; as a stimulant and expectorant, three to five grains; as an alterative, half a grain to two grains. Tincture, twenty to sixty drops.

BOX (BUXUS SEMPERVIRENS).

MEDICINAL PART. *The leaves.*

Description.—Box is a small, dense-leaved, hard-wood evergreen tree. The leaves are ovate, deep shining green, becoming red in autumn; flowers pale yellow; and the fruit a six-seeded globular capsule.

History.—The box tree is a native of the west of Asia, but grows on dry hills and sandy elevations generally in Europe, and but rarely on similar soil in America. A preparation called *Buxina* is obtained from the powdered bark, but the leaves are the parts mainly used in medical practice. They readily impart their virtues to alcohol or water.

Properties and Uses.—It is cathartic, sudorific, and alterative. The preparations of the leaves are excellent for the expulsion of worms, for purging the bowels, and regulating the action of the liver; for breaking fevers, and for purifying the blood and glandular secretions. In syrup it is very valuable as a cure for all diseases of a syphilitic character, and may be used alone to great advantage, where the compound syrup of stillingia cannot be obtained. The stillingia is preferable if it is at all to be had. The dose of a strong decoction, or syrup, of box, is half a fluid ounce, three times a day. In very severe cases the dose may be increased to a fluid ounce; but this should not be undertaken excepting by the advice of a physician. When intestinal worms are to be destroyed or expelled, the powdered leaves are usually administered in, to children, doses of five grains; to adults, in doses of from ten to fifteen grains. It possesses antispasmodic qualities, and has been given with good effect in hysteria, epilepsy, chorea (St. Vitus' Dance), etc. Chips of the wood (decoction) are useful in chronic rheumatism. The chief value of the *Buxus Sempervirens*, however, centres in its antisyphilitic virtues. I combine it with corydalis (Turkey pea) and the compound syrup of stillingia, in such a manner that it will *surely* cure syphilis in the first, second, or third stage; also certain forms of scrofula and scurvy. In other diseases it is no better than many other plants mentioned in this book.

The reader will do well to remember that the common garden box possesses the medical qualities of the *Buxus Sempervirens* to a feeble extent only. The powerful antisyphilitic virtues of which I have spoken can be procured only from the leaves of the tree reared in Asia, the influences of that climate being requisite to perfect them.

BUCHU (BAROSMA CRENATA).

MEDICINAL PART. *The leaves.*

Description.—This plant has a slender, smooth, upright, perennial stem, between two and three feet high. The leaves are opposite, flat, about an inch long, ovate or obovate, acute, serrated, and dotted. The flowers are pink, and fruit an ovate capsule.

History.—The Buchu plant is a native of Southern Africa. It does not grow very prolifically. There are two other varieties from which the leaves are taken, and which are of equal value with the *Barosma Crenata.* The leaves are the parts which are termed official. The Hottentots gather these leaves (which emit a sort of minty odor) and powder them. "The powder," says a traveler, "they have named *Booko*, and they use it for *anointing* their bodies." They also distil the leaves, and obtain from them a strong spirituous liquor somewhat resembling pale brandy, which they not only use for convivial purposes, but for the cure of various diseases, particularly those which are located in the stomach, bladder, bowels, and kidneys. A decoction of the leaves is systematically applied by them, with success, we are told, to wounds; but this is an assertion of which we have no direct proof. As we get them, the leaves are nearly, or quite, an inch in length, and from a sixth to half an inch in width, elliptical, lanceolate, slightly acute, or shorter and obtuse; their margin is serrated and glandular, upper surface smooth, and of a clear shining green, the under surface paler, with scattered oil points. They taste and smell like pennyroyal; but are neither heating nor bitter when chewed. They have to be kept very carefully, if their odor and virtues are desired to be thoroughly preserved for any reasonable length of time. The leaves of all the varieties are somewhat similar, and possess about the same qualities. They yield their volatile oil and extractive (upon which their virtues are mainly dependent) to alcohol or water

Properties and Uses.—Buchu is aromatic and stimulant, diuretic and diaphoretic. It is employed in dyspepsia with a palliative effect, but is chiefly administered in chronic inflammation of the bladder, irritation of the membrane of the urethra, uric acid gravel, diabetes in its first stage, and in incontinence of urine. It is recommended, without good reason, for cutaneous and rheumatic affections. I have no doubt Buchu is of some importance in chronic diseases of the urino-genital organs, for I have tried it; but I am sure that we have many native remedies which are altogether superior, and which are neglected only because the public is so familiar with them that they do not care to give them a fair trial.

Dose.—Of the powder, twenty to thirty grains; infusion, two to four ounces; tincture, one or two drachms; fl. extract, thirty to sixty drops.

BURNING BUSH (EUONYMUS ATROPURPUREUS).

COMMON NAMES. *Wahoo, Spindle Tree, etc.*

MEDICINAL PART. *The bark of the root.*

Description.—Wahoo is a small shrub or bush, with smooth branches, and from five to ten feet high. The leaves are from two to five inches in length, lanceolate, acute, and finely serrate. Flowers dark purple, and the fruit a crimson, five-celled capsule. There is another variety known as *Euonymus Americanus*, which is equally useful medicinally, and this and the foregoing are both known by the name of *Wahoo* better than by any other title.

History.—These plants grow in many sections of the United States, in woods and thickets, and in river bottoms, flowering in June. The bark of the root has a bitter and unpleasant taste in its natural shape, and yields its qualities to water and alcohol. The active principle is *Euonymin.*

Properties and Uses.—It is tonic, laxative, alterative, diuretic, and expectorant. It is serviceable in dyspepsia, torpid liver, constipation, dropsy, and pulmonary diseases. In intermittents it serves a good purpose.

Dose. Of the powder, twenty to thirty grains; tincture, one to four drachms; Euonymin, one-eighth to half a grain.

BUTTER WEED (ERIGERON CANADENSE).

COMMON NAMES. *Colt's Tail, Pride Weed, Horse Weed, Canada Flea Bane.*

MEDICINAL PART. *The whole plant.*

Description.—This is an indigenous, annual herb, with a high bristly, hairy stem, from six inches to nine feet high. The leaves are lanceolate; flowers small, white, and very numerous.

History.—Butterweed is common to the Northern and Middle States, grows in fields and meadows, by road-sides, and flowers from June to September. It should be gathered when in bloom, and carefully dried. It has a feeble odor, somewhat astringent taste, and yields its virtues to alcohol or water.

Properties and Uses.—It is tonic, diuretic, and astringent. It is useful in gravel, diabetes, dropsy, and in many kidney diseases. It can also be employed in diarrhœa, dysentery, etc. The volatile oil may be used instead of the infusion.

Dose.—Of the powder, half a drachm; infusion, two to four ounces; fl. extract, teaspoonful; oil, from four to six drops on sugar.

CAHINCA (Chiococca Racemosa).

Common Name. *Snow Berry.*

Medicinal Part. *The bark of the root.*

Description.—This is a climbing shrub, with a round branched root, and a stem from eight to twelve feet high. The leaves are ovate and smooth; flowers white and odorless, and become yellow and redolent; calyx, five-cleft; corolla, funnel-shaped; stamens, five. The fruit is a small white berry.

History.—This plant is a native of the West Indies, Florida, and South America. The root has a coffee-like taste, of a reddish-brown color, and a disagreeable odor. It affords the *Cahincic Acid*, its most important medicinal agent.

Properties and Uses.—In medium doses it aids the urinary discharge, increases the action of the heart, and promotes perspiration. It has been found efficient in amenorrhœa, rheumatism, syphilis, etc., and is used in Brazil as an antidote to snake-bites.

Dose.—Of the powder, from twenty to sixty grains.

CALICO BUSH (Kalmia Latifolia).

Common Names. *Sheep Laurel, Spoonwood, Mountain Laurel, Lamb-kill.*

Medicinal Part. *The leaves.*

Description.—This handsome plant is a shrub from four to eight feet high, with crooked stems and a rough bark. The leaves are evergreen, ovate, lanceolate, acute at each end, on long petioles, and from two to three inches long. The flowers are white and numerous. The fruit is a dry capsule.

History.—Sheep Laurel inhabits the rocky hills and elevated grounds of most parts of the United States. Its beautiful flowers appear in June and July. The leaves are reputed to be poisonous to sheep and other animals, and it is said that birds which have eaten them will poison those who eat the birds. The leaves are the officinal part. Attention was called to their medicinal virtues by the use which the Indians make of them, viz., a decoction by which they commit suicide.

Properties and Uses.—The plant, in medicinal doses, is antisyphilitic, sedative to the heart, and somewhat astringent. It is a most efficient agent in syphilis, fevers, jaundice, neuralgia, and inflammation. The preparation should be used with great care and prudence. In cases of poisoning with this plant, either man or beast, whiskey is the best antidote. Externally, stewed with lard, it is serviceable as an ointment for various skin diseases.

Dose.—The saturated tincture of the leaves is the best form of administration. It is given in from ten to twenty drops every two or three hours. Powdered leaves, from ten to twenty grains.

CANCER ROOT (OROBANCHE VIRGINIANA).

COMMON NAME. *Beech Drops.*

MEDICINAL PART. *The plant.*

Description.—This is a parasitic plant, with a smooth, leafless stem from a foot to a foot and a half in height, with slender branches given off the whole length of it. The root is scaly and tuberous.

History.—This plant is native to North America, and generally a parasite upon the roots of beech trees, flowering in August and September. The whole plant is of a dull red color, without any verdure. It has a disagreeable, astringent taste. It yields its virtues to water and alcohol.

Properties and Uses.—An eminent astringent. Used with benefit in fluxes and in diarrhœa, but possesses no property of curing cancer. It can be used with advantage in erysipelas. Locally applied to wounds, it prevents or arrests the process of mortification. It is also useful as an application to obstinate ulcers, aphthous ulcerations, etc., etc. It exerts the same influence upon the capillary system as the mineral drug tincture of iron.

CANNABIS INDICA.

COMMON NAME. *Indian Hemp.*

MEDICINAL PART. *The root.*

Description.—This is an herbaceous annual, growing about three feet high, with an erect, branched, angular bright green stem. The leaves are alternate. or opposite, on long lax foot-stalks, roughish, with sharply serrated leaflets tapering into a long, smooth entire point. The male flowers are drooping and long, the females simple and erect. The seeds are small, ash-colored, and inodorous.

History.—Cannabis Indica, or Cannabis Sativa, is a native of the Caucasus, Persia, but grows in the hilly regions of Northern India. It is cultivated in many parts of Europe and Asia; but medicine of value can only be made from the Indian variety, the active principle of the plant being developed only by the heat of the climate of Hindostan. The dried tops and resin are the parts used. The preparations called *Churrus*, *Gunjah*, *Bhang*, *Hashish*, etc., sold in this country, are mostly feeble imitations of the genuine articles, and are comparatively worthless. Even the few specimens of the genuine productions which reach the shops, and are sold at high prices, are crude and inferior, and can in no wise impart the effects which attach to the pure article. It is a matter of great difficulty to procure the genuine article even direct from dealers in India, unless you have had years of experience as a practising herbal physician, and have established business connections in various parts of the world as an importer of rare and pure medicinal herbs, barks, roots, resins, etc.

The *Cannabis Sativa*, or common hemp, possesses similar properties, and can be substituted if the Asiatic hemp is not procurable.

Properties and Uses.—It is narcotic, anodyne, and antispasmodic. It has been successfully employed in gout, neuralgia, rheumatism, locked-jaw, convulsions, chorea, hysteria, and uterine hemorrhage; but it is chiefly valuable as an invigorator of mind and body. Its exhilarating qualities are unequalled, and it is a certain restorative in low mental conditions, as well as in cases of extreme debility and emaciation. In such cases it may be regarded as a real rejuvenator. It should be taken by the advice of one experienced in its uses, in order that its merits may be properly and fairly experienced. The spurious hemp should never be taken, as it produces, what the genuine does not, unpleasant consequences. I have used this article in many a preparation with great success.

CASSIA MARILANDICA.

COMMON NAMES. *American Senna*, *Wild Senna.*

MEDICINAL PART. *The leaves.*

Description.—This is a perennial herb, growing from four to six feet high, with round, smooth, and slightly hairy stems. The leaves have long petioles, ovate at base; each petiole has eight or ten leaflets, which are oblong, smooth, mucronate, an inch or two long, and quite narrow. The flowers are bright yellow, and the fruit is a legume from two to four inches long.

History.—The American Senna is to be found from New England to Carolina, growing in rich soils here and there. It flowers from June to September, and the leaves are gathered, for their medicinal virtues, while the plant is in bloom. They yield their virtues to alcohol or water.

Properties and Uses.—It is one of the most important herbal cathartics furnished by America, and is mentioned here solely on the ground that it is equally valuable as the foreign Senna, or ordinary Senna of the drug-shops, and costs much less. The analysis of the leaves shows that they contain albumen, mucilage, starch, yellow coloring matter, volatile oil, fatty matter, resin, lignin, and salts of potassa, and lime.

Dose.—Of the powder, from a half-drachm to two and a half drachms; infusion, four or five ounces.

CATECHU (ACACIA CATECHU).

COMMON NAMES. *Cutch, Gambir, Terra Japonica.*

MEDICINAL PART. *Extract of the wood.*

Description.—Catechu is a small-sized tree from fifteen to twenty feet high. The bark is thick, and branches spreading. Leaves bipinnate. Flowers numerous, white or pale yellow, and the fruit a legume.

History.—This tree is common to the East Indian continent, thriving in Bengal, and on the Malabar coast. As found in the shops it is in square, round, and irregular pieces, variable in color, friable, odorless, astringent taste. Soluble in hot water, depositing a reddish matter on cooling.

Properties and uses.—This is a strong astringent. In chronic diarrhœa, chronic catarrh, chronic dysentery, it proves beneficial, and it is a valuable agent as a local application in throat diseases, especially such as singers are subject to. The tincture is often useful as a local application to fissured nipples of nursing women.

Dose.—Of the powder, from five to twenty grains; of the tincture from twenty minims to half an ounce.

CEDRON (SIMABA CEDRON).

MEDICINAL PART. *The seed.*

Description.—*Simaba* is a small tree, with an erect stem about half a foot in diameter, branching luxuriantly at the top. Leaves obovate, large, and serrated; flowers sessile, pale brown, and the fruit a solitary drupe.

History.—This tree grows in New Grenada and Central America. Its value as a medicinal agent has long been known in Costa Rica, Trinidad, etc., and from thence was communicated to scientific gentlemen in France. The seed, which is the part used, is about an inch and a half long, nearly an inch broad, and about half an inch thick. It is hard, but can be easily cut by a common knife. It is inodorous, but tastes like quassia or aloes, and yields its properties to water or alcohol. In South America the properties of these seeds were known as early as the year 1700. At that time they were applied more especially as an antidote to the bites of poisonous serpents, and similar affections.

Properties and Uses.—It is an antispasmodic, and one of the most valuable articles of the kind known to educated herbalists. It is very useful in all nervous affections, and is administered in one or two grain doses. As it can only be obtained from those who, like myself, import it especially, it is unnecessary to say that it should not be administered without the advice of competent herbal physicians. To give an idea of its value as an antispasmodic, I mention that it is a *cure* for hydrophobia, and an antidote for the majority of acro-narcotic poisons.

CELANDINE (Chelidonium Majus).

Common Name. *Tetter Wort.*

Medicinal Parts. *Herb and root.*

Description.—This plant is an evergreen perennial, with a stem from one to two feet in height, branched, swelled at the joints, leafy, round, and smooth; the leaves are smooth, spreading, very deeply pinnatified; leaflets in from two to four pairs, from one and a half to two and a half inches long, and about two-thirds as broad, the terminal one largest, all ovate, cuneately incised or lobed; the lateral ones sometimes dilated at the lower margin, near the base almost as if auricled; color of all, a deep shining green; the flowers are bright yellow, umbellate, on long, often hairy stocks.

History.—Celandine is a pale green, fleshy herb, indigenous to Europe and naturalized in the United States; it grows along fences, by-roads, in waste places, etc., and flowers from May to October. If the plant be wounded, a bright yellow, offensive juice flows out, which has a persistent, nauseous, bitter taste, with a biting sensation in the mouth and fauces. The root is the most intensely bitter part of the plant, and is more commonly preferred. Drying diminishes its activity. It yields its virtues to alcohol or water.

Properties and Uses.—It is stimulant, acrid, alterative, diuretic, diaphoretic, purgative, and vulnerary. It is used internally in decoction or tincture, and externally in poultice or ointment for scrofula, cutaneous diseases, and piles. It is likewise good in hepatic affections, or liver complaints, and exerts a special influence on the spleen. As a drastic hydragogue, or purge, it is fully equal to gamboge. The juice, when applied to the skin, produces inflammations, and even vesications. It has long been known as a caustic for the removal of warts; it is also applied to indolent ulcers, fungous growths, etc., and is useful in removing specks and opacities of the cornea of the eye.

Celandine is from the Greek word *Chelidon*, which signifies a swallow. The ancients assert that if you put out the eyes of young swallows when they are in the nest, the old ones will restore their eyes again with this herb. It is said that we may mar the apple of the bird's eye with a needle, and that the old birds will restore their sight again by means of this herb. Never having made any such cruel experiments, I am not prepared to say whether any such miraculous power of healing loss of sight is a virtue of the plant, or whether it is an instinct or gift inherent of the swallow itself.

Celandine is also used in curing salt-rheum, tetter, or ringworm. It is superior to *arnica* as a vulnerary; an alcoholic tincture of the root (three ounces to a pint) will be found an unrivalled application to prevent or subdue traumatic inflammations.

Dose.—Of the powdered root, from half a drachm to one drachm; of the fresh juice, from twenty to forty drops, in some bland liquid; of the tincture, from one to two fluid drachms; of the aqueous extract, from five to ten grains.

CENTAURY (SABBATIA ANGULARIS).

COMMON NAME. *Rose Pink.*

MEDICINAL PART. *The herb.*

Description.—This plant has a yellow fibrous, biennial root, with an erect, smooth, quadrangular stem, with the angles winged, having many opposite branches, and growing from one to two feet in height. The leaves are opposite, fine-veined, smooth, entire, from one to five inches in length, and from half an inch to one and a half inches wide, clasping the stem. The flowers are numerous, from an inch and a quarter to an inch and a half in diameter, of a rich rose or carnation color, standing, as it were, at the tops of one umbril or tuft, very like those of *St. John's wort*, opening themselves in the day-time and closing at night, after which come seeds in little short husks, in forms like unto wheat corn. There are three varieties of the Centaury in England, one kind bearing white flowers, another yellow, and another red. All have medicinal properties, although the American variety is considered preferable to the European Centaury.

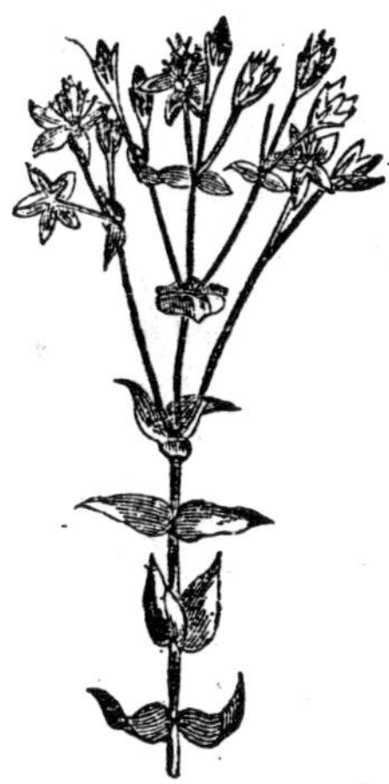

Centaury.

History.—This plant is common to most parts of the United States, growing in moist meadows, among high grass, on the prairies, and in damp, rich soils, flowering from June to September. The whole herb is used. It has a very bitter taste, and yields its virtues to water or alcohol. The best time for gathering it is during the flowering season. In England they use the red Centaury in diseases of the blood, the yellow in choleric diseases, and the white in those of phlegm and water.

Properties and Uses.—It is an excellent tonic. It is used in all fall periodic febrile diseases, both as a preventive and a remedy. It is also serviceable as a bitter tonic in dyspepsia and convalescence from fevers. When administered in warm infusion it is a domestic remedy for worms, and to restore the menstrual secretion.

Dose.—Of the powder, from half a drachm to a drachm; of the cold infusion, a teacupful every two or three hours; of the tincture, a wineglassful; of the extract, from two to six grains.

CENTURY PLANT (AGAVE AMERICANA).

COMMON NAME. *South American Agave.*

MEDICINAL PART. *The inspissated juice.*

Description.—This plant, which is also sometimes called the Century Plant, from an erroneous idea that it blossoms but once in a hundred years, is the largest of all herbaceous plants. It is an evergreen, and does not blossom often.

History.—It flourishes in the warmer latitudes of South America, where its juice is expressed by the natives and allowed to ferment. In this condition it is called *pulque*, and is used as an exhilarating beverage. The natives can drink large quantities of this liquor without getting very much intoxicated; but it is very severe upon those who are not accustomed to it.

Properties and Uses.—The fresh juice is used by the South Americans to regulate the action of the bowels and kidneys, and is considered very valuable for dyspepsia and diseases of the bladder. The South American women use the juice and the decoction to promote menstruation. I can say of my own knowledge that, in proper combination, it is a superior anti-syphilitic, and that in scorbutic affections it is without many superiors. The dose is from half a fluid ounce to two ounces, three times a day.

Chamomile.

The *Agave Virginica*, or *False Aloe*, is not to be confounded with this, as that plant is a laxative and carminative.

CHAMOMILE (ANTHEMIS NOBILIS).

MEDICINAL PART. *The Flowers.*

Description.—This is a perennial herb, with a strong fibrous root. The stems in a wild state are prostrate, but in gardens more upright.

about a span long, round, hollow, furrowed, and downy; the leaves pale green, pinnate, sessile, with thread-shaped leaflets. The flower-heads terminal, rather larger than the daisy, and of yellow color, or whitish.

History.—Chamomile is indigenous to Southern Europe; we have also a common or wild Chamomile (*Matricaria Chamomilla*) growing in the United States, but it is not considered as good as the Roman Chamomile for medicinal purposes, which is the kind I use. The white flowers are the best; they have an aromatic, agreeably bitter taste, and peculiar odor. They yield their properties to alcohol and water.

Properties and Uses.—Chamomile is a tonic; one or two teacupfuls of the warm infusion will usually vomit. The cold infusion is highly useful in dyspepsia, and in all cases of weak or irritable stomachs, also in intermittent and typhoid fevers. The oil is carminative and anti-spasmodic, and is used in flatulency, colic, cramp in the stomach, hysteria, nervous diseases, and painful menstruation.

A poultice of Chamomile will often prevent gangrene, and remove it when present. It is an ingredient in my "Restorative Assimilant," and is a most excellent adjutant and corrigent in that great remedy.

Dose.—Half a drachm to two drachms of the flowers. Of the infusion, half a teacupful to a teacupful; of the oil, five to fifteen drops on sugar.

CHERRY LAUREL (PRUNUS LAUROCERASUS).

MEDICINAL PART. *The leaves.*

Description.—This is a small evergreen shrub or tree with smooth branches. Leaves with short petioles, oval-oblong, serrate, acute, and smooth. Flowers shorter than the leaves, calyx inferior, corolla has five white petals; stamens about twenty; and fruit a round, black, smooth drupe.

Cherry Laurel.

History.—Originally a native of Asia Minor, from whence it was introduced into Europe in 1576, and subsequently from Europe to the United States. It is now common in gardens and shrubberies. The leaves have scarcely any odor until bruised, then they have a bitter almond odor; taste very bitter, aromatic, and slightly astringent. They impart their virtues to water and alcohol.

Properties and Uses.—An excellent sedative. Useful in tic-douloureux, phthisis, spasmodic cough, palpitation of the heart, and in all spasmodic affections.

Dose.—Powdered leaves, four to eight grains; laurel water, ten to thirty drops.

CHICKWEED (STELLARIA MEDIA).

MEDICINAL PART. *The herb.*

Description.—This plant is an annual or biennial weed, from six to fifteen inches in length, with a prostrate, brittle, and leafy stem. The leaves are ovate-cordate; the lower ones on hairy petioles. The flowers are small and white, petals two-parted, stamens three, five, or ten.

History.—It is a common plant in Europe and America, growing in fields and around dwellings, in moist, shady places. It flowers from the beginning of spring till the last of autumn. The seeds are eaten by poultry and birds. The whole herb is used when recent.

Properties and Uses.—It is a cooling demulcent. The fresh leaves bruised and applied as a poultice to indolent, intractable ulcers, even when of many years' standing, will produce most immediate and decided beneficial results, to be changed two or three times a day. The bruised leaves will likewise be found an invaluable application in acute ophthalmia. An ointment made by bruising the recent leaves in fresh lard, may be used as a cooling application to erysipelatous and other forms of ulceration, as well as many forms of cutaneous diseases.

CHOCOLATE ROOT, GEUM RIVALE (*Water Avens*), GEUM VIRGINIANUM (*White Avens*).

COMMON NAMES. *Throat Root, Purple Avens.*

MEDICINAL PART. *The root.*

Description.—GEUM RIVALE, or *Purple Avens*, is a perennial, deep green herb; woody root; leaves nearly lyrate, crenate-dentate, and from four to six inches long. The flowers are few and yellowish purple in color.

GEUM VIRGINIANUM, or *Throat Root*, is also a perennial, with a small, crooked root. The stem is two or three feet high. The leaves are pinnate or lyrate; flowers rather small and white; and the fruit an achenium. The former is common to the United States and Europe, flowering in June or July, and the latter only to the United States, flowering from June to August.

History.—These plants, with other varieties, have long been used in domestic practice. The whole herb contains medicinal properties, but the officinal and most efficient part is the root. Boiling water or alcohol extracts their virtues.

Properties and Uses.—Is tonic and astringent. It is used in passive and chronic hemorrhages, chronic diarrhœa and dysentery, leucorrhœa, dyspepsia, pulmonary affections, congestions of the abdominal viscera, etc.

Dose.—Of the powder, from twenty to thirty grains; of the decoction, from two tablespoonfuls to a wineglassful, three or four times a day.

CINCHONA.

COMMON NAMES. *Peruvian Bark, Jesuits' Bark.*

MEDICINAL PART. *The bark.*

Description.—The bark is obtained from the *Cinchona Calisaya, Cinchona Condaminea, Cinchona Succirubra,* and *Cinchona Lancifolia.* These trees are all evergreen trees or shrubs. Their generic character is to have opposite entire leaves; flowers white, or usually roseate or purplish, and very fragrant; calyx a turbinated tube; corolla salver-shaped; stamens, five; anthers, linear; style, simple; stigma, bifid. The fruit a capsule, ovate or oblong, filled with numerous winged seeds. About thirteen varieties of cinchona are known to commerce, but the above are the most important. Of these species the former three yield respectively the pale, yellow, and red cinchona barks, and the fourth is one of the sources of quinine.

Cinchona.

History.—Cinchona is a very old discovery, and takes its name from the wife of the Spanish viceroy, Count de Cinchon, who was cured of fever by it, at Lima, about the year 1638. For some time after its introduction into Europe, the Jesuits, who received the bark from their brethren in Peru, alone used it, and kept to themselves the secret of its origin; and their use of it was so successful that it received the name which still clings to it of "Jesuits' Bark." The bark richest in the antiperiodic alkaloids is the Cinchona Calisaya. The geographical range of the cinchonas appears to be exclusively confined to the Andes, within the boundaries of Peru, Bolivia, Equador, and New Granada. Thirteen species furnish the barks of commerce, and all of them are found growing from one to ten thousand feet above the level of the sea. The four species we have named at the head of this article are, however, the only ones recognized by the United States Pharmacopœia, and are the favorites everywhere. Since the seventeenth century these barks have been the study of men versed in medical and chemical science, and they and the preparations made from them rank among the most important articles of the Materia Medica. It contains numerous active principles, but the most important, and one chiefly used, is quinine.

Properties and Uses.—Cinchona bark is tonic, antiperiodic, astringent to a moderate extent, and eminently febrifuge. It is topically (or externally) antiseptic, and is of much value when applied to gangrenous ulcerations, or used for gargles and washes in erysipelas, ulcerated sore throat, mouth, etc. I do not recommend the use of the bark in cases where the stomach is *very much* weakened (although it is employed in every disease in which there is deficient tone), because the woody fibre in the powder will most generally disagree. When taken internally it imparts a sensation of warmth to the stomach, which gradually spreads over the whole body; the pulse becomes stronger and is accelerated, and the various organs are gently stimulated. It may be used with benefit in ordinary cases of dyspepsia, general debility, and all febrile, eruptive, and inflammatory diseases, in whatever stage they may be. In all cases of night-sweating, or great feebleness, it is valuable. As an antiperiodic it is not surpassed by anything else used. When it excites nausea, add an aromatic; if purging, opium; if costiveness, rhubarb.

Quinine is a white flocculent powder, inodorous, and has a very bitter taste. It is very sparingly soluble in warm water, still less so in cold water. It is readily soluble in hot alcohol, and tolerably so in ether. It is always best to administer quinine instead of the bark, unless some of the effects of the other principles are desired.

Dose.—Of the powder, half a drachm to a drachm; fluid extract, ten to sixty drops; of quinine, from one to fifteen grains, according to purpose.

CINQUE-FOIL (POTENTILLA CANADENSIS).

COMMON NAME. *Five-Finger.*

MEDICINAL PART. *The root.*

Description.—This perennial plant has a procumbent stem from two to eighteen inches in length. The leaves are palmate, leaflets obovate, and flowers yellow, on solitary pedicels.

There are two varieties of this plant, the *P. Pamilla*, which is very small and delicate, flowering in April and May, and growing in dry, sandy soils, and the *P. Simplex*, a larger plant, growing in richer soils, and flowering from June to August.

History.—Five-finger is common to the United States, growing by road-sides, on meadow banks and waste grounds, and flowering from April to October. The root is the part used. It has a bitterish, styptic taste, and yields its virtues to water.

Properties and Uses.—It is tonic and astringent. A decoction is useful in fevers, bowel complaints, night sweats, menorrhagia, and other hemorrhages. It makes an excellent gargle for spongy, bleeding gums, and ulcerated mouth and throat.

The POTENTILLA TORMENTILLA, or *Sept-Foil* of Europe, possesses similar qualities, and may be used by my readers in that country if the American root is not to be obtained.

CLEAVERS (GALIUM APARINE).

COMMON NAMES. *Goose Grass, Catchweed, Bed-Straw.*

MEDICINAL PART. *The herb.*

Description.—It is an annual succulent plant, with a weak, procumbent, quadrangular, retrosely-prickled stem, which grows from two to six feet high, and is hairy at the joints. The leaves are one or two inches in length, and two or three lines in breadth; rough on the margin and tapering to the base. The flowers are white, small, and scattered.

History.—This plant is common to Europe and the United States, growing in cultivated grounds, moist thickets, and along banks of rivers, and flowering from June to September. In the green state the plant has an unpleasant odor; but it is inodorous when dried, with an acidulous, astringent, and bitter taste. Cold or warm water extracts the virtues of the plant; boiling water destroys them. The roots dye a permanent red.

Properties and Uses.—It is a most valuable refrigerant and diuretic, and will be found very beneficial in many diseases of the urinary organs, as suppression of urine, calculous affections, inflammation of the kidneys and bladder, and in the scalding of urine in gonorrhœa. It is contra-indicated in diseases of a passive character, on account of its refrigerant and sedative effects on the system, but may be used freely in fevers and all acute diseases. An infusion may be made by macerating an ounce and a half of the herb in a pint of warm water for two hours, of which from two to four fluid ounces may be given three or four times a day when cold. It may be sweetened with sugar or honey. It has also been found useful in many cutaneous diseases, as psoriasis, eczema, lichen, cancer, and scrofula, and is more particularly useful in these diseases when they are combined with strumous diathesis. The best form for administration is that of the inspissated juice, which may be in one or two drachm doses, three times a day.

The plant called GALIUM TINCTORIUM, or *Small Cleavers*, is nervine, anti-spasmodic, expectorant, and diaphoretic. It is used successfully in asthma, cough, and chronic bronchitis, exerting its influence principally upon the respiratory organs. The plant has a pungent, aromatic, pleasant, persistent taste. A strong decoction of the herb may be given in doses of from one to four fluid ounces, and repeated two or three times a day, according to circumstances. The root of this plant will also dye a permanent red.

COCA (ERYTHROXYLON COCA).

MEDICINAL PART. *The herb.*

Description.—I first became acquainted with this most remarkable plant many years ago, while traveling in Bolivia, South America, in the beautiful valleys of the Cordilleras. The Coca is a bush which rarely attains six feet in height, and does not often exceed three. Its foliage is of a bright green, its flowers white, and its fruit small and red. When the plants are just about eighteen inches high they are transplanted from the seed-beds into fields called *cocales*. The ripe leaves are gathered with the fingers. They are dried by spreading them in the sun, sometimes on woollen cloths. The operation requires great care, for the plant must be protected from all dampness, which changes its color, and thus diminishes its value. It is then packed in bags, weighing from fifty to one hundred and fifty pounds, which are often transported to great distances. In the Vice-royalty of Lima, in the latter part of the last century, CASTELNAU represents the consumption of the leaf at three and a half millions of pounds, and worth one million and a quarter of Spanish dollars, while at the same time the total consumption in Peru was two and a half millions of dollars. The importance of the Coca trade, however, is diminishing as the Red Man disappears. The Indians mix the Coca with a small quantity of lime, and constantly carry a small bag of it on all their excursions. They take it from three to six times a day. Dr. TSCHUDI [*Travels in Peru*, page 453] mentions an Indian of sixty-two years of age, who was employed by him, and though at very hard work for five days, took no other nourishment, and rested but two hours of the night. Immediately, or soon after this, he accomplished a journey of one hundred miles in two days, and said that he was ready to do the same thing again if they would give him a new supply of Coca. CASTELNAU says he himself knew of instances as extraordinary. In the time of the Incas the Coca was regarded as sacred.

Properties and Uses.—Its physiological actions are as follows :—

1. It stimulates the stomach and promotes digestion.

2. In large doses it augments animal heat and accelerates the pulse and respiration.

3. It induces slight constipation.

4. In moderate doses, from one to four drachms, it stimulates the nervous system, so as to render it more tolerant of muscular fatigue.

5. In larger doses it gives rise to hallucinations and true delirium.

6. Its most precious property is that of inducing the most pleasant visions ("*phantasmagoria*") without any subsequent depression of the nervous energies.

7. Probably it diminishes some of the secretions.

The Coca has doubtless many other medical properties of a high order, and deserves further investigation.

It stimulates powerfully the digestive functions, while at the same time it exercises a calmative influence over the mucous membranes of the stomach and bowels. In this double action upon the stomach—stimulant and calmative—it resembles Columbo.

It is anti-spasmodic, and is of great service in many nervous disorders, and particularly in *spermatorrhœa* and all debilities of the generative organs.

An infusion of the leaves, or a tincture of the flowers, leaves, and berries may be used in all cases of spermatorrhœa and nervous debility. Combined with other remedies it may be used with great advantage in fevers, pneumonia, pleuritis, neuralgia, hysteria, dysmenorrhœa, amenorrhœa, blenorrhœas (including gonorrhœa and leucorrhœa), chorea, epilepsy, paralysis, after-pains, convulsions, dyspepsia, delirium tremens, etc. My course of concentrated herbal remedies, in which Coca is a principal ingredient, will surely cure spermatorrhœa, seminal weakness, impotence, sterility, and barrenness, and I now use it extensively for all disorders arising from sexual debility. It never yet failed to meet my expectations—hundreds of such cases having been radically cured by its truly miraculous medicinal properties.

COLOCYNTH (Cucumis Colocynthis.)

Colocynth.

Common Name. *Bitter Cucumber.*

Medicinal Part. *The fruit divested of its rind.*

Description.—Colocynth is an annual plant, with a whitish root, and prostrate, angular, and hispid stems. The leaves are alternate, cordate, ovate, many-lobed, white with hairs beneath. Flowers yellow and solitary; petals small; and fruit globose, smooth, size of an orange, yellow when ripe, with a thin solid rind, and a very bitterish flesh.

History.—This plant is a native of the south of Europe, Asia, and Africa. The fruit assumes a yellow or orange color externally during the autumn, at which time it is pulled and dried quickly, either in the stove or sun. That which is deprived of its rind, very white, light spongy, and without seeds, is the best article; all others are more or less inferior in quality. It contains, besides oils, resins, and gums, bassorin and the sulphates of lime and magnesia. *Colocynthin* is its active principle.

Properties and Uses.—It is a powerful hydragogue cathartic, producing copious watery evacuations. It should never be used alone, but be combined with other cathartics. It may be used advantageously in passive dropsy and cerebral derangements. In combination with hyoscyamus it loses its irritant properties, and may be so employed whenever its peculiar cathartic effects are desired. Hippocrates used colocynth as a pessary to promote menstruation.

Dose.—Five to ten grains.

COLT'S FOOT (TUSSILAGO FARFARA).

COMMON NAMES. *Cough Wort, Foal's Foot, Horse Hoof, and Bull's Foot.*

MEDICINAL PART. *The leaves.*

Description.—Colt's foot has a long, perennial, creeping, fibrous rhizome. The leaves are erect, cordate, sharply dentate, smooth green above, and pure white and cottony beneath. They do not appear until the flowers are withered, and are from five to eight inches long, and about an inch broad. The flowers are large and bright yellow.

History.—This plant grows in Europe, the Crimea, Persia, Siberia, and the East Indies, from the sea-shore to elevations of nearly eight thousand feet. It also grows in the United States, in wet places, on the sides of brooks, flowering in March and April. Its presence is a certain indication of a clayey soil. The leaves are rather fragrant, and continue so after having been carefully dried. The leaves are the parts used, though all parts of the plant are active, and should always be employed, especially the leaves, flowers, and root. The leaves should be collected at about the period they have nearly reached their full size, the flowers as soon as they commence opening, and the root immediately after the maturity of the leaves. When dried, all parts have a bitter, mucilaginous taste, and yield their properties to water or diluted alcohol.

Properties and Uses.—It is emollient, demulcent, and slightly tonic. The decoction is usually administered in doses of from one to three or four fluid ounces, and is highly serviceable in coughs, asthma, whooping-cough, and other pulmonary complaints; also useful in scrofula. The powdered leaves form a good errhine for giddiness, headache, nasal obstructions, etc. It is also used externally in form of poultice in scrofulous tumors.

COLUMBO (COCCULUS PALMATUS).

MEDICINAL PART. *The root.*

Description.—Columbo, so important in the present practice of medicine, is a climbing plant, with a perennial sort which is quite thick and branching. The root is covered with a thin brown skin, marked with transverse warts. The stems, of which one or two proceed from the same root, are twining, simple in the male plant, branched in the female, round, hairy, and about an inch or an inch and a half in circumference. The leaves stand on rounded glandular-hairy footstalks, and are alternate, distant, cordate, and have three, seven, or nine lobes and nerves. The flowers are small and inconspicuous.

History.—This plant inhabits the forests near the southeastern coast of Africa, in the neighborhood of Mozambique, where the natives call it *Kalumb.* The root is dug up in the dry season in the month of March, and is cut in slices, strung on cords, and hung up to dry. The odor of Columbo is slightly aromatic; the taste bitter, and also mucilaginous. The root is easily pulverized, but spoils by keeping after having been reduced to a powder. It is best to powder it only as it is required for use. The active principle of Columbo is called *Columbin.* The root also yields *Berberin*, an excellent stomachic, which is produced from the Barberry.

Properties and Uses.—It is one of the purest bitter tonics in the world, and in dyspepsia, chronic diarrhœa, and dysentery, as well as in convalescence from febrile and inflammatory diseases, it can hardly be surpassed as a remedial agent. It is most useful in the remittent and intermittent fevers of hot climates. It is used in many combinations, according to indications.

Dose.—Of the powder, ten to thirty grains; of the infusion, one or two ounces; of the tincture, from one to two drachms.

COMFREY (SYMPHYTUM OFFICINALE).

MEDICINAL PART. *The root.*

Description.—Comfrey has an oblong, fleshy, perennial root, black on the outside and whitish within, containing a glutinous or clammy, tasteless juice, with divers very large, hairy, green leaves lying on the ground, so hairy, or so prickly, that if they touch any tender parts of the hands, face, or body, it will cause it to itch. The stalks are hollowed and cornered, very hairy, having leaves that grow below, but less and less up to the top; at the joints of the stalk it is divided into many branches, at the ends of which stand many flowers, in order one above another, which are somewhat long and hollow like the finger of a glove, of a pale, whitish color; after them come small black seeds. There is another sort which bears flowers of a pale purple color, having similar medicinal pro perties.

History.—Comfrey is a native of Europe, but naturalized in the United States, growing on low grounds and moist places, and flowering all summer. The root is officinal and contains a large amount of mucilage which is readily extracted by water.

Properties and Uses.—The plant is demulcent and slightly astringent All mucilaginous agents exert an influence on mucous tissues, hence the cure of many pulmonary and other affections in which these tissues have been chiefly implicated, by their internal use. Physicians must not expect a *serous* disease to yield to remedies which act on mucous membranes only; to determine the true value of a medicinal agent, they must first ascertain the true character of the affection, as well as of the tissues involved. Again, mucilaginous agents are always beneficial in scrofulous and anæmic habits. Comfrey root is very useful in diarrhœa, dysentery, coughs, hemoptysis or bleeding of the lungs, and other pulmonary affections; also in leucorrhœa and female debility: all these being principally affections of mucous membranes.

It may be boiled in water, wine, or made into a syrup, and taken in doses of from a wineglassful to a teacupful of the preparation, two or three times a day.

Externally the fresh root, bruised, forms an excellent application to bruises, ruptures, fresh wounds, sore breasts, ulcers, white swellings, etc.

CUNDURANGO (EQUATORIA GARCIANA).

MEDICINAL PART. *The bark of the vine.*

Description.—Cundurango, or Condor Vine, a name derived from two words, *cundur* and *angu*, whose marvellous medicinal properties have lately been made known to the world, and which is now so greatly interesting the medical profession, is a climbing vine, resembling much in its habits the grape vine of our forests. The vines are from three to five inches diameter. They are quite flexible when fresh, but when dry very brittle. The bark is externally of a greenish-gray color, and has numerous small warty excrescences. The leaves are large, sometimes reaching six inches in length by five in breadth, opposite, simple, entire, dentate, cordate, and of a dark green color. The flowers are small, arranged in complete umbels; stamens five; petals five; sepals five; and filaments small. The fruit is a pair of pods, and seeds numerous and dark brown. It should be more properly called *Cundurangu*, as there is no *o* in the language of the Incas.

History.—This plant is a native of the Andes Mountains in South America, especially the southern portion of Equador, and found most plentifully in the mountains surrounding the city of Loja. It is generally found on the western exposure of the Andes, at an altitude of 4,000 or 5,000 feet. Its virtues were known to the Indians of the locality for a long time. The tradition is that it was regarded by them as poisonous, and that an Indian woman unintentionally cured her husband, who suffered from a very painful cancer, giving him to drink bowlfuls of decoction of Cundurango. believing and hoping it would prove fatal. It was intro duced into medical practice by Dr. Eguiguren, brother of the Governor of the province of Loja, both of whom cured many cases of syphilis and cancerous ulcers in the trial of it. The subject was brought to the notice of our government by our minister at Quito. The Department of State, at once realizing the value of the discovery and the intense interest with which our people would seek after information concerning it, published a circular, setting forth its great value as a remedy. This action of the government at once inspired that confidence to which the plant is entitled. It was tested in a case of cancer afflicting the mother of Vice-President Colfax, and at once asserted its value. It has since been used by progressive physicians, and the success it has given in cancerous and syphilitic affections renders it worthy of the name of a specific, equally as much so as cinchona. It is a singular coincidence that these two specific products of the herbal world should grow in the same regions. The natives insist that there are two varieties of the bark, the *amarillo*, or yellow, and *blanco*, or white; but upon inspection I find they are the same, the difference in color depending upon the strong rays of the sun. When freshly cut the vines give an abundance of milky, viscous juice or sap, the odor of which is balsamic, and flavor decidedly bitter and aromatic. It is not abundant, and hence necessarily of high price.

Properties and Uses.—An unequalled remedy for cancer, syphilis, ulcers, etc. In a short period, when taken, the typical symptoms subside, the pain is diminished, the discharge thickens and becomes less offensive, the tumor becomes softer, the deposits lessen, the expression improves, and a cure is speedily effected. It has also diuretic and tonic powers, and cures many nervous diseases. I have given this remedy competent trials in cases of cancer and syphilis, and the results were so satisfactory as to surprise me, and I am ready to assert that in Cundurango we have a remedy that will rob cancer of its terror, and one that will soon banish it from existence as a disease. Its price is exceedingly high, almost costing its weight in gold; but still that has not deterred me from using it in such cases as I deemed the requirement necessary.

Dose.—Of the powder, one to two drachms; fluid extract, one drachm. (Much that is spurious is sold in market.)

COPAIBA (COPAIFERA OFFICINALIS).

COMMON NAME. *Balsam of Copaiba.*

MEDICINAL PART. *The oleo-resinous juice.*

Description.—Copaiba is a tall and handsome tree, with many small, crooked branches, and a grayish-brown bark. The leaves are large and equally pinnated, leaflets in pairs of from two to five, petioles short. The flowers are white; calyx four-parted; stamens, ten; fruit obovate, two valved, and one-seeded.

History.—There are several species which furnish oil of copaiba, all natives of South America and West Indies. The juice is obtained by deep incisions being made in the trunk during or following the wet season; the balsam (which, however, is not a balsam, as it contains no benzoic acid) flows freely, being clear, transparent, and fluid, but becoming pale yellowish in time. The oil is unpleasant in smell and taste.

Properties and Uses.—In large doses Copaiba is an irritant, but in proper doses it is stimulant, cathartic, and diuretic. It exerts a favorable influence on the mucous tissues of the system, diminishing excessive secretions, and for this purpose it is chiefly employed. Taken internally it gives warmth to the gastric region, and sometimes provokes nausea and emesis. It is especially useful in chronic mucous affections, as gonorrhœa, bronchitis, diseases of the bladder, gleet, chronic catarrh, diarrhœa, and dysentery, etc., etc. It was formerly regarded as a specific for gonorrhœa, but has lost some of its prestige. Locally it is an excellent application to fistulas, chilblains, old ulcers, etc.

Dose.—From twenty to sixty drops in emulsion with yolk of egg and mint or cinnamon water.

CRANBERRY (High).—(VIBURNUM OPULUS.)

MEDICINAL PART. *The bark.*

Description.—It is a nearly smooth and upright shrub, or small tree, usually from five to twelve feet in height, with several stems from the same root branched above; the leaves are three-lobed, three-veined, broadly-wedged shape, and crenately toothed on the side. The flowers are white, or reddish-white; the fruit ovoid, red, very acid, ripens late, and remains upon the bush after the leaves have fallen. It resembles the common cranberry, and is sometimes substituted for it.

History.—It is indigenous to the northern part of the United States and Canadas, being a handsome shrub, growing in low rich lands, woods, and borders of fields, flowering in June, and presenting at this time a very showy appearance. The flowers are succeeded by red and very acid berries, resembling low cranberries, and which remain through the winter. The bark is the officinal part, as met with in drug-stores. It is frequently put up by Shakers, when it is somewhat flattened from pressure. It has no smell, but has a peculiar, not unpleasant, bitterish, and astringent taste. It yields its properties to water or diluted alcohol. *Viburnine* is its active principle.

Properties and Uses.—It is a powerful antispasmodic, and hence generally known among American practitioners as *Cramp Bark.* It is very effective in cramps and spasms of all kinds, as asthma, hysteria, cramps of females during pregnancy, preventing the attacks entirely if used daily for the last two or three months of gestation.

The following forms an excellent preparation for the relief of spasmodic attacks, viz.: take of Cramp bark, two ounces; scull-cap, skunk cabbage, of each one ounce; cloves, half an ounce; capsicum, two drachms. Have all in powder, coarsely bruised, and add to them two quarts of sherry or native wine. *Dose* of this, half a wineglassful two or three times a day.

It may here be remarked that a poultice of the fruit of the *Low* Cranberry is very efficacious in indolent and malignant ulcers, malignant scarlet fever, applied to the throat; in erysipelas, and other similar diseases. Probably the *High* Cranberry will effect the same result.

Dose.—Of the decoction, or vinous tincture, one glassful two or three times a day.

CRANESBILL (Geranium Maculatum).

Common Names. *Dove's Foot, Crow Foot, Alum Root, Spotted Geranium, etc.*

Medicinal Part. *The root.*

Description.—This plant has a perennial, horizontal, thick, rough, and knotty root, with many small fibres. The stems are grayish-green, erect, round, and a foot or two high. The leaves are spreading and hairy, and the blossoms large, and generally purple, mostly in pairs. The Dove's Foot, or Cranebill, which grows in England, is a different plant, bearing many small bright-red flowers of five leaves apiece, though it possesses medicinal properties similar to the American varieties.

History.—Geranium is a native of the United States, growing in nearly all parts of it, in low grounds, open woods, etc., blossoming from April to June. The root is the officinal part. Its virtues are yielded to water or alcohol. *Geranin* is its active principle.

Properties and Uses.—It is a powerful astringent, used in the second stage of dysentery, diarrhœa, and cholera infantum; in infusion, with milk. Both internally and externally it may be used wherever astringents are indicated, in hemorrhages, indolent ulcers, aphthous sore mouth, ophthalmia, leucorrhœa, gleet, hematuria, menorrhagia, diabetes, and excessive chronic mucous discharges; also to cure mercurial salivation. Relaxation of the uvula may be benefited by gargling with a decoction of the root, as well as aphthous ulceration of the mouth and throat. From its freedom from any nauseous or unpleasant qualities, it is well adapted to infants and persons with fastidious stomachs. In cases of bleeding piles, a strong decoction of the root should be injected into the rectum, and retained as long as possible. Troublesome epistaxis, or bleeding from the nose, wounds, or small vessels, and from the extraction of teeth, may be checked effectually by applying the powder to the bleeding orifice, and, if possible, covering with a compress of cotton. With Aletri's Farinosa (*Unicorn root*) in decoction, and taken internally, it has proved of superior efficacy in diabetes and in Bright's disease of the kidneys. A mixture or solution of two parts of hydrastin and one of geranin will be found of unrivalled efficacy in all chronic mucous diseases, as in gleet, leucorrhœa, ophthalmia, gastric affections, catarrh, and ulceration of the bladder, etc. A decoction of two parts of geranium and one of sanguinaria (*Bloodroot*) forms an excellent injection for gleet and leucorrhœa.

Dose of geranium powder, from twenty to thirty grains; of the decoction. a tablespoonful to a wineglassful.

CRAWLEY (CORALLORHIZA ODONTORHIZA).

COMMON NAMES. *Dragon's Claw, Coral root, etc.*

MEDICINAL PART. *The root.*

Description.—This is a singular, leafless plant, with coral-like rootstocks. The root is a collection of small fleshy tubers; the flowers, from ten to twenty in number, are of a brownish-green color, and the fruit a large oblong capsule.

History.—The plant is a native of the United States, growing about the roots of trees, in rich woods, from Maine to Florida, flowering from July to October. The entire plant is destitute of verdure. The root only is used for medical purposes. It is small, dark brown, resembling cloves, or a hen's claws; has a strong, nitrous smell, and a mucilaginous, slightly bitter, astringent taste.

Properties and Uses.—It is probably the most powerful, prompt, and certain diaphoretic in the materia medica; but its scarcity and high price prevents it from coming in general use. It is also sedative, and promotes perspiration without producing any excitement in the system. Its chief value is as a diaphoretic in fevers, especially in typhus, and inflammatory diseases. It has proved effectual in acute erysipelas, cramps, flatulency, pleurisy, and night-sweats; it relieves hectic fever without debilitating the patient. Its virtues are especially marked in the low stages of fevers.

Combined with caulophyllin it forms an excellent agent in amenorrhœa and dysmenorrhœa, or scanty or painful menstruation, and is unsurpassed in after-pains, suppression of lochia, and the febrile symptoms which sometimes occur at the parturient period.

In fevers Crawley may be advantageously combined with leptandrin or podophyllin, when it is found necessary to act upon the bowels or liver; and mixed with dioscorein it will be found almost a specific in flatulent and bilious colic.

Dose.—From twenty to thirty grains of the powdered root, given in water as warm as the patient can drink, and repeated every hour or two, according to circumstances. The powder should always be kept in well-closed vials. It constitutes the *fever powders* of some practitioners.

CROWFOOT (Ranunculus Bulbosus).

Medicinal Parts. *The cormus and herb.*

Description.—This plant is not to be confounded with the *Geranium maculatum*, which is also called Crowfoot. The cormus or root of this herb is a perennial, solid, fleshy, roundish, and depressed, sending out radicles from its under sides. The root sends up annually erect hairy stems, six to eighteen inches in height. The leaves are on long petioles, dentate and hairy. Each stem supports several solitary golden-yellow flowers; sepals, oblong and hairy; petals, five, cordate; stamens numerous and hairy.

History.—This plant is common in Europe and the United States, growing in fields and pastures, and flowering in May, June, and July. There a great many varieties, but all possess similar qualities, and designated by the general name of *Butter-cup*. When any part of these plants is chewed, it occasions much pain, inflammation, excoriation of the mouth, and much heat and pains in the stomach, if it be taken internally.

Properties and Uses.—This plant is too acrid to be used internally, especially when fresh. When applied externally it is powerfully rubefacient and epispastic. It is employed in its recent state in rheumatic neuralgia and other diseases where vesication and counter-irritation are indicated. Its action, however, is generally so violent that it is seldom used. The beggars use it to produce and keep open sores to excite sympathy. It has been used with success in obstinate cases of nursing sore-mouth—an infusion being made by adding two drachms of the recent root, cut into small pieces, to one pint of hot water, when cold a tablespoonful being given two or three times a day, and the mouth frequently washed with a much stronger infusion.

CUBEBS (Piper Cubeba).

Medicinal Part. *The berries.*

Description.—This is a perennial plant, with a climbing stem, round branches, about as thick as a goose-quill, ash-colored, and rooting at the joints. The leaves are from four to six and a half inches long by one and a half to two inches broad, ovate-oblong, acuminate, and very smooth. Flowers arranged in spikes at the end of the branches; fruit, a berry rather longer than that of black pepper.

History.—Cubebs is a native of Java and other islands of the Indian Ocean, growing in the forests without cultivation. The fruit is gathered before fully ripe, and then dried. It affords a volatile oil, which is much used. Cubebs has a pleasant, aromatic odor, and a hot, bitter taste. *Cubebin* is the active principle.

Properties and Uses.—It is mildly stimulant, expectorant, stomachic, and carminative. It acts particularly on mucous tissues, and arrests excessive discharges, especially from the urethra. It exercises an influence over the urinary apparatus, rendering the urine of deeper color. It is successfully employed in gonorrhœa, gleet, leucorrhœa, chronic bladder diseases, bronchial affections, and atony of the stomach and bowels.

Dose.—Of the powder, half a drachm to a drachm; tincture, two fluid drachms; oil, ten to thirty drops.

DAISY (LEUCANTHEMUM VULGARE).

COMMON NAMES. *Ox-eye Daisy, White Weed.*

MEDICINAL PARTS. *The leaves and flowers.*

Description.—This is a perennial herb, having an erect, branching, and furrowed stem, from one to two feet high. The leaves are few, alternate, lanceolate-serrate, the lower ones petiolate; the upper ones small, subulate, and sessile.

History.—The plant was introduced into the United States from Europe, and is a very troublesome weed to farmers in nearly every section. It bears white flowers in June and July. The leaves are odorous and somewhat acid; the flowers are bitterish; they impart their virtues to water.

Properties and Uses.—It is tonic, diuretic, and anti-spasmodic, and, in large doses, emetic. It is used as a tonic instead of Chamomile flowers, and is serviceable in whooping-cough, asthma, and nervous excitability. Very beneficial externally and internally in leucorrhœa. Its internal use is highly recommended in colliquative perspiration. Externally it is a good application to wounds, ulcers, scald-head, and some other cutaneous diseases. Dose of the decoction, from a wineglassful to a teacupful, two or three times a day. The fresh leaves or flowers will destroy or drive away fleas.

DANDELION (LEONTODON TARAXACUM).

MEDICINAL PART. *The root.*

Description.—Dandelion is a perennial, top-shaped herb, having a very milky root. The leaves are all radical, shining green in color, sessile, and pinnate. The scape or flower stem is longer than the leaves, five or six inches in height, and bearing a single yellow flower. The fruit is an achenium.

History.—This plant is a native of Greece, but is now found growing abundantly in Europe and the United States, in fields, gardens, and along road-sides, flowering from April to November. The root only is the officinal part, and should be collected when the plant is in flower. Alcohol or boiling water extracts its properties. The young plant is frequently used as a salad or green, and possesses some slight narcotic properties.

Properties and Uses.—The dried root possesses but little medicinal virtue; but when fresh, is a stomachic and tonic, with slightly diuretic and aperient actions. It has long been supposed to exert an influence upon the biliary organs, removing torpor and engorgement of the liver as well as of the spleen; it is also reputed beneficial in dropsies owing to want of action of the abdominal organs, in uterine obstructions, chronic diseases of the skin, etc. Its virtues, however, are much over-rated.

DEVIL'S BIT (HELONIAS DIOCIA).

COMMON NAMES. *False Unicorn Root*, *Drooping Star Wort*, etc.

MEDICINAL PART. *The root.*

Description.—This is an herbaceous perennial plant, with a large bulbous root, from which arises a very smooth angular stem one or two feet in height. The cauline leaves are lanceolate, acute, and small; the radical leaves (or those springing from the root) are broader and from four to eight inches in length. The flowers are small, very numerous, greenish-white, disposed in long, terminal, nodding racemes, resembling plumes. The fruit is a capsule.

History.—This plant is indigenous to the United States, and is abundant in some of the Western States, growing in woodlands, meadows, and moist situations, and flowering in June and July.

Properties and Uses.—In large doses it is emetic, and when fresh, sialagogue. In doses of ten or fifteen grains of the powdered root, repeated three or four times a day, it has been found very beneficial in dyspepsia, loss of appetite, and for the removal of worms. It is beneficial in colic, and in atony of the generative organs. It is invaluable in uterine diseases, acting as a uterine tonic, and gradually removing abnormal conditions, while at the same time it imparts tone and vigor to the reproductive organs. Hence, it is much used in leucorrhœa, amenorrhœa, dysmenorrhœa, and to remove the tendency to repeated and successive miscarriage. The plant will kill cattle feeding on it, and the decoction, insects, bugs, and lice.

Dose.—Of the powder, from twenty to forty grains; of the decoction, from a wineglassful to a teacupful.

The *Helonias Bullata*, with purple flowers, and probably some other species possess similar medicinal virtues.

DOCK (RUMEX CRISPUS).

MEDICINAL PART. *The root.*

Description.—There are four varieties of Dock which may be used in medicine: the *Rumex Aquaticus* (Great Water Dock); *Rumex Britannica* (Water Dock); *Rumex Abtusifolius* (Blunt-leaved Dock); and the *R. Crispus*, or Yellow Dock. They all possess similar medicinal qualities, but the Yellow Dock is the only one entitled to extensive consideration. It has a deep, spindle-shaped yellow root, with a stem two or three feet high. The leaves are lanceolate, acute, and of a light green color. The flowers are numerous, pale green, drooping, and interspersed with leaves below. The fruit is a nut contracted at each end.

Dock.

History.—The Docks are natives of Europe, excepting the blunt-leaved, which is indigenous, but they have all been introduced into the United States. Yellow Dock grows in cultivated grounds, waste grounds, about rubbish, etc., flowering in June and July. The root has scarcely any odor, but an astringent bitter taste, and yields its virtues to water and alcohol.

Properties and Uses.—Yellow Dock is an alterative, tonic and detergent, and eminently useful in scorbutic, cutaneous, scrofulous, cancerous and syphilitic affections, leprosy, elephantiasis, etc. For all impurities of the blood it has no equal, especially if properly compounded with appropriate adjutants and corrigents. The fresh root bruised in cream, lard, or butter, forms a good ointment for various affections. This admirable alterative is one of the ingredients of my Blood Purifier (see page 471), in which it is associated with other eminent alteratives, making the compound worthy of the reputation it has achieved.

Dogwood.

DOGWOOD (CORNUS FLORIDA).

COMMON NAMES. *Boxwood, Flowering Cornel, Green Ozier.*

MEDICINAL PART. *The bark.*

Description.—Dogwood is a small indigenous tree from twelve to thirty feet high, with a very hard and compact wood, and covered with a rough and brownish bark. The tree is of slow growth. The leaves are opposite, smooth, ovate, acute, dark green above, paler beneath. The flowers are very small, of a greenish yellow color, and constitute the chief beauty of the tree when in bloom. The fruit is an oval drupe of a glossy scarlet color, containing a nut with two cells and two seeds.

History.—This tree grows in various parts of the United States; it flowers in April and May. The fruit matures in autumn. The wood is used for many purposes. The bark yields its virtues to water and alcohol. The chemical qualities are tannic and gallic acids, resin, gum, oil, wax, lignin, lime, potassa, and iron.

Properties and Uses.—It is tonic, astringent, and slightly stimulant. It is an excellent substitute for Peruvian bark, and may be used when the foreign remedy is not to be obtained, or when it fails, or where it cannot be administered. The bark should only be used in its dried state. *Cornine*, its active principle, is much used as a substitute for quinine.

Dogwood, or green ozier, exerts its best virtues in the shape of an ointment. It is detergent in all inflammatory conditions, destructive to morbid growths, and at variance with diseased nutrition. It stimulates granulations, increases the reparative process, induces circulation of healthy blood to the parts, removes effete matter, vitalizes the tissues, and speedily removes pain from the diseased parts. It fulfils these conditions in my great healing remedy, the "Herbal Ointment," see page 472.

Dose.—Of the powder, twenty to sixty grains; extract, five to ten grains; cornine, from one to ten grains.

DRAGON ROOT (ARUM TRIPHYLLUM).

COMMON NAMES. *Wake Robin, Indian Turnip, Jack in the Pulpit, etc.*

MEDICINAL PART. *The cormus or root.*

Description.—This plant has a round, flattened, perennial rhizome; the upper part is tunicated like an onion. The leaves are generally one or two, standing on long, sheathing footstalks; leaflets oval, mostly entire, acuminate, smooth, and paler on the under side.

History.—It inhabits North and South America, is found in wet locations, and flowers from May to June. The whole plant is acrid, but the root is the only part employed. It is of various sizes, turnip-shaped, dark and corrugated externally, and milk-white within, seldom exceeding two and a half inches in diameter. When first dug it is too fiercely acrid for internal employment, as it will leave an impression upon the tongue, lips, and fauces, like that of a severe scald, followed by inflammation and tenderness, which, however, may be somewhat mollified by milk. It exerts no such influence upon the external skin, except upon long and continued application. The root loses its acrimony by age, and should always be used when partially dried. In addition to its acrid principle, it contains a large proportion of starch, with a portion of gum, albumen, and saccharine matter. When the acrid matter is driven off by heat, the root yields a pure, delicate, amylaceous matter, resembling arrow-root, very white and nutritive.

Properties and Uses.—It is acrid, expectorant, and diaphoretic, used in asthma, hooping-cough, chronic bronchitis, chronic rheumatism, pains in the chest, colic, low stages of typhus, and general debility; externally in scrofulous tumors, scald-head, and various skin diseases.

Dose.—Of the grated root, in syrup or mucilage, ten grains, three or four times a day.

ELDER (Sambucus Canadensis).

Medicinal Parts. *The flowers and berries.*

Description.—This is a common, well-known native American plant, from five to twelve feet high, with a shrubby stem, filled with a light and porous pith, especially when young. The bark is rather scabrous and cinereous. The leaves are nearly bipinnate, antiposed. The flowers are numerous, white, in very large level-topped, five-parted cymes, and have a heavy odor. The European Elder, though larger than the American kind, is similar in its general characteristics and properties.

History.—It is an indigenous shrub, growing in all parts of the United States, in low, damp grounds, thickets, and waste places, flowering in June and July, and maturing its berries in September and October. The officinal parts are the flowers, the berries, and the inner bark.

Properties and Uses.—In warm infusion the flowers are diaphoretic and gently stimulant. In cold infusion they are diuretic, alterative, and cooling, and may be used in all diseases requiring such action, as in hepatic derangements of children, erysipelas, erysipelatous diseases, etc. In infusion with Maiden-hair and Beech-drops, they will be found very valuable in all erysipelatous diseases. *The expressed juice of the berries*, evaporated to the consistence of a syrup, is a valuable aperient and alterative; one ounce of it will purge. An infusion of the young leaf-buds is likewise purgative, and sometimes acts with violence. The flowers and expressed juice of the berries have been beneficially employed in scrofula, cutaneous diseases, syphilis, rheumatism, etc. The inner green bark is cathartic; an infusion of it in wine, or the expressed juice, will purge moderately in doses from half a fluid ounce to a fluid ounce. Large doses produce emesis or vomiting. In small doses it produces an efficacious deobstruent, promoting all the fluid secretions, and is much used in dropsy, especially that following scarlatina and other febrile and exanthematous complaints, as well as in many chronic diseases. Beaten up with lard or cream, it forms an excellent discutient ointment, of much value in burns, scalds, and some cutaneous diseases. The juice of the root in half-ounce doses, taken daily, acts as a hydragogue cathartic, and stimulating diuretic, and will be found valuable in all dropsical affections. The inner bark of Elder is hydragogue and emetico-cathartic. Has been successfully used in epilepsy, by taking it from branches one or two years old, scraping off the gray outer bark, and steeping two ounces of it in five ounces of cold or hot water for forty-eight hours. Strain and give a wineglassful every fifteen minutes when the fit is threatening: the patient fasting. Resume it every six or eight days.

ELECAMPANE (INULA HELENIUM).

MEDICINAL PART. *The root.*

Description.—This plant has a thick, top-shaped, aromatic, and perennial root, with a thick, leafy, round, solid stem, from four to six feet high. The leaves are large, ovate, dark green above, downy and hoary beneath, with a fleshy mid-rib. The flowers are of a bright yellow color, and the fruit an achenium.

History.—Elecampane is common in Europe, and cultivated in the United States. It grows in pastures and along road-sides, blossoming from July to September. The root is the part used, and should be gathered in the second year of its development, and during the fall months. It yields its properties to water and alcohol, more especially to the former.

Properties and Uses.—It is aromatic, stimulant, tonic, emmenagogue, diuretic, and diaphoretic. It is much used in chronic pulmonary affections, weakness of the digestive organs, hepatic torpor, dyspepsia, etc.

Dose.—Of the powder, from one scruple to one drachm; of the infusion, one to two fluid ounces.

ERGOT (SECALE CORNUTUM).

COMMON NAMES. *Spurred or Smut Rye.*

MEDICINAL PART. *The degenerated seeds.*

Description.—Ergot is the name given to the fungoid, degenerated seeds of the common rye, which is the result of a parasitic plant called *Oidium Abortifaciens.*

History.—Ergot consists of grains, varying in length, of a violet-black color; odor fishy, peculiar, and nauseous. Their taste is not very marked, but is disagreeable and slightly acrid. They should be gathered previous to harvest.

Properties and Uses.—Ergot has a remarkable effect upon the human system, and when persisted in for a length of time as an article of food manifests certain symptoms termed *ergotism.* Its chief use as a medicine is to promote uterine contractions in slow, natural labors. It is also useful in checking menorrhagia, uterine hemorrhages, and to expel polypi. It is also employed in gonorrhœa, amenorrhœa, paraplegia, paralysis of the bladder, fever and ague.

This is a valuable remedy to the obstetrician and midwife, but its use should not be persisted in too long, as it often produces dangerous symptoms.

Dose.—Of the powder, five, ten, or fifteen grains; fluid extract, thirty drops.

ERYNGO (ERYNGIUM AQUATICUM).

COMMON NAMES. *Buttonsnake Root, Rattlesnake's Master, etc.*

MEDICINAL PART. *The root.*

Description.—This indigenous, perennial herb has a simple stem from one to five feet high. The root is a tuber; the leaves are one or two feet long, half an inch to an inch wide, and taper-pointed. The flowers are white or pale, and inconspicuous.

History.—This plant is indigenous, growing in swamps and low, wet lands from Virginia to Texas, especially on prairie lands, blossoming in August. The root is the officinal part. Water or alcohol extracts its properties.

Properties and Uses.—It is aphrodisiac, exciting venereal desires and strengthening the procreative organs. It is also diuretic, stimulant, diaphoretic, expectorant, and, in large doses, emetic. Very useful in dropsy, nephritic and calculous affections, also in scrofula and syphilis. It is valuable as a diaphoretic and expectorant in pulmonary affections. It is a good substitute for *Senega.* The pulverized root, in doses of two or three grains, is very effectual in hemorrhoids and prolapsus ani. Two ounces of the pulverized root, added to one pint of good Holland gin, is effectual in obstinate cases of gonorrhœa and gleet, to be administered in doses of one or two fluid drachms, three or four times a day. By some practitioners the root is employed as a *specific* in gonorrhœa, gleet, and leucorrhœa; used internally in syrup, decoction, or tincture—and the decoction applied locally by injection. Used externally and internally, it cures the bites of snakes and insects.

Dose.—Of the powder, from twenty to forty grains; of the decoction, which is principally used, from two to four fluid ounces, several times a day.

EYE-BRIGHT (EUPHRASIA OFFICINALIS).

MEDICINAL PART. *The leaves.*

Description.—This is an elegant little annual plant, with a square, downy, leafy stem, from one to five inches in height. The leaves are entirely opposite, ovate or cordate, and downy; the flowers very abundant, inodorous, with a brilliant variety of colors. The fruit is an oblong pod, filled with numerous seeds.

History.—This plant is indigenous to Europe and America, bearing red or white flowers in July. The leaves are commonly employed; they are inodorous, but of a bitter, astringent taste. Water extracts their virtues.

Properties and Virtues.—Slightly tonic and astringent. Useful in form of infusion or poultice, in catarrhal ophthalmia; also of service in all mucous diseases attended with increased discharges; also, in cough, hoarseness, ear-ache, and head-ache, which have supervened upon catarrhal affections. Four fluid ounces of the infusion taken every morning upon an empty stomach, and also every night at bed-time, has been found successful in helping epilepsy.

FERNS (FILICES).

ROYAL FLOWERING FERN. *Osmunda Regalis.*

COMMON NAME. *Buckhorn Brake.*

MEDICINAL PART. *The root.*

Description.—This Fern has a hard, scaly, tuberous root, quite fibrous, and a whitish core in the centre. The fronds are three or four feet high, bright green, and doubly pinnate. The numerous leaflets are sessile and oblong, some of the upper ones cut.

History.—This beautiful Fern is found in meadows, and low, moist grounds, throughout the United States, blossoming in June. The main root or caudex is the officinal part; it is about two inches long, and has the shape of a buck's horn. It contains an abundance of mucilage, which is extracted by boiling water. The roots should be collected in August, or about the latter part of May, and dried with great care, as they are apt to become mouldy.

The *Osmunda Cinnamomea*, or cinnamon-colored Fern, is inferior to the preceding, but is frequently used for the same medical purposes.

Properties and Uses.—Mucilaginous, tonic, and styptic. Used in coughs, diarrhœa, and dysentery; also used as a tonic during convalescence from exhausting diseases. One root, infused in a pint of hot water for half an hour, will convert the whole into a thick jelly, very valuable in leucorrhœa and other female weaknesses. The mucilage mixed with brandy is a popular remedy as an external application for subluxations and debility of the muscles of the back. For internal use the roots may be infused in hot water, sweetened, and ginger, cinnamon, brandy, etc., added, if not contra-indicated.

FEMALE FERN (POLYPODIUM VULGARE).

COMMON NAMES. *Rock Polypod, Brake Root, Common Polypody.*

MEDICINAL PARTS. *The root and tops.*

Description.—This perennial has a creeping, irregular, brown root. The fronds are from six to twelve inches high, green, smooth, and deeply pinnatified. The fruit on the lower surface of the fronds is in large golden dots or capsules.

History.—This fern is common on shady rocks in woods and mountains throughout the United States. The root has a peculiar and rather unpleasant odor, and somewhat sickening taste. Water extracts its properties.

Properties and Uses.—This plant is pectoral, demulcent, purgative, and anthelmintic. A decoction of syrup has been found very valuable in pulmonary and hepatic diseases. A strong decoction is a good purgative, and will expel tenia and other worms. Dose of the powdered plant, from one to four drachms. Of the decoction or syrup, from one to four fluid ounces, three or four times a day.

MALE FERN (ASPIDIUM FILIX MAS).

MEDICINAL PART. *The rhizome.*

Description.—Male Fern has a large, perennial, tufted, scaly rhizome, sending forth yearly several leaves, three or four feet high, erect, oval, lanceolate, acute, pinnate, bright green, and leafy nearly to the bottom; their stalks and midribs having tough, brown, and transparent scales throughout. Leaflets numerous, crowded, oblong, obtuse, and crenate throughout.

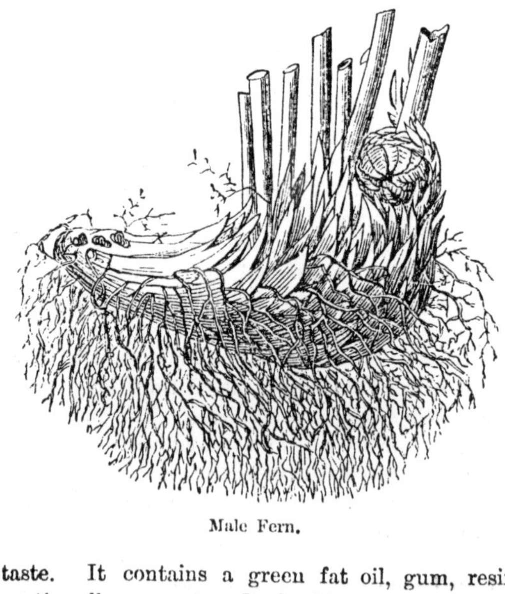

Male Fern.

History.—Male Fern grows in all parts of the United States and Europe. The root has a dark brown epiderm, is almost inodorous, and a nauseous sweet taste. It contains a green fat oil, gum, resin, lignin, tannic acid, pectin, albumen, etc. It should be gathered from June to September. After gathering, it should be carefully prepared, as on the preparation its virtues depend. It loses its virtues in two years if not properly preserved.

Properties and Uses.—It is used for the expulsion of worms, especially tape-worms. It was used as such by Pliny, Dioscorides, Theophrastus, and Galen. It was the celebrated secret remedy of Madame Nouffer, the widow of a Swiss surgeon, who sold her secret to Louis XVI. for 18,000 francs. It is, in fact, a royal anthelmintic, and worthy of all the high commendations it has received from ages past up to the present time. It is one of the ingredients of my "Male Fern Vermifuge." See page 471.

FEVERFEW (PYRETHRUM PARTHENIUM).

MEDICINAL PART. *The herb.*

Description.—Feverfew is a perennial herbaceous plant, with a tapering root, and an erect, round, and leafy stem about two feet high. The leaves are alternate, petiolate, hoary-green, with leaflets inclining to ovate and dentate. The flowers are white and compound, and the fruit a wingless, angular, and uniform achenium.

History.—The plant is a native of Europe, but common in the United States; found occasionally in a wild state, but generally cultivated in gardens, and blossoms in June and July. It imparts its virtues to water, but much better to alcohol.

Properties and Uses.—It is tonic, carminative, emmenagogue, vermifuge, and stimulant. The warm infusion is an excellent remedy in recent colds, flatulency, worms, irregular menstruation, hysteria, suppression of urine, and in some febrile diseases. In hysteria or flatulency, one teaspoonful of the compound spirits of lavender forms a valuable addition to the dose of the infusion, which is from two to four fluid ounces. The cold infusion or extract makes a valuable tonic. The leaves, in poultice, are an excellent local application in severe pain or swelling of the bowels, etc. Bees are said to dislike this plant very much, and a handful of the flower-heads carried where they are will cause them to keep at a distance.

FIGWORT (SCROPHULARIA NODOSA).

MEDICINAL PARTS. *The leaves and root.*

Description.—Figwort has a perennial, whitish, and fibrous root, with a leafy, erect, smooth stem from two to four feet high. The leaves are opposite, ovate; the upper lanceolate, acute, of deep green color, and from three to seven inches in length. The flowers are small, and dark purple in color. The fruit is an ovate-oblong capsule.

History.—This plant is a native of Europe, but is found growing in different parts of the United States, in woods, hedges, damp copses, and banks, blossoming from July to October. The plants known by the names of *Carpenter's Square, Heal All, Square Stalk* etc. (*S. Mari-*

landica and *S. Lanceolata*), are all mere varieties of *Figwort*, possessing similar medicinal properties. The leaves and root are the officinal parts, and yield their virtues to water or alcohol. The leaves have an offensive odor, and a bitter, unpleasant taste; the root is slightly acrid.

Properties and Uses.—It is alterative, diuretic, and anodyne; highly beneficial in hepatic or liver diseases, dropsy, and as a general deobstruent to the glandular system when used in infusion or syrup. Externally, in the form of fomentation or ointment, it is valuable in bruises, inflammation of the mammæ, ringworm, piles, painful swellings, itch, and cutaneous eruptions of a vesicular character. The root, in decoction and drunk freely, will restore the lochial discharge when suppressed, and relieve the pains attending difficult menstruation. This plant possesses many valuable and active medicinal properties.

Dose.—Of the infusion or syrup, from a wineglassful to a teacupful.

FIREWEED (ERECHTHITES HIERACTIFOLIUS).

MEDICINAL PARTS. *The root and herb.*

Description.—This plant has an annual, herbaceous, thick, fleshy, branching, and roughish stem, from one to five feet high. The leaves are simple, alternate, large, lanceolate or oblong, acute, deeply dentate, sessile, and light green. The flowers are whitish, and the fruit an achenium, oblong and hairy.

History.—This indigenous rank weed grows in fields throughout the United States, in moist woods, in recent clearings, and is especially abundant in such as have been burned over. It flowers from July to October, and somewhat resembles the Sowthistle. The whole plant yields its virtues to water or alcohol. It has a peculiar, aromatic, and somewhat fetid odor, and a slightly pungent, bitter, and disagreeable taste.

Properties and Uses.—It is emetic, cathartic, tonic, astringent, and alterative. The latter three qualities are the most valuable. It is an unrivalled medicine in diseases of the mucous tissues. The spirituous extract which I use in my practice is most excellent in cholera and dysentery, promptly arresting the discharges, relieving the pain, and effecting a speedy cure. It is invariably successful in summer complaints of children, even in cases where other means have failed.

FROST-WEED (HELIANTHEMUM CANADENSE).

COMMON NAMES. *Rock Rose, Frost Plant, etc.*

MEDICINAL PART. *The herb.*

Description.—Rock Rose is a perennial herb, with a simple, ascending downy stem, about a foot high. The leaves are alternate, from eight to twelve inches long, about one-fourth as wide; oblong, acute, lanceolate, erect, and entire. The flowers are large and bright yellow, some with petals, and some without petals. The flowers open in sunshine and cast their petals next day.

History.--It is indigenous to all parts of the United States, growing in dry, sandy soils, and blossoming from May to July. The leaves and stems are covered with a white down, hence its name. The whole plant is officinal, having a bitterish, astringent, slightly aromatic taste, and yields its properties to hot water. Prof. Eaton, in his work on botany, records this curious fact of the plant: "In November and December of 1816 I saw hundreds of these plants sending out broad, thin, curved ice crystals, about an inch in breadth from near the roots. These were melted away by day, and renewed every morning for more than twenty-five days in succession."

Rock Rose.

Properties and Uses.—This plant has long been used as a valuable remedy for scrofula, in which disease it performs some astonishing cures. It is used in form of decoction, syrup, or fluid extract, but had better be used in combination with other remedies. In combination with *Corydalis Formosa* and *Stillingia* it forms a most valuable remedy. It is tonic and astringent, as well as antiscrofulous. It can be used with advantage in diarrhœa, as a gargle in scarlatina and aphthous ulcerations, and as a wash in scrofulous ophthalmia. Externally, a poultice of the leaves is applied to scrofulous tumors and ulcers. An *oil* has been procured from the plant which is said to be highly valuable in cancerous affections. This excellent alterative is a constituent of that happy combination of alteratives composing my "Blood Purifier," see page 471.

The *Helianthemum Corymbosum*, or Frost-weed, growing in the pine barrens and sterile lands of the Southern and Middle States, possesses similar qualities, and may be employed if the former frost-weed is not to be had.

FUMITORY (FUMARIA OFFICINALIS).

MEDICINAL PART. *The leaves.*

Description.—Fumitory is an annual, glaucous plant, with a sub-erect, much branched, spreading, leafy and angular stem, growing from ten to fifteen inches high. The leaves are mostly alternate. Culpepper, who knew the plant which is now used, better than anybody else, said that "at the top of the branches stand many small flowers, as it were in a long spike one above another, made like little birds, of a reddish purple color, with whitish bellies, after which come small round husks, containing small black seeds. The root is small, yellow, and not very long, and full of juice when it is young." The fruit, or nut, is ovoid or globose, one-seeded or valveless. The seeds are crestless.

History.—Fumitory is found growing in cultivated soils in Europe and America, and flowers in May, June, and July. The leaves are the parts used. Culpepper recommended the whole plant, but the modern decision is to use the leaves, gathered at the proper times, alone. They have no odor, but taste bitter under all circumstances. They are to be used when fresh, and possess the same qualities as Culpepper affixes to the fresh root, viz. : malate of lime and bitter extractive principles.

Properties and Uses.—Its virtues are chiefly tonic, and those who suffer from diseases of the stomach know too well that a tonic, if properly defined, is, simple as it may be, one of the most important remedies for human ailments nature has provided. Its chief value is found in its action upon the liver. It is used, in combination, with excellent effect in cutaneous diseases, liver complaints, such as jaundice, costiveness, scurvy, and in debility of the stomach. An infusion of the leaves is usually given in a wineglass (full) every four hours. The flowers and tops have been applied, macerated in wine, to dyspepsia, with partial good effect.

GAMBIR PLANT (UNCARIA GAMBIR).

MEDICINAL PART. *Extract of the leaves and young shoots.*

Description.—Gambir is a stout climbing shrub with round branches. Leaves ovate, lanceolate, acute, smooth, and have short petioles. Flowers in loose heads, green and pink; calyx short, corolla funnel-shaped; stamens five, and the fruit a two-celled capsule.

History.—It is an inhabitant of the East Indian Archipelago, where it is extensively cultivated. On the island of Bingtang alone there are 60,000 Gambir plantations. It affords what is known as *pale catechu.* It is chiefly imported from Singapore. It is found in cubes which float on water, externally brown, internally pale brick red, breaking easily. Taste bitter, very astringent, and mucilaginous. Boiling water almost completely dissolves it. It is used in the arts for tanning.

Properties and Uses.—It is employed as an astringent. In various affections of the mouth it is an efficacious astringent. It is also excellent as a stomachic in dyspeptic complaints, especially when accompanied with pyrosis. It should be used just before taking food. It is an excellent astringent in chronic diarrhœa and dysentery.

Dose.—From ten to forty grains

GELSEMIN (GELSEMINUM SEMPERVIRENS).

COMMON NAMES. *Yellow Jessamine, Woodbine, Wild Jessamine.*

MEDICINAL PART. *The root.*

Description.—This plant has a twining, smooth, glabrous stem, with opposite, perennial, lanceolate, entire leaves, which are dark green above and pale beneath. The flowers are yellow, and have an agreeable odor. Calyx is very small, with five sepals, corolla funnel-shaped, stamens five, pistils two, and the fruit a two-celled capsule.

History.—Yellow jessamine abounds throughout the Southern States, growing luxuriantly, and climbing from tree to tree, forming an agreeable shade. It is cultivated as an ornamental vine, and flowers from March to May. The root yields its virtues to water and alcohol. *Gelsemin* is its active principle. It also contains a fixed oil, acrid resin, yellow coloring matter, a heavy volatile oil, a crystalline substance, and salts of potassa, lime, magnesia, iron, and silica.

Properties and Uses.—It is an unrivalled febrifuge, possessing relaxing and antispasmodic properties. It is efficacious in nervous and bilious headache, colds, pneumonia, hemorrhages, leucorrhœa, ague-cake, but especially in all kinds of fevers, quieting all nervous irritability and excitement, equalizing the circulation, promoting perspiration, and rectifying the various secretions, without causing nausea, vomiting, and purging, and is adapted to any stage of the disease. It may follow any preceding treatment with safety. Its effects are clouded vision, double-sightedness, or even complete prostration, and inability to open the eyes. These, however, pass completely off in a few hours, leaving the patient refreshed, and completely restored. When the effects are induced no more of the remedy is required. It is also of great service in various cardiac diseases, spermatorrhœa, and other genital diseases; but its use should be confined entirely to the advice of the physician.

Dose.—The tincture is the form in which it is employed. The dose is from ten to fifty drops in a wineglass half full of water; to be repeated every two hours, as long as required.

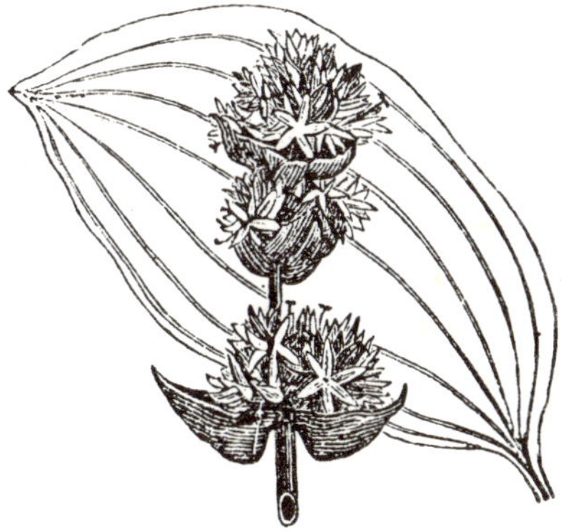

Gentian.

GENTIAN (GENTIANA LUTEA).

MEDICINAL PART. *The root.*

Description.—This plant has a long, thick, cylindrical, wrinkled, ringed, forked, perennial root, brown externally, and yellow within, with a stem three or four feet high, hollow, stout, and erect; leaves ovate-oblong, five-veined, pale, bright green; the blossoms are large, of a bright yellow, in many-flowered whorls; and the fruit is a capsule, stalked, oblong, and two-valved.

History.—This plant is common in Central and Southern Europe, especially on the Pyrenees and Alps, being found from 3,000 to 5,000 feet above the level of the sea. The root affords the medicinal portion, and is brought to America chiefly from Havre and Marseilles. It has a feeble aromatic odor, and a taste at first faintly sweetish, and then purely, intensely, and permanently bitter. It imparts its virtues readily to cold or hot water, alcohol, wine, spirits, or sulphuric ether.

Properties and Uses.—Is a powerful tonic, improves the appetite, strengthens digestion, gives force to the circulation, and slightly elevates the heat of the body. Very useful in debility, exhaustion, dyspepsia, gout, amenorrhœa, hysteria, scrofula, intermittents, worms, and diarrhœa.

Dose.—Of the powder, ten to thirty grains; of the extract, one to ten grains; of the infusion, a tablespoonful to a wineglassful; of the tincture, one or two teaspoonfuls.

Uncrystallized gentianin is a most valuable substitute for quinia, acting as readily and efficaciously on the spleen, in doses of from fifteen to thirty grains, twice a day.

GENTIANA CATESBEI, or the *Blue*, or *American Gentian*, has a perennial, branching, somewhat fleshy root, with a simple, erect, rough stem, eight or ten inches in height, and bears large blue flowers. It grows in the grassy swamps and meadows of North and South Carolina, blossoming from September to December. The root is little inferior to the foreign gentian, and may be used as a substitute for it in all cases, in the same doses and preparations.

GENTIANA QUINQUEFLORA, or *Five-flowered Gentian*, sometimes called Gall-weed, on account of its intense bitterness, is very useful in headache, liver complaint, jaundice, etc. The plant is found from Vermont to Pennsylvania, and a variety of it is common throughout the Western States. It grows in woods and pastures, and flowers in September and October. It may be regarded as a valuable tonic and cholagogue, and deserves further investigation of its therapeutic properties.

There is another kind of gentian (*Gentiana Ochroleuca*), known by the names of Marsh Gentian, Yellowish-white Gentian, Straw-colored Gentian, and Sampson Snake-weed. It has a stout, smoothish, ascending stem, one or two inches in height, its leaves two to four inches long, and three-fourths to an inch and a half in width, with straw-colored flowers two inches long by three-quarters thick, disposed in a dense, terminal cyme, and often in axillary cymes. It is found in Canada and the Southern and Western States, though rarely in the latter, blossoming in September and October; the root is the officinal part, although the tops are often employed. They are bitter, tonic, anthelmintic, and astringent. Used in dyspepsia, intermittents, dysentery, and all diseases of periodicity.

To two ounces of the tops and roots pour on a pint and a half of boiling water, and when nearly cold add a half-pint of brandy. Dose, from one to three tablespoonfuls every half-hour, gradually increasing as the stomach can bear it, lengthening the intervals between the doses. It is also used for bites of snakes, etc.

GILLENIA (Gillenia Trifoliata).

Common Name. *Indian Physic.*

Medicinal Part. *The bark of the root.*

Description.—Gillenia is an indigenous, perennial herb, with an irregular, brownish, somewhat tuberous root, having many long, knotted, stringy fibres. The several stems are from the same root, about two or three feet high, erect, slender, smooth, and of a reddish or brownish color. The leaves are alternate, subsessile; leaflets lanceolate, acuminate, sharply dentated; flowers are white, with a reddish tinge; and the fruit a two-valved, one-celled capsule. Seeds are oblong, brown, and bitter.

History.—This species is found scattered over the United States from Canada to Florida, on the eastern side of the Alleghanies, occurring in open hilly woods, in light gravelly soil. The period of flowering is in May, and the fruit is matured in August. The root yields its virtues to boiling water and alcohol.

Properties and Uses.—It is emetic, cathartic, diaphoretic, expectorant, and tonic. It resembles ipecac in action. It is useful in amenorrhœa, rheumatism, dropsy, costiveness, dyspepsia, worms, and intermittent fever. It may be used in all fevers where emetics are required.

Dose.—As an emetic, twenty to thirty-five grains of the powder, as often as required; as a tonic, two to four grains; as a diaphoretic, six grains in cold water, and repeated at intervals of two or three hours.

GOSSYPIUM HERBACEUM.

Common Name. *Cotton.*

Medicinal Part. *The inner bark of the root.*

Description.—Cotton is a biennial or triennial herb, with a fusiform root, with a round pubescent branching stem about five feet high. The leaves are hoary, palmate, with five sub-lanceolate, rather acute lobes; flowers are yellow; calyx cup-shaped, petals five, deciduous, with a purple spot near the base; stigmas, three or five; and the fruit a three or five-celled capsule, with three or five seeds involved in cotton.

History.—It is a native of Asia; but is cultivatea extensively in many parts of the world, and in the Southern portions of America more successfully than anywhere else. The inner bark of the recent root is the part chiefly used in medicine. Its active principle, which is that administered by all educated herbal physicians, is called *Gossypiin.*

Properties and Uses.—The preparation *Gossypiin* is most excellent for diseases of the utero-genital organs. In these diseases it evinces its sole and only virtues, and it ought, on every occasion where it can be procured in its purity, to be used in the stead of *ergot*, or smut rye, in cases of difficult labor. The latter will produce uterine inflammation, and puerperal fever, while gossypiin will achieve the beneficial effects for which ergot is usually administered, and leave the system perfectly free from any prejudicial after-results. The active principle of fresh cotton root forms a most wonderful uterine tonic, and, if correctly prepared, will be found invaluable in sterility, vaginitis, whites, menstrual irregularities, green sickness, etc. I do not recommend the use of the decoction of the root by inexperienced persons. The seeds are said to possess superior anti-periodic properties.

GLOBE FLOWER (CEPHALANTHUS OCCIDENTALIS).

COMMON NAMES. *Button Bush, Pond Dogwood, etc.*

MEDICINAL PART.—*The bark.*

Description.—This is a handsome shrub, growing from six to twelve or more feet high, with a rough bark on the stem, but smooth on the branches. The leaves are opposite, oval, acuminate, in whorls of three, from three to five inches long by two to three wide. The flowers are white, and resemble those of the sycamore, and the fruit a hard and dry capsule.

History.—This plant is indigenous, and found in damp places, along the margins of rivers, ponds, etc., flowering from June to September. The bark is very bitter, and yields its virtues to water and alcohol.

Properties and Uses.—Tonic, febrifuge, aperient, and diuretic. It is used with much success in intermittent and remittent fevers. The inner bark of the root forms an agreeable bitter, and is employed in coughs and gravel. It deserves more notice than it receives, for my experience with it teaches me that it is a valuable medicinal plant.

GOLDEN SEAL (HYDRASTIS CANADENSIS).

COMMON NAMES. *Yellow Puccoon, Ground Raspberry, Turmeric Root, etc.*

MEDICINAL PART. *The root.*

Description.—This indigenous plant has a perennial root or rhizome, which is tortuous, knotty, creeping, internally of a bright yellow color, with long fibres. The stem is erect, simple, herbaceous, rounded, from six to twelve inches high, bearing two unequal terminal leaves. The two leaves are alternate, palmate, having from three to five lobes, hairy, dark-green, cordate at base, from four to nine inches wide when full grown. The flower is a solitary one, small, white or rose-colored, and the fruit resembles a raspberry, is red, and consists of many two-seeded drupes.

History.—Golden seal is found growing in shady woods, in rich soils, and damp meadows in different parts of the United States and Canada, but is more abundant west of the Alleghanies. It flowers in May and June. The root is the officinal part. Its virtues are imparted to water or alcohol. The root is of a beautiful yellow color, and when fresh is juicy, and used by the Indians to color their clothing, etc.

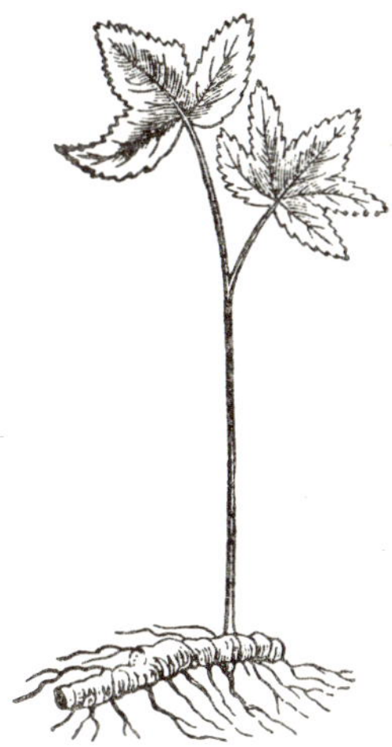

Golden Seal.

Properties and Uses.—The root is a powerful tonic, at the same time exerting an especial influence upon the mucous surfaces and tissues, with which it comes in contact. Internally, it is successfully administered in dyspepsia, chronic affections of the mucous coats of the stomach, erysipelas; remittent, intermittent, and typhoid fevers; torpor of the liver, and wherever tonics are required. In some instances it proves laxative, but without any astringency, and seems to rank in therapeutical action between rhubarb and blood-root.

A strong decoction of two parts of Golden Seal and one part of Geranium or Cranebill, is very valuable in gleet, chronic gonorrhœa, and leucorrhœa, used in *injection.* It is likewise of much benefit in *incipient stricture*, *spermatorrhœa*, and *inflammation* and *ulceration of the internal coat of the bladder.* Ulceration of the internal coat of the bladder may be cured by the decoction of Golden Seal alone. It must be injected into the bladder, and held there as long as the patient can conveniently retain it. To be repeated three or four times a day, immediately after emptying the bladder.

Dose.—Of the powder, from ten to thirty grains; of the tincture, from one to two fluid drachms.

GOLD THREAD (Coptis Trifolia).

Common Name. *Mouth-root.*

Medicinal Part. *The root.*

Description.—This plant has a small, creeping, perennial root, of a bright yellow color; the stems are round, slender, and at the base are invested with ovate, acuminate, yellowish scales. The leaves are evergreen, on long, slender petioles; leaflets roundish, acute at base, small and smooth, and veiny and sessile. The flower is a small starry white one, and the fruit an oblong capsule, containing many small black seeds.

History.—Goldthread is found growing in dark swamps and sphagnous woods in the northern parts of the United States, and in Canada, Greenland, Iceland, and Siberia. It flowers early in the spring to July. The root is the medicinal part, and autumn is the season for collecting it.

Properties and Uses.—It is a pure and powerful bitter tonic, somewhat like quassia, gentian, and columbo, without any astringency. It may be beneficially used in all cases where a *bitter* tonic is required, and is decidedly efficacious as a wash or gargle, when a decoction, in various ulcerations of the mouth. In dyspepsia, and in chronic inflammation of the stomach, equal parts of goldthread and golden seal, made into a decoction, with elixir vitriol added in proper quantity, will not only prove effectual, but in many instances will permanently destroy the appetite for alcoholic beverages.

Dose.—Of the powder or tincture, from half a drachm to a drachm; of the decoction, the dose is from one wineglassful to a teacupful. The tincture, made by adding an ounce of the powdered root to a pint of diluted alcohol, is preferable to the powder. The dose is from twenty drops to a teaspoonful, three times a day.

GUAIAC (GUAIACUM OFFICINALE).

COMMON NAME. *Lignum Vitæ.*

MEDICINAL PARTS. *The wood and resin.*

Description.—This is a tree of slow growth, attaining a height of from thirty to forty feet; stem commonly crooked; bark furrowed; wood very hard, heavy, the fibres crossing each other diagonally. Leaves bijugate; leaflets obovate or oval, obtuse, and evergreen. Flowers light blue, and the fruit an obcordate capsule.

History.—This tree is an inhabitant of the West Indian Islands, and on the neighboring part of the continent. The wood is used by turners for making block-sheaves, pestles, etc., and is very hard and durable. Both the wood and resin are used in medicine. Alcohol is the best solvent.

Properties and Uses.—The wood or resin, taken internally, commonly excites a warmth in the stomach, a dryness of mouth, or thirst. It is an acrid stimulant, and increases the heat of the body and accelerates the circulation. If the body be kept warm while using the decoction, it is diaphoretic; if cool, it is diuretic.

It is used in chronic rheumatism, cutaneous diseases, scrofula, and syphilitic diseases.

Dose.—Decoction of the wood, two to four ounces; of powdered resin, five to twenty grains; tincture, one to four fluid drachms.

HAZEL (WITCH) (HAMAMELIS VIRGINICA).

COMMON NAMES. *Winterbloom, Snapping-hazelnut, Spotted Alder.*

MEDICINAL PARTS. *The bark and leaves.*

Description.—This indigenous shrub consists of several crooked, branching stems, from the same root, from four to six inches in diameter and ten to twelve feet high, covered with a smooth gray bark. The leaves are on short petioles, alternate, oval or obovate; flowers yellow; calyx small, petals four, and the fruit a nut-like capsule or pod.

History.—It grows in damp woods, in nearly all parts of the United States, flowering from September to November, when the leaves are falling, and maturing its seeds the next summer. The barks and leaves are the parts used in medicine. They possess a degree of fragrance, and when chewed are at first somewhat bitter, very sensibly astringent, and then leave a pungent sweetish taste, which remains for a considerable time. Water extracts their virtues. The shoots are used as *divining rods* to discover water and metals under ground by certain adepts in the occult arts.

Properties and Uses.—It is tonic, astringent, and sedative. A decoction of the bark is very useful in hemoptysis, hematemesis, and other hemorrhages or bleedings, as well as in diarrhœa, dysentery, and excessive mucous discharges. It is employed with great advantage in incipient phthisis or consumption, in which it is supposed to unite anodyne influences with its others.

The Indians use it in the form of poultice, in external inflammations, swellings, and all tumors of a painful character.

The decoction may be advantageously used as a wash or injection for sore mouth, painful tumors, external inflammations, bowel complaints, prolapsus ani and uteri, leucorrhœa, gleet, and ophthalmia.

An *Ointment* made with lard, and a decoction of white-oak bark, apple-tree bark, and witch-hazel, is a very valuable remedy for hemorrhoids or piles.

The following forms a useful preparation: Take equal parts of witch-hazel bark, golden seal, and lobelia leaves, the two first made into a strong decoction, after which add the lobelia to the hot liquid, and cover; when cold, strain. This decoction, as a collyrium, will frequently and speedily cure the most obstinate and long-standing cases of ophthalmia.

Dose of the witch-hazel decoction alone, from a wineglassful to a teacupful, three or four times a day.

HELLEBORE (AMERICAN) (VERATRUM VIRIDE).

COMMON NAMES. *Swamp Hellebore, Indian Poke, Itch-weed.*
MEDICINAL PART. *The rhizome.*

Description.—This plant has a perennial, thick, and fleshy rhizome, tunicated at the upper part, sending off a multitude of large whitish roots. The stem is from three to five feet high; lower leaves from six inches to a foot long, oval, acuminate; upper leaves gradually narrower, linear, lanceolate, and all alternate. The flowers are numerous and green, part of them barren.

Hellebore.

History.—American Hellebore is native to the United States, growing in swamps, low grounds, and moist meadows, blossoming in June and July. The roots should be gathered in autumn, and as it rapidly loses its virtues, it should be gathered annually and kept in well-closed vessels. When fresh, it has a very strong, unpleasant odor, but when dried is inodorous. It has a sweetish-bitter taste, succeeded by a persistent acridity.

Properties and Uses.—It has many very valuable properties. It is slightly acrid, confining this action to the mouth and fauces. It is unsurpassed by any article as an expectorant. As a diaphoretic, it is one of the most certain of the whole materia medica, often exciting great coolness and coldness of the surface. In suitable doses it can be relied upon to bring the pulse down from a hundred and fifty beats in a minute to forty, or even to thirty. Sometimes it renders the skin merely soft and moist, and at others produces free and abundant perspiration. In fevers, in some diseases of the heart, acute rheumatism, and in many other conditions which involve an excited state of the circulation, it is of exceeding great value. As a deobstruent or alterative, it far surpasses iodine, and therefore used with great advantage in the treatment of cancer, scrofula, and consumption. It is nervine, and never narcotic, which property renders it of great value in all painful diseases, or such as are accompanied with spasmodic action, convulsions, morbid irritability and irritative mobility, as in chorea, epilepsy or fits, pneumonia, puerperal fever, neuralgia, etc., producing these effects without stupefying and torpifying the system, as opium is known to do. As an emetic, it is slow, but certain and efficient, rousing the liver to action, and vomits without occasioning prostration or exhaustion like other emetics, being the more valuable in not being cathartic. It is peculiarly adapted as an emetic in whooping-cough, croup, asthma, scarlet fever, and in all cases where there is much febrile or inflammatory action. As an arterial sedative it stands unparalleled and unequalled, while in small doses it creates and promotes appetite beyond any agent known to medical men. It has recently come into use, and may be justly regarded as one of the most valuable contributions to the list of medicines in a hundred years.

Dose.—Veratrum is usually given in the form of a tincture, the formula being of the dried root, eight ounces to sixteen ounces diluted .835 alcohol, macerating for two weeks, then to be expressed and filtered. To an adult eight drops are given, which should be repeated every three hours, increasing the dose one or two drops every time until nausea or vomiting, or reduction of the pulse to sixty-five or seventy, ensue, then reduce to one-half in all cases. Females and persons from fourteen to eighteen should commence with six drops and increase as above. For children, from two to five years, begin with two drops, and increase one drop only. Below two years of age, one drop is sufficient. If taken in so large a dose as to produce vomiting or too much depression, a full dose of morphine or opium, in a little brandy or ginger, is a complete antidote. In pneumonia, typhoid fever, and many other diseases, it must be continued from three to seven days after the symptoms have subsided. In typhoid fever, while using the veratrum, quinia is absolutely inadmissible. It is administered in a little sweetened water, and its employment in moderate doses, or short of nausea, may be continued indefinitely without the least inconvenience.

Helleborus Niger.

The HELLEBORUS NIGER, *Black Hellebore*, inhabiting the subalpine and southern parts of Europe, was formerly much used in palsy, insanity, apoplexy, dropsy, epilepsy, etc., but is now more or less discarded. It has diuretic and emmenagogue properties, but as it is very toxical in effects, its use is not to be advised in domestic practice.

HENBANE (HYOSCYAMUS NIGER).

MEDICINAL PARTS. *The leaves and seeds.*

Description.—Henbane is a biennial plant. It has a long, thick, spindle-shaped, corrugated root, which is of a brown color externally, but whitish internally. The stem sometimes reaches the height of two feet, but often stops at an altitude of six inches. The leaves are large, oblong, acute, alternate, and of a pale, dull green color. They have long, glandular hairs upon the midrib. The flowers are funnel-shaped, of a dull yellow color, with purple veins and orifice. The seeds are many, small, obovate, and brownish.

History.—Henbane is original with Europe, but has been naturalized in America. It grows in waste grounds, and flowers from July to September. The leaves and seeds are the parts medicinally used. The leaves are collected in the second year, when the plant is in flower; the seeds are gathered when perfectly ripe. It grows more plentifully than elsewhere in America, in the waste grounds of old settlements, in graveyards, and around the foundations of ruined houses. Bruise the recent leaves, and they emit a strong narcotic odor, like tobacco. Dry them, and they have little smell or taste. Their virtues are completely extracted by diluted alcohol. The active principle of Henbane is called *Hyosciamia*, but all the recognized preparations are now known by the general name of *Hyoscyamus.*

Properties and Uses.—Henbane is a powerful narcotic, but, unless improperly and injudiciously used, it is not "dangerously" poisonous, as we learn from King. All narcotics are "dangerously" poisonous if dangerously administered. Nature grows wild her most potent medicinal herbs, and those which, if used by persons who understand them, are curative of the very worst afflictions of the human race, are also destructive to a small extent if applied and administered by parties who have not thoroughly studied their properties. Medicinally used, Henbane is calmative, hypnotic, anodyne, and antispasmodic. It is much better than opium, as it does not produce constipation. It is always given, where opium does not agree, with the very best effects. I use it principally to cause sleep, and remove irregular nervous action. Combined with other preparations mentioned in many parts of this volume, it is most excellent for gout, rheumatism, asthma, chronic cough, neuralgia, irritations of the urinary organs, etc. The leaves make fine external preparations for glandular swellings or ulcers, etc. I instruct my patients never to use it, under any circumstances, without the advice of a good herbal physician.

HOARHOUND (MARRUBIUM VULGARE).

MEDICINAL PART. *The herb.*

Description.—This well-known herb has a fibrous, perennial root and numerous annual, bushy stems, leafy, and branching from the bottom to one or two feet in height. The leaves are roundish-ovate, rough and veiny above, woolly on the under surface, one or two inches in diameter; the flowers small and white.

History.—Hoarhound is a native of Europe, but has been naturalized in the United States, where it is very common. It grows on dry, sandy fields, waste grounds, and road-sides, flowering from June to September. The entire plant has a white or hoary appearance; the whole herb is medicinal, and should be gathered before its efflorescence. It has a peculiar, rather agreeable, vinous, balsamic odor, and a very bitter, aromatic, somewhat acrid and persistent taste. Its virtues are imparted to alcohol or water.

Properties and Uses.—A stimulant, tonic, expectorant, and diuretic. It is used in the form of *syrup*, in coughs, colds, chronic catarrh, asthma, and all pulmonary affections. The *warm* infusion will produce perspiration and flow of urine, and is used with great benefit in jaundice, asthma, hoarseness, amenorrhœa, and hysteria. The cold infusion is an excellent tonic in some forms of dyspepsia. It will expel worms and act as a purgative in large doses. It enters into the composition of several syrups and candies.

Dose.—Of the powder, one drachm; of the infusion or syrup, from half to a teacupful.

HOUND'S TONGUE (Cynoglossum Officinale).

Medicinal Parts. *The leaves and root.*

Description.—This biennial plant has an erect stem one or two feet high. The leaves are hoary, with soft down on both sides, acute, lanceolate, radical ones petiolate, cauline ones sessile, with cordate bases. The flowers are in clusters, calyx downy, corolla reddish purple, and fruit a depressed achenium.

History.—Cynoglossum Officinale grows on the road-sides and waste places of both Europe and America. The leaves and the root are the parts used in medicine; but the preference I give to the root. This, upon being gathered, emits an unpleasant and somewhat heavy odor, which vanishes when it is dried. Its taste is bitter and mawkish. The fresh root is spoken of by several herbalists as being better than the desiccated or dried, but this probably arises from the fact that the roots they used had not been gathered at the proper time, dried in the correct way, or kept in a skilful manner. The dried root is quite as active as the fresh, if prepared by a person who knows its qualities.

Properties and Uses.—It is chiefly valuable for coughs, catarrhs, bleeding from the lungs, and other disorganizations of the respiratory apparatus. The leaves and root are both applied, with great benefit, as a poultice to old ulcers, scrofulous tumors, burns, goitre, and recent bruises and abrasions. In my several remedies the values of many of the plants described at length in these pages are most thoroughly embraced. The object in giving such plants a descriptive space each is to enable the reader, in extraordinary emergencies, to be *his own physician* until he can get a better one, and to show him that what he treads on may, without his knowledge, contain the germs of his rejuvenation.

CYNOGLOSSUM MORRISONI, or *Virginia Mouse-ear*, *Beggars' Lice*, *Dysentery Weed*, etc., is an annual weed with an erect hairy, leafy stem, two to four feet high. Leaves three to four inches long, oblong, lanceolate; flowers very small, white, or pale blue. It grows in rocky grounds and among rubbish. The whole plant has an unpleasant odor. The root is the medicinal part. It is very efficacious in diarrhœa and dysentery. The root may be chewed or given in powder or infusion *ad libitum*.

HOPS (HUMULUS LUPULUS).

MEDICINAL PART. *The strobiles or cones.*

Description.—This well-known twining plant has a perennial root, with many annual angular stems. The leaves are opposite, deep green, serrated, venated, and very rough. The flowers are numerous and of a greenish color. Fruit a strobile.

History.—This plant is found in China, the Canary Islands, all parts of Europe, and in many places in the United States. It is largely cultivated in England and the United States for its cones or strobiles, which are used medicinally, and in the manufacture of beer, ale, and porter. the odor of hops is peculiar and somewhat agreeable, their taste slightly astringent and exceedingly bitter. They yield their virtues to boiling water, but a better solvent than water is diluted alcohol. Lupulin is the yellow powder procured by beating or rubbing the strobiles, and then sifting out the grains, which form about one-seventh part of the Hops. Lupulin is in globose kidney-shaped grains, golden yellow and somewhat transparent, and preferable to the Hops itself. *Lupulite* is the bitter principle of Hops, and is obtained by making an aqueous solution of *Lupulin*.

Properties and Uses.—Hops are tonic, hypnotic, febrifuge, antilithic, and anthelmintic. They are principally used for their sedative or hypnotic action—producing sleep, removing restlessness, and abating pain, but sometimes failing to do so. A pillow stuffed with Hops is a favorite way for obtaining sleep. The *lupulin* or its tincture is used in delirium tremens, nervous irritation, anxiety, exhaustion, and does not disorder the stomach, nor cause constipation, as with opium. It is also useful in after-pains, to prevent chordee, suppress venereal desires, etc. Externally, in the form of a fomentation alone, or combined with Boneset or other bitter herbs, it has proved beneficial in pneumonia, pleurisy, gastritis, enteritis, and as an application to painful swellings and tumors. An *ointment*, made by boiling two parts of Stramonium leaves and one of Hops in lard, is an excellent application in salt rheum, ulcers, and painful tumors. It is a powerful antaphrodisiac, composing the genital organs, quieting painful erections in gonorrhœa, etc.

Dose.—Fluid extract, half a drachm to a drachm; solid extract, five to twenty grains; tincture (two and a half ounces of hops to one pint of alcohol), three to six drachms; *infusion* (four drachms to one pint of hot water), a wineglass to a cupful of *Lupulin*, the dose six to ten grains; *tinct.* of Lupulin (two ounces of Lupulin to one pint of alcohol), one to two teaspoonfuls in sweetened water. Fifteen to twenty grains well rubbed up with white sugar in a mortar is very efficacious in priapism, chordee, and spermatorrhœa.

HOUSE-LEEK (SEMPERVIVUM TECTORUM).

MEDICINAL PART. *The leaves.*

Description.—House-leek has a fibrous root, with several tufts of oblong, acute, extremely succulent leaves. The stem from the centre of these tufts is about a foot high, erect, round, and downy; flowers large, pale rose-colored, and scentless. Offsets spreading.

History.—This perennial plant is a native of Europe, and is so succulent that it will grow on dry walls, roofs of houses, etc. It flowers in August. It is much cultivated in some places. The leaves contain super-malate of lime.

Properties and Uses.—The fresh leaves are useful as a refrigerant when bruised, and applied as a poultice in erysipelatous affections, burns, stings of insects, and other inflammatory conditions of the skin. The leaves, sliced in two, and the inner surface applied to warts is a positive cure for them. It can be used for many skin diseases. The leaves also possess an astringent property, serviceable in many cases.

HYSSOP (HYSSOPUS OFFICINALIS).

MEDICINAL PARTS. *The tops and leaves.*

Description.—Hyssop is a perennial herb, with square stems, woody at the base, and a foot or two in height, with rod-like branches. The leaves are opposite, sessile, linear, and lanceolate, green on each side; flowers, bluish-purple, seldom white; stamens four.

History.—It is an inhabitant of Europe and this country, being raised principally in gardens, and flowers in July. The taste of the leaves is hot, spicy, and somewhat bitter, and yield their virtues to water and alcohol. They contain yellow oil and sulphur.

Properties and Uses.—Stimulant, aromatic, carminative, and tonic. Generally used in quinsy and other sore-throats, as a gargle with sage. As an expectorant it is beneficial in asthma, coughs, etc. The leaves applied to bruises speedily relieve the pain and remove the discoloration

IBERIS AMARA.

COMMON NAME. *Bitter Candy Tuft.*

MEDICINAL PART. *The seeds.*

Description.—This plant has a herbaceous stem, about a foot in height, with acute, toothed leaves, and bright white flowers.

History.—The leaves, stem, root, and seeds are used; the seeds especially. The plant is an annual, carefully cultivated in Europe, but grows wild also. It flowers in June and July.

Properties and Uses.—The ancients employed it in gout, rheumatism, and diseases of a kindred nature. We use it, compounded with other herbal preparations, for such diseases in their worst forms, and we also use it by itself, in certain proportions, to allay excited action of the heart, particularly where the heart is enlarged. In asthma, bronchitis, and dropsy it is now considered one of the most excellent ingredients of certain cures for those afflictions. The dose is from one to five grains of the powdered seeds.

ICELAND MOSS (CETRARIA ISLANDICA).

MEDICINAL PART. *The plant.*

Description and History.—Iceland Moss is a perennial, foliaceous plant from two to four inches high; a native of Britain and the northern countries of Europe, particularly Iceland. It is diversified in its color, being brownish or grayish-white in some parts, and of a reddish hue in others. It is without odor, with a mucilaginous, bitter, somewhat astringent taste, and when dry the lichen is crisp, cartilaginous, and coriaceous, and is convertible into a grayish-white powder. It swells up in water, absorbing more than its own weight of that fluid, and communicating a portion of its bitterness to it, as well as a little mucilage; when long chewed it is converted into a mucilaginous pulp, and when boiled in water the decoction becomes a firm jelly on cooling.

Properties and Uses.—It is demulcent, tonic, and nutritious. Used as a demulcent in chronic catarrh, chronic dysentery, and diarrhœa, and as a tonic in dyspepsia, convalescence, and exhausting diseases. Boiled with milk it forms an excellent nutritive and tonic in phthisis and general debility. Its tonic virtues depend upon its *cetrarin*, which, if removed, renders the lichen merely nutritious.

IRON WEED (VERNONIA FASCICULATA).

MEDICINAL PART. *The root.*

Description.—This is an indigenous, perennial, coarse, purplish-green weed, with a stem from three to ten feet high. The leaves are from four to eight inches long, one or two broad, lanceolate, tapering to each end. Corolla showy, and dark purple.

History.—This is a very common plant to the Western States, growing in woods and prairies, and along rivers and streams, flowering from July to September. The root is bitter, and imparts its virtues to water and alcohol.

Properties and Uses.—It is a bitter tonic, deobstruent, and alterative. In powder or decoction the root is beneficial in amenorrhœa, dysmenorrhœa, leucorrhœa, and menorrhagia. It is useful in scrofula and some cutaneous diseases.

Dose.—Of the decoction, one or two fluid ounces; of the tincture, one or two fluid drachms. The leaves or powdered root make an excellent discutient application to tumors.

IVY (AMERICAN) (AMPELOPSIS QUINQUEFOLIA).

COMMON NAMES. *Woodbine, Virginia Creeper, Five Leaves, False Grape, Wild wood-vine.*

MEDICINAL PARTS. *The bark and twigs.*

Description.—This is a woody vine, with a creeping stem, digitate leaves; leaflets acuminate, petiolate, dentate, and smooth; flowers inconspicuous, greenish, or white; and the fruit a berry, acid, dark blue, and small.

History.—The American Ivy is a common, familiar, shrubby vine, climbing extensively, and, by means of its radiating tendrils, supporting itself firmly on trees, stone walls, churches, etc., and ascending to the height of from fifty to a hundred feet. The bark and the twigs are the parts usually used. Its taste is acrid and persistent, though not unpleasant, and its decoction is mucilaginous. The bark should be collected after the berries have ripened. It is like the ivy of England and other countries.

Properties and Uses.—Alterative, tonic, astringent, and expectorant. It is used principally in form of syrup in scrofula, dropsy, bronchitis, and other pulmonary complaints. An old author affirms that there is a very great antipathy between wine and ivy, and therefore it is a remedy to preserve against drunkenness, and to relieve or cure intoxication by drinking a draught of wine in which a handful of bruised ivy leaves have been boiled.

Dose.—Of the decoction of syrup, from one to four tablespoonfuls, three times a day.

JALAP (IPOMŒA JALAPA).

MEDICINAL PART. *The root.*

Description.—Jalap has a fleshy, tuberous root, with numerous roundish tubercles. It has several stems, which are smooth, brownish, slightly rough, with a tendency to twine. The leaves are on long petioles, the first hastate, succeeding ones cordate, acuminate, and mucronate. The calyx has no bracts; corolla funnel-shaped, purple, and long. Fruit a capsule.

Jalap.

History.—This plant grows in Mexico. at an elevation of nearly six thousand feet above the level of the sea, near Chicanquiaco and Xalapa, from which it is exported, and from which last-named place it also receives its name. It is generally imported in bags, containing one or two hundred pounds. The worm-eaten root is the most energetic, as the active part is untouched by them. It is soluble in water and alcohol.

Properties and Uses.—Jalap is irritant and cathartic, operating energetically, and produces liquid stools. It is chiefly employed when it is desired to produce an energetic influence on the bowels, or to obtain large evacuations. In intestinal inflammations it should not be used.

Dose.—Powder, ten grains.

JAMESTOWN WEED (DATURA STRAMONIUM).

COMMON NAMES. *Thorn-Apple, Stinkweed, Apple-peru, etc.*

MEDICINAL PARTS. *The leaves and seeds.*

Description.—This plant is a bushy, smooth, fetid, annual plant, two or three feet in height, and in rich soil even more. The root is rather large, of a whitish color, giving off many fibres. The stem is much branched, forked, spreading, leafy, of a yellowish-green color. The leaves are large and smooth, from the forks of the stem, and are uneven at the base. The flowers are about three inches long, erect, large, and white. The fruit is a large, dry, prickly capsule, with four valves and numerous black reniform seeds. There is the *Datura Tatula*, or purple Stramonium, which differs from the above in having a deep purple stem, etc.

History.—Stramonium is a well-known poisonous weed, growing upon waste grounds and road-sides, in all parts of the United States. It is found in very many parts of the world. The whole plant has a fetid, narcotic odor, which diminishes as it dries. Almost every part of the plant is possessed of medicinal properties, but the officinal parts are the leaves and seeds. The leaves should be gathered when the flowers are full-blown, and carefully dried in the shade. They impart their properties to water, alcohol, and the fixed oils. The seeds are small, reniform, compressed, roughish, dark brown or black when ripe, grayish-brown when unripe. They yield what is called *Daturia*, which may be obtained by exhausting the bruised seeds with boiling rectified alcohol, and then proceeding as for the active principle of other seeds of a similar character.

Properties and Uses.—In large doses it is an energetic narcotic poison. The victims of this poison suffer the most intense agonies, and die in maniacal delirium. In medicinal doses it is an anodyne, antispasmodic, and is often used as a substitute for opium. It is used with fair effect in cases of mania, epilepsy, gastritis, delirium tremens, and enteritis; also in neuralgia, rheumatism, and all periodic pains. The dried and smoked leaves are useful in spasmodic asthma, but as there are other means much more certain to cure, and less dangerous, I, and other herbalists, seldom or never recommend them. Daturia is seldom employed in medicine, being a very active and powerful poison. I should advise my readers never to employ it, unless they be physicians; but I deemed proper to give it a place in this work, as its medicinal qualities are quite important, if its use is intrusted to proper and educated persons.

JUNIPER (Juniperus Communis).

Medicinal Part. *The berries.*

Description.—This is a small evergreen shrub, never attaining the height of a tree, with many very close branches. The leaves are attached to the stem in threes. The fruit is fleshy, of dark-purplish color, ripening the second year from the flower.

History.—Juniper grows in dry woods and hills, and flowers in May. The American berries contain less virtue than those imported from Europe. The oil is contained in the spirituous liquor called Holland gin. The berries yield their properties to hot water and alcohol.

Properties and Uses.—The berries and oil are stimulating, carminative, and diuretic. It is especially useful in averting mucous discharges, especially from the urethra.

Dose.—Of the berries, from one to two drachms; of the oil, from four to twenty minims.

KINO (Pterocarpus Marsupium).

Medicinal Part. *Concrete juice.*

Description.—Kino is a leafy tree, with the outer coat of the bark brown, and the inner red, fibrous, and astringent. Branches smooth, leaves alternate; leaflets, from five to seven, alternate, elliptical, and rather emarginate; flowers very numerous, white, with a tinge of yellow; fruit a legume on a long petiole.

History.—Kino is the juice of the tree, obtained by making longitudinal incisions in the bark. It flows freely, is of a red color, and by drying it in the sun it cracks into irregular angular masses. The fragments are reddish, black, translucent, and ruby-red on the edges, inodorous, and very astringent. When chewed it tinges the saliva blood-red. Alcohol dissolves about two-thirds of it. It is chiefly imported from Malabar. It inhabits the Circur mountains and forests of the Malabar coast.

Properties and Uses.—Employed in medicine as an energetic astringent only, principally in obstinate chronic diarrhœa. It is also administered as an astringent in leucorrhœa and sanguineous exudations. As a topical remedy, it is applied to flabby ulcers, and used as a gargle, injection, and wash.

Dose.—Of the powder, from ten to thirty grains.

KIDNEY LIVER-LEAF (HEPATICA AMERICANA).

MEDICINAL PART. *The plant.*

Description.—This is a perennial plant, the root of which consists of numerous strong fibres. The leaves are all radical, on long, hairy petioles, smooth, evergreen, cordate at base, the new ones appearing later than the flowers. The flowers appear almost as soon as the snow leaves the ground in the spring. Fruit an ovate achenium.

HEPATICA ACUTALOBA, or *Heart Liver-leaf*, which possesses the same medicinal qualities, differs from the above in having the leaves with three ovate, pointed lobes, or sometimes five-lobed. They both bear white, blue, or purplish flowers, which appear late in March or early in April.

History.—These plants are common to the United States, growing in woods and upon elevated situations—the former, which is the most common, being found on sides of hills, exposed to the north, and the latter on the southern aspect. The plants yield their virtues to water.

Properties and Uses.—It is a mild, mucilaginous astringent, and is freely used in infusion, in fevers, diseases of the liver; and for bleeding from the lungs, coughs, etc., it is a most valuable curative.

Dose.—Infusion taken *ad libitum.*

KOUSSO (BRAYERA ANTHELMINTICA).

MEDICINAL PART. *The leaves.*

Description.—This is a tree, growing about twenty feet high, with round rusty branches. The leaves are crowded, alternate; leaflets oblong, acute, and serrate; flowers small, greenish, and becoming purple; the fruit so far unknown.

History.—This tree grows upon the table-lands of Northeastern Abyssinia, at an elevation of several thousand feet. The flowers are the parts used. They are gathered when in full bloom, and are used in their fresh state, but are equally valuable when properly dried. After drying they are powdered, and in this form they are mixed with warm water and administered. The value of this medicine has been known for a long time, having been introduced in the French practice over forty years ago. It is quite difficult to procure even the adulterated or spurious article in America or England; the genuine is not to be obtained at any price in the drug-stores. In the stores, however, can be obtained, at great cost, an active resinous principle, extracted from the flowers, and sometimes the unripe fruit, to which the names of *Tœniin* and *Koussin* have been given. The dose of this is set down at twenty grains.

Kousso.

Properties and Uses.—In large doses it will produce heat of the stomach, nausea, and sometimes vomiting, and occasionally will act powerfully on the bowels; but this is only when injudiciously taken. Its chief property is developed in the destruction and expulsion of worms, *especially the tape-worm.* It is the surest of all remedies for that distressing affliction, when compounded with other ingredients which I have mentioned elsewhere. Taken in the proper dose, it seems to have no general effect, but operates wholly and solely upon the worms. The dose of the powdered flowers in infusion is half an ounce to half a pint of warm water. It must be reduced for children. If the medicine does not operate in four hours, use castor-oil. It is one of the ingredients of my Male Fern Vermifuge. (See page 471.)

LADIES' SLIPPER (CYPRIPEDIUM PUBESCENS).

COMMON NAMES. *American Valerian, Umbel, Nerve-root, Yellow Moccasin flower, Noah's Ark.*

MEDICINAL PART. *The root.*

Description.—This indigenous plant has a perennial, fibrous, fleshy root, from which arise several round leafy stems, from twelve to eighteen inches high. The leaves are from three to six inches long, by two or three broad, oblong, lanceolate, acuminate, pubescent, alternate, generally the same number on each side. Flowers large and very showy, and pale yellow.

History.—This plant grows here in rich woods and meadows, and flowers in May and June. There are several varieties of it, but as they all possess the same medicinal properties, a description of each is not requisite or desirable.

Properties and Uses.—The fibrous roots are the parts used in medicine, and they should be gathered and carefully cleansed in August or September. The properties and uses are various. The preparations made from these roots are tonic and stimulant, diaphoretic, and antispasmodic, and are considered to be unequalled in remedying hysteria, chorea, nervous headache, and all cases of nervous irritability. Combined with a certain foreign plant of a mucilaginous character, and growing near the sea-shore, it is an unfailing cure of fever and ague. The preparation has, however, to be skilfully compounded. Any one afflicted by fever and ague may write to me for particulars and I will gladly and promptly furnish them. They are also used for delirium, neuralgia, and hypochondria. The form of preparation is an alcoholic extract.

Dose.—From ten to twenty grains; tincture, from one to three fluid drachms; infusion, from one to four fluid ounces. When made into powder, one drachm in warm water is a dose, and may be repeated, in season, as often as may be required.

LARCH (Abies Larix).

Medicinal Part. *Resinous exudation.*

Description.—Larch is a very lofty and graceful tree, with wide-spreading branches. The buds are alternate, perennial, cup-shaped, scaly, producing annually a pencil-like tuft. Male flowers drooping, about half an inch long, yellow; female flowers erect, larger than the male flowers, and variegated with green and pink; cones erect, ovate, about an inch long, purple when young, reddish-brown when ripe.

History.—The Larch grows in the mountainous regions of Europe, and yields the article of use and commerce known as *Venice turpentine.* The bark contains a large amount of tannic acid.

Properties and Uses.—The medicinal properties are those known to be confined to turpentine.

LARGE FLOWERING SPURGE (Euphorbia Corollata).

Common Names. *Blooming Spurge, Milk-weed, Bowman's Root, etc.*

Medicinal Part. *The bark of the root.*

Description.—This is a perennial plant with a round, slender, erect stem, one or two feet high, with a yellowish, large, and branching root. The leaves are scattered, sessile, oblong-obovate, smooth in some plants.

very hairy in others, and from one to two inches in length. Flowers white and showy, and fruit a three-celled capsule.

History.—This plant grows plentifully in Canada and the United States, in dry fields and woods, and flowers from June to September. The bark of the root is the part used. The plant is readily detected by a milky fluid which exudes from the stem, when that is broken. This fluid, if applied to warts or wens, is of great benefit, in most cases banishing the offensive excrescences.

Properties and Uses.—It is emetic, diaphoretic, expectorant, and epispastic. As an emetic the powdered bark of the root (say from fifteen to twenty grains) is mild, pleasant, and efficacious.

Dose.—As an expectorant it is administered three grains at a time, mixed with honey, molasses, or sugar; as a cathartic, from four to ten grains are required. It is regarded, in doses of fifteen or twenty grains, as one of the very best remedies ever discovered for the dropsy. It has cured hydrothorax and ascites when all other means have failed.

LARKSPUR (DELPHINUM CONSOLIDA).

MEDICINAL PARTS. *The root and seeds.*

Description.—Larkspur is an annual herb, with a simple slender root, a leafy stem, from a foot and a half to two feet high, with alternate spreading branches. The leaves are sessile; flowers bright blue and purple.

DELPHINUM STAPHISAGRIA, or *Stavesacre*, which possesses the same properties as Larkspur, but to a greater degree, is an elegant upright herb, about the same height as Larkspur. Leaves broad, palmate, and petioled. Flowers bluish-gray. Fruit a capsule.

History.—Larkspur is a native of Europe, but has become naturalized in the United States, growing in woods and fields. Stavesacre is native to Europe, growing in waste places.

Properties and Uses.—In medicinal doses emetic, cathartic, and narcotic. It has also vermifuge properties. The whole plant contains an acid principle which is sure death to all kinds of domestic vermin. The flowers and leaves were extensively used in the United States army during the rebellion, to kill lice, and it is pretty well authenticated that the same substance forms the basis of the many preparations offered for the destruction of all noxious insects whose room is better than their company. The flowers are emmenagogue, diuretic, and vermifuge. A tincture of the seeds, it is said, will cure asthma and dropsy. Also a specific for cholera morbus.

Dose.—Two ounces of the seed added to one quart of diluted alcohol makes the tincture, of which ten drops may be given three times a day. This, however, should be used only in extreme cases.

LAVENDER (Lavandula Vera and Lavandula Spica).

Medicinal Part. *The flowers.*

Description.—Lavandula Vera is a small shrub from one to two feet high, but sometimes attaining six feet. The leaves are oblong linear or lanceolate, entire, opposite, and sessile. The flowers are of lilac color, small and in whorls.

Lavandula Spica is more dwarfish and more hoary than the last. Leaves oblong-lanceolate. This plant is not used in medicine, but furnishes the *oil of spike*, much used in the preparation of artistical varnishes and by porcelain painters.

History.—Lavandula Vera grows in the dry soils of Southern Europe, and flowers in July and August. It is largely cultivated in this country. The whole plant is aromatic, but the flowers are the parts used, and should be gathered shortly after their appearance, and carefully dried. The disease to which this plant is subject can only be prevented by not allowing them to grow too closely together.

Properties and Uses.—It is a tonic, stimulant, and carminative, useful mostly in diseases of the nervous system.

LEVER-WOOD (Astrya Virginica).

Common Names. *Iron-wood, Hop-hornbeam.*

Medicinal Part. *The inner wood.*

Description.—This small tree of from twenty-five to thirty feet in height is remarkable for its fine, narrow, brownish bark. The wood is white, hard, and strong; leaves oblong-ovate, acuminate, serrate, and somewhat downy. Flowers, fertile and sterile, green, and appear with the leaves.

History.—The inner wood and bark are the parts in which reside the curative virtues, and the latter, which are immense, readily yield to water. The tree flowers in April and May, and is common to the United States. The bark and wood should be gathered in August or September.

Properties and Uses.—Lever-wood is anti-periodic, tonic, and alterative. It is very good in cases of intermittent fever, neuralgia, nervous debility, scrofula, and dyspepsia. It is sometimes administered, with fair success, as a remedy for fever and ague.

Dose.—Decoction, one or two fluid ounces, three or four times a day.

LIFE-ROOT (Senecio Aureus).

Common Names. *Squaw-weed, Ragwort, False Valerian, Golden Senecio,* and *Female Regulator.*

Medicinal Parts. *The root and herb.*

Description.—Life-root has an erect, smoothish stem, one or two feet high. Radical leaves are simple and rounded, mostly cordate and long petioled, lower cauline leaves lyrate, upper ones few, dentate and sessile. Flowers golden-yellow.

History.—The plant is perennial and indigenous, growing on low marshy grounds, and on the banks of creeks. The northern and western parts of Europe are where it is mostly found, and the flowers culminate in May and June. The root and herb are the parts employed for medical purposes. There are several varieties of this plant, but as all possess the same medicinal properties, it is unnecessary to specify them. The whole herb is used of all the varieties.

Properties and Uses.—It is diuretic, pectoral, diaphoretic, and tonic, and exerts a very powerful and peculiar influence upon the reproductive organs of females. This has given it the name of *Female Regulator.* Combined with the Lily, and other native and foreign plants, it is one of the most certain cures in the world for aggravated cases of leucorrhœa; also in cases of menstrual suppression. It will operate excellently in gravel, and other urinary affections.

Dose.—Ordinary decoction, four ounces.

LILY (MEADOW) (LILIUM CANDIDUM).

MEDICINAL PART. *The root.*

Description.—The thick stem of this plant is from three to four feet high, and arises from a perennial bulb or root. Leaves scattered, lanceolate, and narrowed at the base. Flowers are large, snow-white, and smooth inside.

History.—The Meadow Lily is an exotic. It is a native of Syria and Asia Minor. The flowers are regarded as being very beautiful, but are not used for medical purposes. The plant is principally cultivated for the flowers. The bulb is the part used for its curative properties. Water extracts its virtues.

Properties and Uses.—It is mucilaginous, demulcent, tonic, and astringent. It is chosen by some of our best botanical practitioners as a certain remedy for leucorrhœa and falling of the womb, and for those affections, when combined with Life-Root and other herbal preparations, is without an equal. Sometimes the recent root is used to advantage in dropsy. Boiled in milk, it is also useful for ulcers, inflammations, fever-sores, etc. I use it in combination with other indicated plants as an injection in leucorrhœa, with very gratifying success.

LION'S FOOT (NABULUS ALBUS).

COMMON NAMES. *White Lettuce, Rattle-snake Root.*

MEDICINAL PART. *The plant.*

Description.—This indigenous perennial herb has a smooth stem, stout and purplish, from two to four feet high. Radical leaves angular-hastate, cauline ones lanceolate, and all irregularly dentate.

History.—This plant grows plentifully in moist woods and in rich soils, from New England to Iowa, and from Canada to Carolina. The root, leaves, and juice of the plant are employed.

Properties and Uses.—A decoction of the root taken internally will operate most favorably in cases of dysentery. The milky juice of the plant is taken internally, while the leaves, steeped in water, are applied as a poultice (and frequently changed) for the bite of a serpent.

LOBELIA (LOBELIA INFLATA).

COMMON NAMES. *Indian Tobacco, Wild Tobacco.*

MEDICINAL PARTS. *The leaves and seeds.*

Description.—Lobelia is an annual or biennial indigenous plant, with a fibrous root, and an erect, angular, very hairy stem, from six inches to three feet in height. The leaves are alternate, ovate-lanceolate, serrate, veiny, and hairy; flowers small, numerous, pale-blue; fruit a two-celled ovoid capsule, containing numerous small brown seeds.

Lobelia.

History.—Lobelia flowers from July to November, and grows in nearly all parts of the United States, in fields, woods, and meadows. The whole plant is active, and the stalks are used indiscriminately with the leaves by those who are best acquainted with its properties. The root is supposed to be more energetic, medicinally, than any other part of the plant. The proper time for gathering is from the last of July to the middle of October. The plant should be dried in the shade, and then be preserved in packages or covered vessels, more especially if it be reduced to powder. It was used in domestic practice by the people of New England long before the time of Samuel Thompson, its assumed discoverer.

Properties and Uses.—Administered internally it is emetic, nauseant, expectorant, relaxant, sedative, anti-spasmodic, and secondarily cathartic, diaphoretic, and astringent. It is extensively used to subdue spasms, and will give relief in epilepsy, tetanus, cramps, hysteria, chorea, and convulsions; but it is merely a temporary relief when administered internally, and if not used with great skill and caution in that way, may do as much harm as good. Applied externally, in the form of an ointment, combined with healing and soothing barks and roots, it is decidedly the best counter-irritant known to mankind. In this shape its equal has never been discovered, and probably never will be. This is one of the ingredients of the "Herbal Ointment," a full description of which will be found on page 472 of this work. There are any number of officinal preparations of Lobelia, but it is the opinion of the author that its chief value consists in being made into an ointment, with other rare and potent ingredients. There is nothing in nature that can favorably compare with it in this form. In other shapes it may be useful; but it is also dangerous unless given with care.

LOUSEWORT (GERARDIA PEDICULARIA).

COMMON NAMES. *Fever-weed, American Foxglove, etc.*

MEDICINAL PART. *The herb.*

Description.—The stem of this plant is bushy, tall, two or three feet in height. The leaves are numerous, opposite, ovate-lanceolate; flowers large, yellow, and trumpet-shaped; calyx five-cleft, corolla yellow, and fruit a two-celled capsule.

History.—This most elegant plant grows in dry copses, pine ridges, and barren woods and mountains, from Canada to Georgia, flowering in August and September. Water or alcohol extracts its virtues.

Properties and Uses.—It is diaphoretic, antiseptic, and sedative. Used principally in febrile and inflammatory diseases; a warm infusion produces a free and copious perspiration in a short time. Very valuable in ephemeral fever.

Dose.—Of the infusion, from one to three fluid ounces.

LUNGWORT (PULMONARIA OFFICINALIS).

MEDICINAL PART. *The leaves.*

Description.—This rough plant has a stem about one foot high. The radical leaves ovate, cordate; cauline one, ovate and sessile. Flowers, blue; calyx, five-angled; corolla, funnel-shaped; stigma, emarginate; and the fruit a roundish, obtuse achenium. (See Illustration, page 16.)

History.—Lungwort is a herbaceous perennial, growing in Europe and this country in northern latitudes. In Europe it is a rough-leaved plant, but in this country the entire plant is smooth, which exhibits the peculiar climatic influence. It is showy, and freely cultivated. It flowers in May. The leaves are used for medical purposes. They are without any particular odor. Water extracts their properties.

Properties and Uses.—It is demulcent and mucilaginous, and in decoction very useful in bleeding from the lungs, and bronchial and catarrhal affections, and other disorders of the respiratory organs. Its virtues seem to be entirely expended upon the lungs, and it is certainly an efficacious remedial agent for all morbid conditions of those organs. It is an ingredient in the "Acacian Balsam," see page 470.

MADDER (RUBIA TINCTORUM).

MEDICINAL PART. *The root.*

Description.—This plant has a perennial, long, cylindrical root, about the thickness of a quill, and deep reddish-brown. It has several herbaceous, brittle stems. The leaves are from four to six in a whorl, lanceolate, mucronate, two or three inches long, and about one-third as wide. Flowers small and yellow.

History.—Madder is a native of the Mediterranean and Southern European countries. The drug is chiefly imported from Holland and France. The root is collected in the third year of the plant, when it is freed from its outer covering and dried. It is valued as a dye-stuff for its red and purple.

Properties and Uses.—It is sometimes used to promote the menstrual and urinary discharges, but is not in very great favor. Combined in a preparation with other ingredients, it is of some considerable remedial value.

Dose.—Thirty grains, three or four times a day. If used frequently, it will color the bones red.

MAD-DOG WEED (ALISMA PLANTAGO).

COMMON NAME. *Water Plantain.*

MEDICINAL PART. *The leaves.*

Description.—This perennial herb has all radical, oval, oblong, or lanceolate leaves, from four to six inches in length, on long radical petioles. The flowers are small and white, and the fruit a three-cornered achenium.

History.—It inhabits the North American continent as well as Europe, grows in watery places, and flowers in July.

Properties and Uses.—It was once considered a capital remedy for hydrophobia, hence its name; but experience has demonstrated that as a cure for this horrible infliction it is impotent. In urinary diseases and affections, an infusion of the leaves, which must be dried and powdered, is very efficacious.

Dose.—Of the infusion above mentioned, from four to six fluid ounces, three or four times a day. The fresh leaves, when bruised, form a very good but mild counter-irritant.

MAIDENHAIR (ADIANTUM PEDATUM).

MEDICINAL PART. *The herb.*

Description.—This is a most delicate and graceful fern, growing from twelve to fifteen inches high, with a slender, polished stalk. Frond pedate, with pinnate branches.

History.—Maidenhair is perennial, and grows throughout the United

States in deep woods, on moist, rich soil. The leaves are bitterish and somewhat aromatic, and part with their virtues upon being immersed in boiling water.

Properties and Uses.—It is refrigerant, expectorant, tonic, and sub-astringent. A decoction of the plant is most gratefully cooling in febrile diseases, and it is a great benefit in coughs, catarrh, hoarseness, influenza, asthma, pleurisy, etc. The decoction, or syrup, can be used freely.

MAGNOLIA (MAGNOLIA GLAUCA).

COMMON NAMES. *White Bay, Beaver-tree, Sweet Magnolia, Swamp Sassafras, etc.*

MEDICINAL PART. *The bark.*

Description.—This tree varies in height from six to thirty feet, being taller in the South than in the North. The leaves are alternate, petioled, entire, and of elliptical shape. The flowers are large and solitary, and of grateful odor. The fruit is a cone.

History.—The therapeutical virtues of these trees are found in the bark and fruit. The bark of both the trunk and the root is employed. The odor is aromatic, and the taste bitterish, warm, and pungent. It is gathered during the spring and summer. It has smooth and ash-colored bark, elegant, odoriferous, cream-colored flowers, and can be found in morasses from Massachusetts to the Gulf of Mexico. It flowers from May to August. There are other varieties which do not require especial mention or description.

Properties and Uses.—The bark is an aromatic, tonic bitter, and is also anti-periodic. It is used much in the stead of cinchona, and will remedy the intermittent fevers when cinchona has failed. It is used frequently as a substitute for Peruvian Bark, as it can be continued for a longer time and with more safety. Properly prepared it may be used as a substitute for tobacco, and will break the habit of tobacco-chewing.

Dose.—In powder, half-drachm or drachm doses, five or six times a day. The infusion is taken in wineglassful doses, five or six times a day. The tincture, made by adding two ounces of the cones to a pint of brandy, will be found beneficial in dyspepsia and chronic rheumatism.

MALLOW (COMMON) (MALVA SYLVESTRIS).

COMMON NAME. *High-mallow.*

MEDICINAL PART. *The Herb.*

Description.—This plant is a perennial, and has a round stem two or three feet high, and a tapering, branching, whitish root. The leaves are alternate, deep green, soft, and downy. The flowers are large, numerous, and of purple color; calyx five-cleft; petals five; stamens indefinite; pollen large, whitish.

History.—The mallow is a native of Europe, but is naturalized in this country. It grows abundantly in fields, waysides, and waste places, and flowers from May to October. The whole plant, especially the root, abounds in mucilage.

Properties and Uses.—It possesses the properties common to mucilaginous herbs, and an infusion thereof forms an excellent demulcent in coughs, irritations of the air-passages, flux, affections of the kidney and bladder, etc. In inflammatory conditions of the external parts, the bruised herb forms an excellent application, making, as it does, a natural emollient cataplasm.

MALVA ROTUNDIFOLIA, or *Low-mallow*, called by children, who are fond of eating the fruit, *cheeses*, possesses similar qualities.

MANDRAKE (PODOPHYLLUM PELTATUM).

COMMON NAMES. *May-Apple, Wild Lemon, Raccoon-berry, Wild Mandrake.*

MEDICINAL PART. *The root.*

Description.—This plant, which is illustrated by a cut, is an indigenous perennial herb, with a jointed, dark-brown root, about half the size of the finger, very fibrous, and internally yellow. The stem is simple, round, smooth, erect, about a foot high, dividing at the top into two petioles, from three to six inches long, each supporting a leaf. The leaves are large, palmate, oftener cordate, smooth, yellowish-green on top, paler beneath. The flower is solitary in the fork of the stem, large, white, and somewhat fragrant. The fruit is fleshy, of a lemon color, and in flavor resembles the strawberry.

Mandrake.

There is another plant called *mandrake*, but which is the *Atropa Mandragora*, a plant belonging to the night-shade family. The cut I give of this plant is quite truthful. It is not used in medicine. It inhabits the shores of the Mediterranean, and found lurking in dark woods, in the gloomy thickets on the banks of sluggish rivers. It is fetid, poisonous, and repulsive. Even its golden fruit has this nauseous odor. How, then, came it ever to usurp its dominion over men? Its strong narcotic powers may have had some influence; but the peculiar form of its root, in which the resemblance of the human shape, as will be observed, is quite apparent, probably led to its use in magic.

In popular belief, it became invested with half-human attributes; and cries and groans attested its pain when torn from the ground. Gathered with peculiar rites under the shadow of a gallows, it caused money to multiply, but death overtook the daring searcher for mandrake who committed an error in the ritual. There is nothing new under the sun, and as no small number of the old-time magical effects are renewed under new names, our book may reach some spot where the mandrake has been brought forward by some new schemer, and play its part in deluding the silly.

Atropa Mandragora.

History. — The Mandrake is found throughout the United States, in low, shady situations, rich woods, and fields, and flowers in May and June. The fruit matures in September and October. It is scarcer in New England than elsewhere. The Indians were well acquainted with the virtues of this plant. The proper time for collecting the root is in the latter part of October or early part of November, soon after the fruit has ripened. Its active principle is *Podophyllin*, which acts upon the liver in the same manner, but far superior to mercury, and with intelligent physicians it has dethroned that noxious mineral as a cholagogue.

Properties and Uses.—Mandrake is cathartic, emetic, alterative, anthelmintic, hydragogue, and sialagogue. It is an active and certain cathartic. As a deobstruent it has no superior, acting through and upon all the tissues of the system, and its action continues for a long time. In bilious and typhoid febrile diseases it is very valuable as an emeto-cathartic, breaking up the disease quickly. In chronic liver diseases it has no equal in the whole range of medicine. It can also be used as an alterative. In constipation it acts upon the bowels without disposing them to subsequent costiveness. It is also very beneficial in uterine diseases, and its office as a great remedy is extensive. It is one of the ingredients of my "Renovating Pill." See page 473.

Dose.—Of the powdered root, as a cathartic, from ten to thirty grains; of the tincture, from ten to forty drops.

MATICO (PIPER ANGUSTIFOLIUM).

MEDICINAL PART. *The leaves.*

Description.—This is a tall shrub, presenting a singular appearance from its pointed stem and branches. The leaves are harsh, short-stalked, oblong-lanceolate, and acuminate. Flowers hermaphrodite.

Matico Leaf.

History.—This plant grows at Huanaco and elsewhere in Peru. The dried leaves are the parts used, and have a strong fragrant odor, and a warm, aromatic taste. They contain a dark-green resin, chlorophyll, brown and yellow coloring matter, gum, nitrate of potassa, *maticine*, a volatile oil, salts, and lignin. The plant has long been used by the Indians of Peru in venereal diseases, but mostly for diseases of the mucous membranes, over which it has a complete mastery. Having been employed as a mechanical agent to stanch blood by a soldier, it has received the name of *Soldiers' Herb.*

Properties and Uses.—Matico is an aromatic stimulant. It is extremely useful to arrest discharges from mucous surfaces, leucorrhœa, gonorrhœa, and catarrh of the bladder. As a topical agent for stanching blood it is excellent, and is used by surgeons to arrest venous hemorrhage. For the above affections Matico serves its office well, but its greatest use and efficacy is exhibited in nasal catarrh. It is an absolute specific for this disease. I have long employed it—even before it was admitted in the various pharmacopœias—in my special treatment for catarrh, and I have yet to find a case in which it failed. I use it both internally and topically, and combine it with such other remedial agents as are suggested by the character of each individual case. Catarrh (see page 232) has long been regarded by the profession as incurable, but in this remedy the incontrovertible aphorism that "every disease has its specific" is still further exemplified, and human progress will ere long complete the analogy, if they but investigate the majestic tree, the lowly shrub, or creeping herb.

MECHAMECK (CONVOLVULUS PANDURATUS).

COMMON NAMES. *Wild Julap, Man-in-the-Earth, Man-in-the-Ground, Wild Potato.*

MEDICINAL PART. *The root.*

Description.—This has a perennial, very large tapering root, from which arise several long, round, slender, purplish stems, from four to eight feet high. The leaves are cordate at base, alternate, and acuminate, and about two or three inches long. Flowers large and white, opening in the forenoon; fruit an oblong, two-celled capsule.

History.—Mechameck belongs to the United States, and grows in light, sandy soils. It flowers from June to August, but is rarely found in northern latitudes. The root is the officinal part. Its best solvent is alcohol or spirits. Water will extract its active properties.

Properties and Uses.—It is a cathartic if powdered and taken in doses of from forty to sixty grains. The infusion, taken in wineglassful doses every hour, is useful in dropsy, strangury, and calculous affections. It seems to exert an influence over the lungs, liver, and kidneys, without excessive diuresis or catharsis. The milky juice of the root is said to be a protection against the bite of the rattlesnake.

MEADOW SAFFRON (Colchicum Autumnale).

Medicinal Parts. *The cormus and seeds.*

Description.—The cormus of this plant is large, ovate, and fleshy. The leaves are dark-green, very smooth, obtuse, above a foot long, an inch and a half broad, keeled, produced in the spring along with the capsules. Flowers several, bright-purple, with a white tube appearing in the autumn without the leaves. Fruit a capsule, seeds whitish and polished.

History.—It grows in meadows and low, rich soils in many parts of Europe, and is common in England. The plant is annual or perennial, according to the manner in which it is propagated. The root resembles that of the tulip, and contains a white acrid juice. The bulb should be gathered about the beginning of July, and the seeds early in August. *Colchicia* is the active principle.

Properties and Uses.—It is sedative, cathartic, diuretic, and emetic. Used in gout and gouty rheumatism, dropsy, palpitation of the heart; care should be used in its employment. The tincture is the best form of administration, of which the dose is from twenty to sixty drops.

MONKSHOOD (Aconitum Napellus).

Common Name. *Wolf's-bane.*

Medicinal Parts. *Leaves and root.*

Description.—This plant has a small napiform root, and simple, straight, erect stems, about five feet high. The leaves are alternate, petioled, dark-green above, paler beneath. The flowers are large, deep bluish-purple, sometimes white, and hairy; fruit a capsule.

History.—This perennial herb is a native of most parts of Europe, growing in wooded hills and plains, and is much cultivated in gardens. It flowers in May and June. All parts of the plant contain powerfully poisonous properties; but the root is the part most generally employed for medical purposes. It yields *Aconitina.*

Properties and Uses.—Although Aconite in the hands of the intelligent physician is of great service, it should not be used in domestic practice. In improper doses all preparations of aconite act as an energetic acro-narcotic poison. As a sedative and anodyne, it is useful in all febrile and inflammatory diseases, and, indeed, in all affections in which there is an increase of nervous, vascular, or muscular action. In acute rheumatism, pneumonia, peritonitis, gastritis, and many other acute disorders, it has been used with the most decided advantage. Its action is more especially displayed in the highest grades of fever and inflammation.

Dose.—The best preparation is the alcoholic extract, formed by evaporating a tincture made of a pound of aconite and a quart of alcohol. The dose of this is one-eighth of a grain.

MOSS (CORSICAN), (FUCUS HELMINTHICORTON).

MEDICINAL PART. *The whole plant.*

Description.—This marine plant has a cartilaginous, tufted, entangled frond, with branches marked indistinctly with transverse streaks. The lower part is dirty-yellow, the branches more or less purple.

History.—It is found growing on the Mediterranean coast, and especially on the Island of Corsica. It is cartilaginous in consistence, is of a dull and reddish-brown color, has a bitter, salt, and nauseous taste, but its odor is rather pleasant. Water dissolves its active principles.

Properties and Uses.—It is an excellent anthelmintic. The influence it exercises upon the economy is entirely inappreciable, but it acts very powerfully on intestinal worms. Dr. Johnson says: "It destroys any worms domiciliating in the bowels as effectually as choke-damps would destroy the life of a miner." This excellent vermifuge plant is one of the ingredients of my Male Fern Vermifuge, see page 471.

Dose.—From ten to sixty grains, mixed with molasses or syrup, or in infusion.

The FUCUS VESICULOSIS, *Sea-wrack*, or *Bladder Fucus*, possesses analogous properties.

MOTHERWORT (LEONURUS CARDIACA).

MEDICINAL PARTS. *The tops and leaves.*

Description.—This perennial plant has stems from two to five feet in height. The leaves are opposite, dark-green, rough, and downy. The flowers are purplish or whitish-red; calyx, rigid and bristly; corolla, purplish; anthers in pairs, and fruit an oblong achenium.

History.—Motherwort is an exotic plant, but extensively introduced into the United States, growing in fields and pastures, and flowering from May to September. It has a peculiar, aromatic, not disagreeable odor, and a slightly aromatic bitter taste. It yields its properties to water and alcohol.

Properties and Uses.—It is antispasmodic, emmenagogue, nervine, and laxative. In amenorrhœa from colds it is excellent, if given in warm infusion. It is very useful in hysteria, nervous complaints, pains peculiar to females, delirium tremens, wakefulness, liver affections, etc., etc. It is a very valuable remedy for many purposes, and deserves greater attention than it receives.

Dose.—Decoction, two to four ounces; extract, three to six grains.

MULLEIN (VERBASCUM THAPSUS).

MEDICINAL PARTS. *The leaves and flowers.*

Description.—This biennial plant has a straight, tall, stout, woolly, simple stem. The leaves are alternate, oblong, acute, and rough on both sides. The flowers are of a golden-yellow color; calyx, five-parted; corolla, five-lobed; stamens, five; and fruit, a capsule or pod.

History.—Mullein is common in the United States, but was undoubtedly introduced from Europe. It grows in recent clearings, slovenly fields, and along the side of roads, flowering from June to August. The leaves and the flowers are the parts used. They have a faint, rather pleasant odor, and a somewhat bitterish, albuminous taste, and yield their virtues to boiling water.

Properties and Uses.—It is demulcent, diuretic, anodyne, and antispasmodic, the infusion being useful in coughs, catarrh, bleeding from the mouth or lungs, diarrhœa, dysentery, and piles. It may be boiled in milk, sweetened, and rendered more palatable by aromatics, for internal use, especially bowel complaints. A fomentation of the leaves in hot vinegar and water forms an excellent local application for inflamed piles, ulcers, and tumors, mumps, acute inflammation of the tonsils, malignant sore throat, etc. A handful of them may be also placed in an old teapot, with hot water, and the steam be inhaled through the spout, in the same complaints.

MYRRH (BALSAMODENDRON MYRRHA).

MEDICINAL PART. *The resinous exudation.*

Description.—This plant has a shrubby, arborescent stem, spinescent branches, a very pale gray bark, and yellowish-white wood. The leaves are ternate, on short petioles; leaflets, obovate; flowers, unknown.

History.—The Myrrh-tree grows in Arabia, and in the regions between Abyssinia and the Red Sea. The juice flows naturally, like cherry-tree gum, upon the bark. At first it is soft and pale yellow, but by drying becomes hard, darker and redder, and forms the medicinal *Gum Myrrh.* It is readily powdered, and has a peculiar, agreeable, balsamic odor, and a bitter, aromatic, not unpleasant taste.

Properties and Uses.—It is a stimulant of the mucous tissues, and used to promote expectoration, as well as menstruation; and is highly useful in enfeebled conditions of the body, excessive mucous secretion, chronic catarrh, leucorrhœa, etc. Also in laryngitis, bronchitis, humoral asthma, and other diseases of the air-tubes, accompanied with profuse secretion, but expelled with difficulty. It is valuable in suppressed menses and cases of anæmia; also as a local application to indolent sores, gangrenous ulcers, aphthous or sloughy sore throat, spongy and ulcerated condition of the gum, caries of the teeth, etc.

Dose.—In powder and pill, ten to thirty grains; of the tincture, from half to two teaspoonfuls.

NARROW LEAF VIRGINIA THYME (PYCANTHEMUM VIRGINICUM).

COMMON NAME. *Prairie Hyssop.*

MEDICINAL PART. *The plant.*

Description.—This pubescent plant has a simple stem, growing from one to two feet high. The leaves are sessile, entire, and linear; flowers are white, and fruit an achenium.

History.—It is found in low grounds, dry hills, and plains, from Ohio and Illinois extending southward, and flowering in July and August. The whole plant is used, and has the taste and odor peculiar to the mint family.

Properties and Uses.—It is diaphoretic, stimulant, antispasmodic, carminative, and tonic. A warm infusion is very useful in puerperal, remittent, and other forms of fever, coughs, colds, catarrhs, etc., and is also of much benefit in spasmodic diseases, especially colic, cramp of the stomach, and spasms of infants. The cold infusion is a good tonic and stimulant during convalescence from exhausting diseases. It forms a most certain remedy for catarrh when combined with other native and foreign herbs and roots.

Dose.—From one to four fluid ounces of the warm or cold infusion, several times a day.

The *P. Pilosum*, *P. Aristatum* or *Wild Basil*, and *P. Incanum*, have similar properties.

NETTLE (URTICA DIOCA).

COMMON NAME. *Great Stinging Nettle.*

MEDICINAL PARTS. *The root and leaves.*

Description.—This is a perennial, herbaceous, dull-green plant, armed with small prickles, which emit an acrid fluid when pressed. The stem is from two to four feet high; root creeping and branching. The leaves are opposite, cordate, lance-ovate, and conspicuously acuminate. Flowers are small and green.

History.—The Common Nettle is well known both in America and in

Europe, and grows in waste places, beside hedges and in gardens, flowering from June to September. The leaves and root are the parts used. The prickles of the Common Nettle contain Formic Acid. The young shoots have been boiled and eaten as a remedy for scurvy.

Properties and Uses.—It is astringent, tonic, and diuretic. In decoction they are valuable in diarrhœa, dysentery, and piles; also in hemorrhages, scorbutic and febrile affections, gravel, and other nephritic complaints. The leaves of the fresh Common Nettle stimulate, inflame, and raise blisters upon those portions of the skin to which they may be applied, and they have, as a natural consequence, often been used as a powerful rubefacient. They are also an excellent styptic, checking the flow of blood from surfaces almost immediately upon their application. The seeds and flowers are given in wine for agues.

Dose.—Of the powdered root or leaves, from twenty to forty grains; of the decoction, from two to four fluid ounces.

URTICA URENS, or *Dwarf Nettle*, possesses similar qualities, and is very efficacious in uterine hemorrhage.

URTICA PAMILA, *Cool-weed*, *Rich-weed*, or *Stingless Nettle*, has also active properties. It gives relief in inflammations, painful swellings, erysipelas, and the topical poison of rhus.

NET LEAF PLANTAIN (GOODYERA PUBESCENS).

COMMON NAMES. *Scrofula-weed*, *Adder's Violet*, *Rattle-snake Leaf*, *etc.*

MEDICINAL PART. *The leaves.*

Description.—The scape or stem of this plant is from eight to twelve inches high, springing from a perennial root. The leaves are radical, ovate, and dark green. The flowers are white, numerous, and pubescent.

History.—This herb grows in various parts of the United States, in rich woods and under evergreens, and is commoner southward than northward, although there is a variety (*Goodyera Repens*) which is plentiful in colder regions of America. It bears yellowish-white flowers in July and August. The leaves are the parts employed, and yield their virtues to boiling water.

Properties and Uses.—It is anti-scrofulous, and is known to have cured severe cases of scrofula. The fresh leaves are steeped in milk and applied to scrofulous ulcers as a poultice, or the bruised leaves may be laid on them, and in either case they must be removed every three hours; at the same time an infusion must be taken as freely as the stomach will allow. It is also good as a wash in scrofulous ophthalmia. In my opinion scrofula is one of the most obstinate and many-shaped afflictions to which the human race is subjected, but in the production of this and other native and foreign plants, nature has shown her great charity and kindness towards us.

NIGHTSHADE (GARDEN) (SOLANUM NIGRUM).

MEDICINAL PART. *The leaves.*

Description.—This is a fetid, narcotic, bushy herb, with a fibrous root, and an erect, branching, thornless stem, one or two feet high. Leaves are ovate, dentated, smooth, and the margins have the appearance as if gnawed by insects. Flowers white or pale-violet; fruit, a berry.

History.—This plant is also called Deadly Nightshade, but is not to be confounded with Belladonna. It is found growing along old walls, fences, and in gardens, in various parts of the United States, flowering in July and August. The leaves yield their virtues to water and alcohol.

Properties and Uses.—It is a narcotic and sedative, producing, when given in large doses, sickness and vertigo. One to three grains of the leaves, infused in water, will produce a copious perspiration and purge on the day following. They have been freely used in cancer, scurvy, and scrofulous affections, in the form of an ointment. Very small doses are taken internally. These should always be prescribed, and their effects watched by a physician. It is better to use the plant only in the form of an ointment. The berries are poisonous, and will produce torpor, insensibility, and death.

NORWAY PINE (ABIES EXCELSA).

MEDICINAL PART. *The concrete juice.*

Description.—This is a large tree, often having a diameter exceeding four feet, and attaining an altitude of one hundred and forty feet Leaves are short, scattered, mucronate, dark-green, and glossy above.

History.—It is an inhabitant of Germany, Russia, and Norway, and other northern parts of Europe, as well as of Asia. It affords the *Frankincense* of commerce, which, when boiled in water and strained, forms the officinal *Burgundy Pitch.*

Properties and Uses.—Burgundy Pitch is generally used externally to produce a redness of the surface, with a slight serous exhalation. It is employed as a counter-irritant in chronic diseases of the lungs, stomach, intestines, etc , and is regarded with favor as a local application in rheumatic affections.

NUX VOMICA (STRYCHNOS NUX VOMICA).

MEDICINAL PART. *The seeds.*

Description.—This is a moderate-sized tree, with a short and pretty thick trunk. The wood is white, hard, and bitter. The leaves are opposite, oval, and smooth on both sides. Flowers small, greenish-white, funnel-shaped, and have a disagreeable odor. The fruit is a berry, round, and about the size of a large apple, enclosing five whitish seeds.

Nux Vomica.

History.—It is an inhabitant of Coromandel, Ceylon, and other parts of the East Indies. The active principles of the seeds are *strychnine* and *brucia.*

Properties and Uses.—It is an energetic poison, exerting its influence chiefly upon the cerebro-spinal system. It is supposed to affect the spinal cord principally. It is a favorite medicine for paralysis and nervous debility generally. If a poisonous dose is given it will produce spasms like tetanus or lock-jaw. It is tonic, and increases the action of various excretory organs. Where want of nervous energy exists it is an admirable remedy. Its range of service is quite extensive, and valuable for many indications; but as great caution is required in its administration, it should only be employed by the educated physician.

OAK—WHITE, RED, AND BLACK (QUERCUS ALBA, RUBRA, AND TINCTORIA).

MEDICINAL PART. *The bark.*

Description.—These forest-trees vary in size, according to the climate and soil. In diameter they are from three to six feet; in height, from sixty to a hundred feet. They are too well known to require any botanical description.

History.—Quercus is a very extensive and valuable genus, consisting of many species, a large proportion of which grow in the United States. Their usual character is that of astringent, and the three above described are those which have been more particularly employed in medicine. The bark of the tree is the portion used. White oak bark is the one chiefly used in medicine. It is of a pale brownish color, faintly odorous, very astringent, with a slight bitterness, tough, breaking with a stringy or fibrous fracture, and not readily powdered. It contains a very large proportion of tannic acid. Black oak bark is also used as an astringent externally, but is rarely employed internally, as it is liable to derange the bowels. It is also used in tanning and for dyeing. Red oak bark also contains considerable tannin, and is chiefly applied externally in the treatment of cancers, indolent ulcers, etc.

Properties and Uses.—The bark is slightly tonic, powerfully astringent, and antiseptic. It is useful internally in chronic diarrhœa, chronic mucous discharges, passive hemorrhages, and wherever an internal astringent is required. In colliquative sweats the decoction is usually combined with lime-water. The gargle and injection are extensively used for sore throat, whites, piles, etc. A bath of the decoction is often advantageous in cutaneous diseases, but should only be used when ordered by a physician.

Dose.—Of the decoction, one or two fluid ounces; of the extract, from five to twenty grains.

QUERCUS INFECTORIA, or *Dyers' Oak*, is a small shrub, which furnishes the morbid excrescences, *Galls*, which, or the gallic acid obtained from them, may be used wherever an astringent is called for.

OLD MAN'S BEARD (CHIONANTHUS VIRGINICA).

COMMON NAMES. *Fringe Tree, Poison Ash.*

MEDICINAL PART. *Bark of the root.*

Description.—This is a shrub or small tree, growing from eight to twenty-five feet high. The leaves are opposite, oval, oblong, veiny, and smooth; flowers are in dense panicles; calyx very small; corolla snow-white, consisting of four petals; and fruit a fleshy, oval, purple drupe.

History.—This plant is very ornamental, and is much cultivated in gardens, from Pennsylvania to Tennessee. It grows on river-banks and on elevated places, presenting clusters of snow-white flowers in May and June. The bark of the root, which imparts its properties to water or alcohol, is the part used.

Properties and Uses.—The bark is aperient, alterative, and diuretic, with some narcotic properties. An infusion is recommended for bilious, typhoid, and intermittent fevers. To convalescents who are suffering from the effects of exhaustive diseases it is an excellent tonic and restorative. It can be used to advantage as a poultice for ulcers, wounds, and external inflammations.

Dose.—Of the infusion, from the half a fluid ounce to two fluid ounces, repeated several times through the day, according to the influence it exerts upon the system.

OLD FIELD BALSAM (GNAPHALIUM POLYCEPHALUM).

COMMON NAMES. *Indian Posy, Sweet-scented Life Everlasting, White Balsam, etc.*

MEDICINAL PART. *The herb.*

Description.—This indigenous herbaceous annual has an erect, whitish, woolly, and much branched stem, one or two feet high. The leaves are alternate, sessile, lanceolate, acute, and entire; flowers tubular and yellow.

History.—Old Field Balsam is found in Canada and various parts of the United States, growing in old fields and on dry barren lands, flower ing in July and August. The leaves have a pleasant, aromatic smell, and are the parts used. They readily yield their properties to water.

Properties and Uses.—It is an astringent. Ulcerations of the mouth and throat are relieved by chewing the leaves and blossoms. In fevers a warm infusion is found to be very serviceable; also in quinsy, and pulmonary and bronchial complaints. It is also valuable, in infusion, for diseases of the bowels and hemorrhages; and the leaves, applied to bruises, indolent tumors, and other local affections, are very efficacious.

ANTEMARIA MARGARITACEA, or *Pearl-flowered Life Everlasting*, a perennial, possesses similar medicinal qualities.

OPIUM (PAPAVER SOMNIFERUM).

COMMON NAME. *Poppy.*

MEDICINAL PART. *Concrete juice of unripe capsule.*

Description.—An annual herb, with an erect, round, green, smooth stem, from two to four feet high. Leaves large, oblong, green; margins wavy, incised, and toothed; teeth sometimes tipped with a rigid hair. Flowers large, calyx smooth, and the fruit a large, smooth, globose capsule. There are two varieties, the *black* and *white.*

History.—A native of Asia and Egypt. It grows apparently wild in some parts of Europe and in England, but has escaped the gardens. Cultivated in Asia Minor, Egypt, Persia, and India, for the opium obtained from it. The white variety is cultivated on the plains of India, and the black in the Himalayas. Its virtues have been known to the ancients; for Homer speaks of the poppy growing in gardens. Poppy capsules contain a small quantity of the principles found in opium, and the effect is similar, but much weaker than it possesses. They are used medicinally; but opium is almost universally used.

Properties and Uses.—Opium is a narcotic and stimulant, acting under various circumstances as a sedative, antispasmodic, febrifuge, and diaphoretic. It is anodyne, and extensively used for that purpose It contains many active principles, morphia and codeia being, however, the most important. There is no herbal medicine more extensively used, as well as abused, than Opium, and though a valuable remedy, its indiscriminate use is pernicious, as it is capable of doing great harm. Laudanum and paregoric are the forms mostly used in domestic practice, but the "soothing syrups" and "carminatives" found in every nursery and household all contain Opium in some form, and work a great deal of mischief.

Dose.—Opium, one grain; laudanum, twenty drops; paregoric, a teaspoonful.

PAPOOSE ROOT (CAULOPHYLLUM THALICTROIDES)

COMMON NAMES. *Blue Cohosh, Squaw Root, etc.*

MEDICINAL PART. *The root.*

Description.—This is a smooth, glaucous plant, purple when young, with a high, round stem, one to three feet high. Leaves biternate or triternate, leaflets oval, petiolate, pale beneath, and from two to three inches long. The flowers appear in May or June.

History.—It is a handsome perennial plant, growing in all parts of the United States, near running streams, and in low, moist, rich grounds; also in swamps and on islands. The seeds, which ripen in August, make a decoction which closely resembles coffee. The berries are dry and rather mawkish. Its active principle is *Caulophyllin.*

Properties and Uses.—It is principally used as an emmenagogue, parturient, and antispasmodic. It also possesses diuretic, diaphoretic, and anthelmintic properties. It is employed in rheumatism, colic, cramps, hiccough, epilepsy, hysteria, uterine inflammation, etc. It is a valuable remedy in all chronic uterine diseases, but should be given in combination with such other remedies as the case requires.

Dose.—Of the decoction, from two to four fluid ounces, three or four times a day.

PAREIRA BRAVA (CISSAMPELOS PAREIRA).

COMMON NAMES. *Velvet Leaf, Ice Vine.*

MEDICINAL PART. *The root.*

Description.—This plant is a shrub, with a round woody root and smooth stems. Leaves roundish, peltate, subcordate, and smooth above when full grown. Flowers small, and the fruit a scarlet, round, reniform, shrivelled berry.

History.—This is a native of the West India Islands and the Spanish Main. It is sometimes imported under the name of *abuta* or *butua* root. It comes in cylindrical pieces, sometimes flattened, and some as thick as a child's arm, and a foot or more in length. The alkaloid obtained from it has been called *Cissampelin*, or *Pelosin.*

Properties and Uses.—Tonic, diuretic, and aperient. Used in chronic inflammation of the bladder, and various disorders of the urinary organs. It is also serviceable in leucorrhœa and gonorrhœa. It is highly beneficial in calculous affections, rheumatism, and jaundice.

Dose.—Of the infusion, one to four ounces; extract, ten to twenty grains.

PARSLEY (PETROSELINUM SATIVUM).

MEDICINAL PART. *The root.*

Description.—This biennial plant has a fleshy, spindle-shaped root, and an erect, smooth, branching stem. The radical leaves are biternate, bright green, and on long petioles; leaflets wedge-shaped. Flowers white or greenish, and petals rounded and barely emarginate.

History.—Although Parsley is reared in all parts of the civilized world as a culinary vegetable, it is a native of Europe. The root is the officinal part. From the seeds French chemists have succeeded in obtaining an essential oil, named *Apiol*, which has proved to be a good substitute for quinia in intermittent fevers, and for ergot as a parturient.

Properties and Uses.—It is diuretic, and very excellent in dropsy, especially that following scarlatina and other exanthematous diseases. It is also frequently used to remedy retention of urine, strangury, and gonorrhœa. The seeds are sometimes used as carminatives. They kill vermin in the head. The leaves, bruised, are a good application for contusions, swelled breasts, and enlarged glands. The bruised leaves applied to the breasts are used by wet-nurses to "dry up" the milk.

Dose.—Of the oil, for diuretic purposes, three or four drops a day; of the infusion, two to four fluid ounces, three or four times a day.

PARTRIDGE BERRY (MITCHELLA REPENS).

COMMON NAMES. *One Berry, Checkerberry, Winter Clover, Deerberry, Squaw-vine, etc.*

MEDICINAL PART. *The vine.*

Description.—This indigenous evergreen herb has a perennial root, from which arises a smooth and creeping stem. The leaves are ovate, slightly cordate, opposite, flat and dark-green; flowers are white, often tinged with red, in pairs, very fragrant, and have united ovaries. Calyx four-parted; corolla funnel-shaped; stamens four, inserted on the corolla. The fruit is a dry berry-like double drupe.

History.—Partridge Berry is indigenous to the United States. It grows both in dry woods and swampy places, and flowers in June and July. The berry is bright scarlet and edible, but nearly tasteless. The leaves, which look something like clover, remain green throughout the winter. The whole plant is used, readily imparting its virtues to alcohol or boiling water.

Properties and Uses.—Partridge Berry is parturient (producing or promoting child-birth, or labor), diuretic, and astringent. In all uterine diseases it is highly beneficial. The Indian women use it for weeks before confinement, in order to render parturition safe and easy. Ladies who wish to use it for that purpose, however, should consult an herbal physician of experience for a proper, safe, and effectual preparation. The remedy is exclusively American, not being used, or even noticed, by European practitioners.

Dose.—Of a strong decoction, from two to four fluid ounces, three or four times a day. The berries are good for dysentery. They are also highly spoken of as a cure for sore nipples. The application for the nipples is made by boiling a strong decoction of the leaves down to a thick liquid, and then adding cream to it. It is not, however, equal to the Herbal Ointment, for an account of which see page 472.

PENNYROYAL (HEDEOMA PULEGIOIDES).

COMMON NAMES. *Tickweed, Squawmint, etc.*

MEDICINAL PART. *The herb.*

Description.—This is an indigenous annual plant, with a fibrous, yellowish root, and an erect, branching stem, from six to twelve inches high. The leaves are half an inch or more long, opposite, oblong, and on short petioles; floral leaves similar. The flowers are quite small and light-blue in color.

History.—This plant should not be confounded with the *Mentha pulegioides*, or *European Pennyroyal.* It grows in barren woods and dry fields, and particularly in limestone countries, flowering from June to September and October, rendering the air fragrant to some distance around it. It is common to nearly all parts of the United States. It is said to be very obnoxious to fleas.

Properties and Uses.—It is stimulant, diaphoretic, emmenagogue, and carminative. The warm infusion, used freely, will promote perspiration, restore suppressed lochia or after-flow, and excite the menstrual discharge when recently checked. It is very much used by females for this last purpose—a large draught being taken at bedtime, the feet being previously bathed in hot water.

PEONY (PÆONIA OFFICINALIS).

MEDICINAL PART. *The root.*

Description.—Peony has many thick, long-spreading, perennial roots, running deep into the ground, with an erect, herbaceous, large, green, and branching stem, about two or three feet high. The leaves are large; leaflets ovate-lanceolate and smooth. The flowers are large, red, and solitary; and fruit a many-seeded, fleshy follicle.

History.—This plant is indigenous to Southern Europe, and is cultivated in gardens in the United States and elsewhere, on account of the elegance of its large flowers, which appear from May to August. The root is the officinal part. This, with the seeds and flowers, yields its virtues to diluted spirits.

Properties and Uses.—It is antispasmodic and tonic, and can be advantageously employed in chorea, epilepsy, spasms, and various nervous affections. An infusion of value is made by adding an ounce of the root, in coarse powder, to a pint of a boiling liquid, composed of one part of *good* gin and two parts of water.

Dose.—Two or three fluid ounces (sweetened), three or four times a day.

PERUVIAN BALSAM (MYROSPERMUM PERUIFERUM).

MEDICINAL PART. *The balsamic exudation.*

Description.—The tree from which this is procured is large, with a thick, straight, smooth trunk, and a coarse, gray, compact, heavy, granulated bark. The bark is of a pale straw color, filled with resin, which, according to its quantity changes the color to citron, yellow, red, or dark chestnut; smell and taste grateful, balsamic, and aromatic. The leaves are pinnate; leaflets alternate, oblong or ovate, acuminate, and emarginate. The flowers are in axillary racemes, and the fruit is a pendulous, straw-colored samara.

History.—The tree is common to the forests of Peru, and flowers from July to October. The natives call it *Quinquino.* It contains a large amount of balsamic juice, which yields copiously when the bark is incised. Balsam of Peru, in thin layers, has a dark, reddish-brown color; in bulk it is black, or of the color of molasses. The natives steep the fruit in rum, call the liquid *balsamito*, and use it largely for medical purposes.

Properties and Uses.—It is expectorant and stimulant, acting especially on mucous tissues. Its reparative action on the lungs in consumption is decided, removing the secretions, healing the ulcers, and expelling the tuberculous matter. In all chronic diseases of the lungs and bronchial tubes it is without a superior. Externally it can be applied to old ulcers, wounds, ringworm, etc.

This valuable remedy is one of the ingredients of my "Acacian Balsam," wherein it is properly combined with many other valuable associates.

PINKROOT (SPIGELIA MARILANDICA).

COMMON NAMES. *Carolina Pink* or *Worm Grass.*
MEDICINAL PART. *The root.*

Description.—This herbaceous, indigenous plant has a perennial, very fibrous, yellow root, which sends up several erect, smooth stems of purplish color, from six to twenty inches high. The leaves are opposite, sessile, ovate-lanceolate, acute, or acuminate, entire, and smooth. Flowers few in number and club-shaped. Fruit a double capsule.

Pinkroot.

History.—It inhabits the Southern States, and is seldom found north of the Potomac. It was used by the Indians as an anthelmintic before the discovery of America, and was formerly collected for the market by the Creeks and

Cherokees in the northern part of Georgia, but since their removal the supply comes from the far Southwest.

Properties and Uses.—It is an active and certain vermifuge, especially among children. Given alone it is very apt to produce various unpleasant symptoms, increased action of the heart, dizziness, etc. I extract from the root a resinous principle, to which I have given the name of *Spigeliin*, which has all of the virtues of the root, but does not produce any derangement. I employ the Spigeliin in my "Male Fern Vermifuge." See page 471.

PIPSISSEWA (CHIMAPHILA UMBELLATA).

COMMON NAMES. *Wintergreen, Prince's Pine, Ground Holly, etc.*
MEDICINAL PART. *The whole plant.*

Description.—This is a small evergreen, nearly herbaceous, perennial herb with a creeping rhizome, from which spring several erect stems, woody at their base, and from four to eight inches high. The leaves are from two to three inches long, on short petioles, and of dark green-color, paler below. The flowers are of light-purple color, and exhale a fragrant odor. The pollen is white, and the fruit is an erect five-celled capsule.

Pipsissewa.

History.—This plant is indigenous to the north temperate regions of both hemispheres, and is met with in dry, shady woods, flowering from May to August. The leaves have no odor when dried, but when fresh and rubbed they are rather fragrant. Boiling water or alcohol extracts their virtues. They contain resin, gum, lignin, and saline substances.

Properties and Uses.—It is diuretic, tonic, alterative, and astringent It is especially useful in scrofula and chronic rheumatism. In diseases of the kidneys and dropsy it exerts a decided curative power. In urinary diseases it is preferable to uva ursi, on account of being less obnoxious to the stomach. In dropsy it cannot be so well depended upon without the use of some more active measures in combination with it.

PLEURISY ROOT (ASCLEPIAS TUBEROSA).

COMMON NAMES. *Butterfly-weed, Wind-root, Tuber-root.*
MEDICINAL PART. *The root.*

Description.—This plant has a perennial, large, fleshy, white, fusiform root, from which numerous stems arise, growing from one to three feet high, which are more or less erect, round, hairy, green or red. and growing in bunches from the root. The leaves are alternate, lanceolate, hairy, dark green above, and paler beneath. The flowers are numerous, erect, and of a beautifully bright orange color. The fruit is a long, narrow, green follicle. Seeds are ovate, and terminate in long silken hairs.

Pleurisy Root.

History.—It is a native of the United States, more particularly of the Southern States, inhabiting gravelly and sandy soils, and flowering in July and August. The root is the medicinal part. When fresh it has a disagreeable, slightly acrimonious taste. but when dried the taste is slightly bitter. Boiling water extracts its virtues. *Asclepin* is the active principle.

Properties and Uses.—Pleurisy Root is much used in decoction or infusion, for the purpose of promoting perspiration and expectoration in diseases of the respiratory organs, especially pleurisy, inflammation of the lungs, catarrhal affections, consumption, etc. It is likewise carminative, tonic, diuretic, and antispasmodic, but does not stimulate. Acute rheumatism, fever, dysentery, etc., are benefited by a free use of the warm infusion. It is also highly efficacious in some cases of dyspepsia. In uterine difficulties it has also been found of great value. Its chief use, however, is in bronchial and pulmonary complaints, and it serves its indications in these complaints most admirably. It is one of the ingredients of my Acacian Balsam. See page 470.

Dose.—Of the powder, twenty to sixty grains, three or four times a day. Of a *strong* tincture, one or two wineglasses full four or five times a day, until perspiration is produced.

POKE (PHYTOLACCA DECANDRA).

COMMON NAMES. *Pigeon-berry, Garget, Scoke, Coakum, etc.*

MEDICINAL PARTS. *The root, leaves, and berries.*

Description.—This indigenous plant has a perennial root of large size, frequently exceeding a man's leg in diameter, fleshy, fibrous, easily cut or broken, and covered with a thin brownish bark. The stems are annual, about an inch in diameter, round, smooth, when young green, and grow from five to nine feet in height. The leaves are scattered, petiolate, smooth on both sides, and about five inches long and three broad. The flowers are numerous, small, and greenish-white in color; and the berries are round, dark-purple, and in long clusters.

History.—This plant is common in many parts of the country, growing in dry fields, hillsides, and roadsides, and flowering in July and August. It is also found in Europe and northern parts of Africa. The leaves should be gathered just previous to the ripening of the berries. The berries are collected when fully matured. *Phytolaccin* is its active principle.

Properties and Uses.—Poke is emetic, cathartic, alterative, and slightly narcotic. The root excites the whole glandular system, and is very useful in syphilitic, scrofulous, rheumatic, and cutaneous diseases. It is an excellent remedy for the removal of mercurio-syphilitic affections. Very few, if any, of the alteratives have superior power to Poke, if it is properly gathered and prepared for medicinal use. It is an ingredient in my "Blood Purifier," which will be found fully described on page 471.

POMEGRANATE (PUNICA GRANATUM).

MEDICINAL PARTS. *The rind of the fruit, and bark of the root.*

Description.—This is a small tree or shrub. The leaves are opposite, entire, smooth, and two or three inches long. The flowers are large, red, two or three, and nearly sessile. Calyx five-cleft, corolla consists of five much crumpled petals. The fruit is a large pericarp, quite pleasant in flavor, and quite watery.

History.—The Pomegranate is Asiatic, but has been naturalized in the West Indies and the Southern States.

Properties and Uses.—The flowers and rind of the fruit are astringent, and are used for the arrest of mucous discharges, hemorrhages, night-sweats, and diarrhœa accompanying consumption. They are also very good for intermittent fever and tape-worm. The bark of the root is used as a specific for tape-worm, but its chief virtues are healing and balsamic, if taken for ulcerations of the lungs.

Dose.—The dose of the rind or flowers in powder is from one to two scruples, and in decoction from one to three fluid ounces.

Prickly Ash.

PRICKLY ASH (XANTHOXYLUM FRAXINEUM).

COMMON NAMES. *Yellow-wood, Toothache-bush, etc.*

MEDICINAL PARTS. *The bark and berries.*

Description.—This indigenous shrub has a stem ten or twelve feet high, with alternate branches, which are armed with strong conical prickles. The leaves are alternate and pinnate;

leaflets ovate and acute. The flowers are small, greenish, and appear before the leaves. The fruit is an oval capsule, varying from green to red in color.

History.—It is a native of North America, growing from Canada to Virginia, and west to the Mississippi, in woods, thickets, and on river banks, and flowering in April and May. The medicinal parts render their virtues to water and alcohol. *Xanthoxyline* is its active principle.

Properties and Uses.—Prickly Ash is stimulant, tonic, alterative, and sialagogue. It is used as a stimulant in languid states of the system, and as a sialagogue in paralysis of the tongue and mouth. It is highly beneficial in chronic rheumatism, colic, syphilis, hepatic derangements, and wherever a stimulating alterative is required. Dose of the powder, from ten to thirty grains, three times a day. The berries are stimulant, carminative, and antispasmodic, acting especially on the mucous tissues.

The *Aralia Spinosa*, or Southern Prickly Ash, differs from Xanthoxy lum, both in botanical character and medicinal virtues.

PRIVET (LIGUSTRUM VULGARE).

COMMON NAMES. *Privy, Prim, etc.*

MEDICINAL PART. *The leaves.*

Description.—This is a smooth shrub, growing five or six feet high. The leaves are dark-green, one or two inches in length, about half as wide, entire, smooth, lanceolate, and on short petioles. The flowers are small, white, and numerous, and fruit a spherical black berry. In England the Privet is carried up with many slender branches to a reasonable height and breadth, to cover arbors, bowers, and banqueting houses, and brought or wrought into many fantastic forms, as birds, men, horses.

History.—It is supposed to have been introduced into America from England but it is indigenous to Missouri, and found growing in wild woods and thickets from New England to Virginia and Ohio. It is also cultivated in American gardens. The leaves are used for medicinal purposes. They have but little odor, and an agreeable bitterish and astringent taste. They yield their virtues to water or alcohol. The berries are reputed cathartic, and the bark is said to be as effectual as the leaves, as it contains sugar, mannite, starch, bitter resin, bitter extractive, albumen, salts, and a peculiar substance called *Ligustrin.*

Properties and Uses.—The leaves are astringent. A decoction of them is valuable in chronic bowel complaints, ulcerations of stomach and bowels, or as a gargle for ulcers of mouth and throat. It is also good as an injection for ulcerated ears with offensive discharges, leucorrhœa, etc. This ingredient I use in a wash for leucorrhœa, which never fails to cure.

Dose.—Of the powdered leaves thirty to sixty grains, three times a day; of the decoction two to four teacupfuls.

QUASSIA (PICRÆNIA EXCELSA).

COMMON NAMES. *Bitter-wood, Bitter-ash.*

MEDICINAL PART. *The wood.*

Description.—This is a tree growing from fifty to one hundred feet high, with an erect stem, three or more feet in diameter at the stem. The bark is grayish and smooth. The leaves are alternate, unequally pinnate; leaflets opposite, oblong, acuminate, and unequal at the base. Flowers are small, pale or yellowish-green. Fruit three drupes, about the size of a pea. The *Quassia Amara*, or bitter quassia, is a shrub, or moderately-sized branching tree, having a grayish bark.

History.—*Quassia Amara* inhabits Surinam, Guiana, Colombia, Panama, and the West India Islands. It flowers in November and December. The bark, wood, and root, which are intensely bitter, are used to the greatest advantage in malignant fevers. For the medicinal parts of this tree, as they seldom reach England or America, we get as a substitute the *Picræna Excelsa* of Jamaica and other neighboring islands, which flowers in October and November, and in the two succeeding months matures its fruit.

Properties and Uses.—Quassia is tonic, febrifuge, and anthelmintic. Cups made of the wood have been used for many years by persons requiring a powerful tonic. Any liquid standing in one of these vessels a few moments will become thoroughly impregnated by its peculiar medicinal qualities. Wherever a bitter tonic is required, Quassia is an excellent remedy.

Dose.—Of the powder, thirty grains; of the infusion, from one to three fluid ounces; of the tincture, one or two fluid drachms, and of the extract, from two to ten grains.

QUEEN OF THE MEADOW (EUPATORIUM PURPUREUM).

COMMON NAMES. *Gravel-root, Joe-pie, Trumpet-weed.*

MEDICINAL PART. *The root.*

Description.—This is a herbaceous plant, with a perennial, woody root, with many long dark-brown fibres, sending up one or more solid green, sometimes purplish, stems, five or six feet in height. The leaves are oblong-ovate or lanceolate, coarsely serrate, and from three to six in a whorl. The flowers are tubular, purple, often varying to whitish.

History.—Queen of the Meadow grows in low places, dry woods or meadows, in the Northern, Western, and Middle States of the American Union, and flowers in August and September. The root is the officinal part It has a smell resembling old hay, and a slightly bitter, aromatic taste, which is faintly astringent but not unpleasant. It yields its properties to water by decoction or spirits.

Properties and Uses.—It is diuretic, stimulant, astringent, and tonic. It is used in all chronic urinary disorders, as well as in hematuria, gout, and rheumatism, with moderate good effect.

Dose.—Of the decoction, from two to four fluid ounces, three or four times a day.

RAGGED CUP (SILPHIUM PERFOLIATUM).

COMMON NAME. *Indian Cup-plant.*

MEDICINAL PART. *The root.*

Description.—This plant has a perennial, horizontal, pitted rhizome, and a large smooth herbaceous stem, from four to seven feet high. The leaves are opposite, ovate, from eight to fourteen inches long by four to seven wide. The flowers are yellowish, and the fruit a broadly ovate winged achenium.

History.—This plant is common to the Western States, and is found growing in rich bottoms, bearing numerous yellow flowers, which are perfected in August. It has a large, long, and crooked root, which is the part used medicinally, and which readily imparts its properties to alcohol or water. It will yield a bitterish gum, somewhat similar to frankincense, which is frequently used to sweeten the breath.

Properties and Uses.—It is tonic, diaphoretic, and alterative. A strong infusion of the root, made by long steeping, or an extract, is said to be one of the best remedies for the removal of ague-cake, or enlarged spleen. It is also useful in intermittent and remittent fevers, internal bruises, debility, ulcers, liver affections, and as a general alterative restorative. The gum is said to be stimulant and antispasmodic. The spleen is an organ whose functions the very best of the old-school physicians cannot define; but that it is the seat of very many most distressing diseases is a fact which not one of them will pretend to deny. It is, as nearly as can be ascertained by the most laborious research. a dependent of the liver and stomach, and what deranges it deranges both the stomach and the liver.

SILPHIUM GUMMIFERUM, or *Rosin-weed*, and SILPHIUM LACINIATUM, or *Compass-weed*, are used in intermittent fever, and are beneficial in dry, obstinate coughs. They often cure the heaves in horses.

RATTLE BUSH (BAPTISIA TINCTORIA).

COMMON NAMES. *Wild Indigo, Horsefly Weed.*

MEDICINAL PART. *The bark of the root and leaves.*

Description.—The blackish and wood root of this perennial plant sends up a stem which is very much branched, round, smooth, and from two to three feet high. The leaves are small and alternate, leaflets rounded at their extremity; calyx four-cleft, and fruit a short, bluish-black legume.

History.—This small shrub grows in dry places in many parts of the United States, and bears bright yellow flowers in July and August. The fruit is of a bluish-black color in the form of an oblong pod, and contains indigo, tannin, an acid, and *baptisin.* Any portion of the plant, when dried, yields a blue dye, which is, however, not equal in value to indigo. If the shoots are used after they acquire a green color they will cause drastic purgation. Alcohol or water will take up the active properties of this plant. Medicinally, both the root and the leaves are valuable, and deserve to be better known than they are at present as remedial agents. The virtues of the root reside chiefly in the bark.

Properties and Uses.—It is purgative, emetic, astringent, and antiseptic. For its antiseptic qualities or properties it is more highly esteemed than for any other. A decoction of the bark of the root is efficacious in the cure of all kinds of external sores and ulcerations. It is used in decoction or syrup, for scarlatina, typhus, and all cases where there is a tendency to putrescency. As a fomentation it is very useful in ulcers, tumors, sore nipples, etc., and may be so used if you cannot get a superior remedy, as the Herbal Ointment.

Dose.—Of the decoction, one tablespoonful every two or four hours, as required. The decoction is made by boiling one ounce of the powdered bark in two pints of water until they are reduced to one pint.

RED RASPBERRY (RUBUS STRIGOSUS.)

MEDICINAL PARTS. *The bark of the root, and leaves.*

Description.—This is a shrubby, strongly hispid plant, about four feet high. Leaves, pinnate; leaflets, oblong-ovate. Flowers, white; corolla, cup-shaped; and fruit, a red berry, of a rich delicious flavor.

History.—The Red Raspberry grows wild, and is common to Canada and the Northern and Middle United States. It grows in hedges and thickets, and upon neglected fields. It flowers in May, and its fruit ripens from June to August. The leaves and bark of the root are the parts used medicinally. They impart their properties to water, giving to the infusion an odor and flavor somewhat similar to black tea.

Properties and Uses.—It is very useful as an astringent. An infusion or decoction of the leaves has been found an excellent remedy in diarrhœa, dysentery, and cholera infantum, and all diseases of a kindred nature. It is somewhat freely used as a wash and injection for leucorrhœa, gleet, gonorrhœa, and prolapsus uteri and ani. The decoction of the leaves combined with cream will suppress nausea and vomiting It is sometimes used as an aid in labor, and has been efficacious in promoting uterine contractions when *ergot* has failed. This plant is one of the ingredients of my prepared remedy for the above diseases.

Dose.—Of the decoction, from one to four fluid ounces, several times a day. Of the pulverized root bark, which is sometimes used, from twenty to thirty grains.

The *Rubus Trivialis*, or *Dewberry*, and *Rubus Villosus*, or *Blackberry*, contain similar medical qualities, and may be used instead.

RED ROOT (CEANOTHUS AMERICANUS).

COMMON NAMES. *New Jersey Tea, Wild Snow-ball.*

MEDICINAL PART. *The bark of the root.*

Description.—This plant has a large root with a red or brownish bark, tolerably thick, and body of dark-red color. The stems are from two to four feet high, slender, with many reddish, round, smooth branches. The leaves are ovate or oblong-ovate, serrate, acuminate, rather smooth above, and cordate at the base. The flowers are minute and white, and fruit a dry capsule.

History.—This plant is very abundant in the United States, especially in the western portions thereof. It grows in dry woodlands, bowers, etc., and flowers from June to August. The leaves are sometimes used as a substitute for Chinese tea, which, when dried, they much resemble. The root, which is officinal, contains a large amount of Prussic acid. *Ceanothine* is the name that has been given to its active principle.

Properties and Uses.—Red Root is astringent, expectorant, sedative, anti-spasmodic, and anti-syphilitic. It is used with great good effect in dysentery, asthma, chronic bronchitis, whooping-cough, and consumption. It is also successfully used as a gargle in aphthæ of children, sore mouth subsequent to fevers, and sore throats.

Dose.—Of decoction, one tablespoonful three times a day.

RHATANY (KRAMERIA TRIANDRIA).

MEDICINAL PART. *The root.*

Description.—The root of this plant is horizontal, very long, with a thick bark. The stem is round and procumbent, branches two or three feet long; when young, white and silky; when old, dark and naked. The leaves are alternate, sessile, oblong and obovate, hoary and entire. The flowers are red on short stalks. Calyx has four sepals, and corolla four petals. The fruit is a dry, hairy drupe.

History.—Rhatany flowers all the year round, and grows upon the sandy, dry, and gravelly hills of Peru. The root is the officinal part, and is dug up in large quantities after the rains. It was made officinal in 1780 by Ruiz, but long before that the natives had used it as a strong astringent for various diseases, afflictions, maladies, and complaints. In Portugal, to which the Peruvians send the bulk of the roots gathered, it is used to adulterate red wines. The best method of extracting the medicinal qualities of the root, is to put it powdered in a displacer and pass water through. This will bring a brick-red aqueous solution, which will embrace all the medicinal virtues. There is a false Rhatany, the source of which is unknown.

Properties and Uses.—It is a powerful astringent, and slightly tonic. It is beneficial wherever powerful astringents are required, and may be used to advantage, if properly prepared, for all diseases which call for the application of a decided astringent.

RHEUMATISM ROOT (JEFFERSONIA DIPHYLLA).

COMMON NAMES. *Twin-leaf, Ground-Squirrel Pea.*

MEDICINAL PART. *The root.*

Description.—This plant is perennial, and has a horizontal *rhizoma* or fleshy root, with matted fibrous radicles. The stem is simple, naked, one-flowered, and from eight to fourteen inches in height. The leaves are in pairs, broader than long, ending in an obtuse point, smooth and petioled; flowers, large and white; and fruit an obovate capsule.

History.—This plant is found from New York to Maryland and Virginia, and in many parts of the Western States. It grows chiefly in limestone soil, but also is found in woods and near rivers, irrespective of limestone, and flowers in April and May. The root is the part used, and its virtues are extracted by water or alcohol. A chemical analysis of this plant showed it to contain tannic acid, gum, starch, pectin, fatty resin, bitter matter, similar to polygalic acid, carbonate and sulphate of potassa, lime, iron, magnesia, silica, etc.

Properties and Uses.—It is diuretic, alterative, antispasmodic, and a stimulating diaphoretic. It is successfully used in chronic rheumatism, secondary or mercurio-syphilis, dropsy, in many nervous affections spasms, cramps, nervous excitability, etc. As a gargle it is useful in diseases of the throat.

Dose.—Of the decoction, from two to four fluid ounces, three or four times a day. Of the saturated tincture, from one to three fluid drachms three times a day.

RHUBARB (RHEUM PALMATUM).

MEDICINAL PART. *The root.*

Description.—The scientific world happens to be in much argument as to the exact plant or plants from which Rhubarb is produced. It is, however, well known to all instructed herbalists that Rhubarb is the root of a Rheum, and that the plant from which the drug of the shops is obtained chiefly inhabits Chinese Tartary, and grows wild on the mountains and highlands of that section of the globe. That the truth of its botanical identity is not elicited is owing to a severe prohibition of the Chinese government. Every sacrifice to obtain the true plant or the seed has been in vain.

Rheum Palmatum.

History.—There are several varieties met with in commerce termed the Russian, Chinese, English, and French Rhubarb, among which the Russian is considered the best. The names are given, not that they are produced in indicated countries, but of the channels by which they are thrown upon the market. Rhubarb has a peculiar aromatic odor, bitter, faintly astringent taste, and when chewed tinges the saliva yellow. It contains oxalate of lime in abundance.

Properties and Uses.—Rhubarb is cathartic. astringent, and tonic; as a cathartic it acts by increasing the muscular action of the bowels rather than augmenting their secretions. It is much used as a laxative for infants, its mildness and tonic qualities making it peculiarly applicable. It is a valuable medicine.

Dose.—Of the powder, as a purgative, from ten to thirty grains. As a laxative, from five to ten grains. As a tonic, from one to five grains. Of the tincture or syrup, one to two fluid drachms.

ROSEMARY (ROSMARINUS OFFICINALIS).

MEDICINAL PART. *The tops.*

Description.—Rosemary is an erect, perennial, evergreen shrub, two to four feet high, with numerous branches of an ash color, and densely leafy. The leaves are sessile, opposite, and linear, over an inch in length, dark-green and shining above, and downy. The flowers are few, bright blue or white. Calyx purplish.

History.—Rosemary is a native of the countries surrounding the Mediterranean, and is cultivated in nearly every garden for its fragrance and beauty. It flowers in April and May. The parts used in medicine are the flowering tops.

Properties and Uses.—It is stimulant, antispasmodic, and emmenagogue. The oil is principally employed as a perfume for ointments, liniments, and embrocations.

Dose.—Of the oil, internally, from three to six drops.

PYROLA (ROUND-LEAVED) (PYROLA ROTUNDIFOLIA).

COMMON NAMES. *False Wintergreen, Shin-leaf, Canker-Lettuce, Pear-leaf Wintergreen, etc.*

MEDICINAL PART. *The herb.*

Description.—This is a low, perennial, evergreen herb. The leaves are radical, ovate, nearly two inches in diameter, smooth, shining, and thick. The petioles are much longer than the leaf. The flowers are many, large, fragrant, white, and drooping. The fruit is a five-called, many-seeded capsule.

History.—This plant is common in damp and shady woods in various parts of the United States, flowering in June and July. The whole plant is used, and imparts its medicinal properties to water.

Properties and Uses.—It is astringent, diuretic, tonic, and antispasmodic. The decoction is much used in all skin diseases, and is good to eradicate a scrofulous taint from the system. It is used in injection for whites and various diseases of the womb. The herb is applied with profit as a poultice to ulcers, swellings, boils, felons, and inflammations. The decoction will be found beneficial as a gargle for sore throat and mouth, and as a wash for sore or ophthalmic eyes. Administer it internally for gravel, ulceration of the bladder, bloody urine, and other urinary diseases; also, for epilepsy and other nervous affections.

Dose.—Of the decoction, one fluid ounce, three times a day; of the extract, two to four grains.

SAFFRON (DYERS') (CARTHAMUS TINCTORIUS).

COMMON NAMES. *Safflower, Bastard Saffron.*

MEDICINAL PART. *The flowers.*

Description.—This annual plant has a smooth, striate stem, from one to two feet high, and branching at the top. The leaves are alternate, ovate-lanceolate, sessile, smooth, and shining. The flowers are numerous, long, slender, and orange-colored. Corolla five-cleft.

History.—This plant is cultivated in England and America, although it is a native of Egypt and the countries surrounding the Mediterranean. The orange-red florets are the officinal parts. The cultivated Safflower is usually sold in the shops, and contains two coloring matters: the first of which is yellow and soluble in water; the second a beautiful red, and readily soluble in alkaline solutions only.

Properties and Uses.—It will restore the menstrual discharge when the latter has been recently suppressed by cold, if used in warm infusion. It will also, when taken in the same form, produce an action of the bowels. In measles, scarlet fever, and other eruptive maladies, it is also considered an excellent diaphoretic. The seeds are sometimes used as purgative and emmenagogue, but, in my opinion, are of no great value. The infusion is made by boiling a drachm or two of the flowers in water, and may be taken tolerably freely.

SAGE (SALVIA OFFICINALIS).

COMMON NAME. *Garden Sage.*

MEDICINAL PART. *The leaves.*

Description.—Sage is a plant with a pubescent stem, erect branches, hoary with down, leafy at the base, about a foot or foot and a half long. The leaves are opposite, entire, petioled, ovate-lanceolate, the lowermost white, with wool beneath. The flowers are blue and in whorls.

History.—Sage is a native of Southern Europe, and has been naturalized for very many years in this country as a garden plant. The leaves and tops should be carefully gathered and dried during its flowering season, which is in June and July. They have a peculiar, strong, aromatic, camphorous odor, and a sharp, warm, slightly bitter taste, which properties are owing to its volatile oil, which may be obtained by distilling the plant with water. It imparts its virtues to boiling water in infusion, but more especially to alcohol.

Properties and Uses.—It is feebly tonic, and astringent, expectorant, diaphoretic, and having properties common to aromatics. The infusion is much valued in cases of gastric debility, checking flatulency with speed and certainty.

The warm infusion will cause active diuresis by checking its diaphoretic tendency. It is called by some a most capital remedy for spermatorrhœa, and for excessive venereal desire, and I am one of those who know from experience in my practice that it is grand for what is termed sexual debility when its use is indicated. The infusion is much used as a gargle for inflammation and ulceration of the throat and relaxed uvula, either alone or combined with vinegar, honey, or sumach.

ST. IGNATIUS' BEAN (IGNATIUS AMARA).

Description.—The Ignatius Amara is a branching tree with long, taper, smooth, scrambling branches. The leaves are veiny, smooth, and a span long. The flowers are long, nodding, and white, and smell like jasmine. The fruit is small and pear-shaped, and the seeds number about twenty, are angular, and are imbedded in a soft pulp.

History.—The tree is indigenous to the Philippine Islands, and the seeds thereof are the St. Ignatius' Bean of the drug-shops. The bean yields its properties best to alcohol, but will also yield them to water. It contains about one-third more strychnia than nux-vomica, but is seldom used for the production of strychnia on account of its extreme scarcity.

Properties and Uses.—Very similar to nux-vomica seeds, but more energetic. It is used in nervous debility, amenorrhœa, chlorosis, epilepsy, worms, etc., with partial good effect, but is a dangerous article however well prepared, and should be used only by the advice of a professional gentleman, upon whose truth and ability you may place the utmost confidence. It should not be employed in domestic practice.

Dose.—Of the powdered seed, one grain; of the alcoholic extract, one-eighth of a grain.

ST. JOHN'S WORT (HYPERICUM PERFORATUM).

MEDICINAL PARTS. *The tops and flowers.*

Description.—This is a beautiful shrub, and is a great ornament to our meadows. It has a hard and woody root, which abides in the ground many years, shooting anew every year. The stalks run up about two feet high, spreading many branches, having deep-green, ovate, obtuse, and opposite leaves, which are full of small holes, which are plainly seen when the leaf is held up to the light. At the tops of the stalks and branches stand yellow flowers of five leaves apiece, with many yellow threads in the middle, which, being bruised, yield a reddish juice, like blood, after which come small, round heads, wherein is contained small blackish seed, smelling like resin. The fruit is a three-celled capsule.

History.—This plant grows abundantly in this country and Europe, and proves exceedingly annoying to farmers. It flowers from June to August. It has a peculiar terebinthine odor, and a balsamic, bitterish taste. It yields its properties to water, alcohol, and ether.

Properties and Uses.—It is astringent, sedative, and diuretic. It suppresses the urine, and is very applicable in chronic urinary affections, diarrhœa, dysentery, jaundice, menorrhagia, hysteria, nervous affections, hemoptysis, and other hemorrhages. Externally, in fomentation, or used as an ointment, it is serviceable in dispelling hard tumors, caked breasts, bruises, etc.

Dose.—Of the powder, from half a drachm to two drachms; infusion, one to two ounces.

SANICLE (SANICULA MARILANDICA).

COMMON NAME. *Black-snake Root.*

MEDICINAL PART. *The root.*

Description.—Sanicle is an indigenous, perennial herb, with a smooth, furrowed stem, from one to three feet high. The leaves are digitate, mostly radical, and on petioles from six to twelve inches long. Cauline leaves few, and nearly sessile. The flowers are mostly barren, white, sometimes yellowish, fertile ones sessile.

History.—It is common to the United States and Canada, and is found in low woods and thickets, flowering in June. The fibrous root is aromatic in taste and odor. It imparts its virtues to water and alcohol.

Properties and Uses.—In its action upon the system it resembles valerian very much, possessing nervine and anodyne properties. Domestically, it is used with advantage in intermittent fevers, sore-throat, erysipelas, and cutaneous affections. It is very efficacious in chorea, and is very beneficially employed in various nervous affections.

Dose.—Powder, one drachm; decoction, from one to four ounces.

SARSAPARILLA (SMILAX OFFICINALIS).

MEDICINAL PART. *The root.*

Description.—The stem of this plant is twining, angular, and prickly, the young shoots being unarmed. The leaves are ovate-oblong, acute, cordate, smooth, and about a foot long. The petioles are an inch long, bearing tendrils above the base. Botanically, nothing is known of the flowers. This plant grows in New Granada, on the banks of the Magdaline, near Bajorque. Great quantities are sent to Mompox and Carthagena, and from thence to Jamaica and Cadiz.

The *Smilax Syphilitica*, *S. Papyracea*, *S. Medica*, *S. China*, and *S. Sarsaparilla* are all members of the same family of plants; their medicinal qualities are similar, and they form the Sarsaparilla of commerce, with the exception of the S. Sarsaparilla, which is native to the United States, flowering from May to August. The American plant is regarded by some as inert, but why so I do not know. The plant extensively known in the South as *Bamboo Brier*, which is but a species of Sarsaparilla, certainly possesses medicinal qualities equal, if not superior, to commercial Sarsaparilla. Professionally, I employ the Honduras Sarsaparilla, which I regard as the best.

History.—The Sarsaparilla of commerce consists of very long roots, having a thick bark of a grayish or brownish color. They have scarcely any odor, but possess a mucilaginous taste. Those roots that have a deep orange tint are the best, and the stronger the acrid and nauseous qualities, the better are the properties of the root. Water and alcohol extract its medicinal qualities. By chemical analysis it contains *salseparin*, a coloring matter, starch, chloride of potassium, an essential oil, bassorin, albumen, pectic and acetic acid, and the several salts of lime, potassa, magnesia, and oxide of iron.

Properties and Uses.—An alterative. When properly prepared it exerts a favorable change over the system. It has great repute in syphilitic diseases. In several chronic diseases, as of the skin, rheumatic affections, passive dropsy, etc., it is of service. Its chief use, however, is an adjuvant to other alteratives; its individual properties being too feeble to answer all the conditions required of an alterative.

Dose.—Of the powder, thirty grains; of the infusion or syrup, four fluid ounces

SASSAFRAS (LAURUS SASSAFRAS).

MEDICINAL PART. *The bark of the root.*

Description.—This is a small tree, varying in height from ten to forty feet. The bark is rough and grayish, that of the twigs smooth and green. The leaves are alternate, petiolate, bright green, very variable in form, smooth above and downy beneath. The flowers appear before the leaves, are small, greenish-yellow; fruit an oval succulent drupe.

History.—Indigenous to North America, and common to the woods from Canada to Florida, and flowering in the latter part of April or early in May. The bark has an aromatic, agreeable taste, and similar odor. It yields its properties to hot water by infusion, and to alcohol.

Properties and Uses.—It is a warm, aromatic stimulant, alterative, diaphoretic, and diuretic. It is much used in alterative compounds as a flavoring adjuvant. In domestic practice it enjoys a wide field of application and use, especially as a so-called spring-renovator of the blood.

SAVORY (SUMMER) (SATUREJA HORTENSIS).

MEDICINAL PART. *The leaves.*

Description.—This annual plant has a branching, bushy stem, about eighteen inches in height, woody at the base, frequently changing to purple. The leaves are numerous, small, entire, and acute at the end. The flowers are pink-colored. Calyx tubular, corolla bilabiate, stamens diverging.

History.—It is a native of the south of France. It is extensively cultivated for culinary purposes in Europe and America, and flowers in July and August. The leaves are the part employed. They have an aromatic odor and taste analogous to those of thyme.

Properties and Uses.—It is a stimulant, carminative, and emmenagogue. A warm infusion is beneficial in colds, menstrual suppression, and wind colic, for which it is a specific. The oil inserted into the carious teeth will often relieve the tooth-ache.

SATUREJA MONTANA, or *Winter Savory*, possesses similar qualities.

Dose.—From two to four ounces of the infusion, several times a day.

SCULL-CAP (SCUTELLARIA LATERIFLORA).

COMMON NAMES. *Blue Scull-Cap*, *Side-Flowering Scull-Cap*, *Mad-Dogweed*, and *Hood-wort*.

MEDICINAL PART. *The whole plant.*

Description.—Scull-cap has a small, fibrous, yellow, perennial root, with an erect and very branching stem, from one to three feet in height. The leaves are on petioles about an inch long, opposite, thin, subcordate on the stem, ovate on branches, acuminate, acute, and coarsely serrate The flowers are small, and of a pale-blue color.

History.—It is an indigenous herb, growing in damp places, meadows, ditches, and by the side of ponds, flowering in July and August. The whole plant is medicinal, and should be gathered while in flower, dried in the shade, and kept in well-closed tin vessels. Chemically it contains an essential oil, a yellowish-green fixed oil, chlorophyll, a volatile matter, albumen, an astringent principle, lignin, chloride of soda, salts of iron, silica, etc.

Properties and Uses.—It is a valuable nervine, tonic, and antispasmodic, used in chorea, convulsions, fits, delirium tremens, and all nervous affections, supporting the nerves, quieting and strengthening the system. In delirium tremens an infusion drunk freely will soon produce a calm sleep. In all cases of nervous excitability, restlessness, or wakefulness, etc., it exerts beneficial results.

Dose.—Of the fluid extract, from half to a teaspoonful; of the tincture (four ounces scull-cap to a pint of diluted alcohol), one to two teaspoonfuls; of the infusion, a wineglassful, three times a day.

SENEKA (POLYGALA SENEGA).

COMMON NAME. *Seneca Snake-Root.*

MEDICINAL PART. *The root.*

Description.—This indigenous plant has a perennial, firm, hard, branching root, with a thick bark, and sends up several annual stems, which are erect, smooth, from eight to fourteen inches high, occasionally tinged with red. The leaves are alternate, nearly sessile, lanceolate, with a sharpish point, smooth; flowers white; calyx consists of five sepals, corolla of three petals; and capsules are small, two-celled and two-valved.

History.—It is found in various parts of the United States, in rocky woods and on hill-sides, flowering in July. It is more abundant in the West and South than in the East. The officinal root varies in size from two to four or five lines in diameter, crooked, and a carinate line extends the whole length of it. Its chemical constituents are polygalic. virgineic, pectic, and tannic acids, coloring matter, an oil, cerin, gum, albumen, salts of alumina, silica, magnesia, and iron.

Properties and Uses.—In large doses emetic and cathartic; in ordinary doses it stimulates the secretions, acting particularly as a sialagogue, expectorant, diuretic, diaphoretic, and emmenagogue. In active inflammatory diseases it should not be employed. In protracted pneumonia, commencing stages of croup, humoral asthma, etc., it is a good expectorant.

Dose.—Powder, five to twenty grains; infusion or syrup, half an ounce to two ounces; polygalic acid, one-fourth to one-half grain.

SKUNK CABBAGE (Symplocarpus Fœtidus).

COMMON NAMES. *Skunk-weed, Pole-cat weed, Meadow Cabbage.*

MEDICINAL PARTS. *The roots and seeds.*

Description.—This plant has been a troublesome one for botanists to classify; but the term *Symplocarpus* is now generally preferred. It is perennial, having a large, abrupt root, or tuber, with numerous crowded, fleshy fibres, which extend some distance into the ground. The *spathe* appears before the leaves, is ovate, spotted, and striped, purple and yellowish-green, the edges folded inward, and at length coalescing. The flowers are numerous, of a dull purple within the spathe, on a short, oval spadix. Calyx consists of four fleshy, wedge-shaped sepals; corolla, none; stamens, four; seeds round and fleshy, and about as large as a pea.

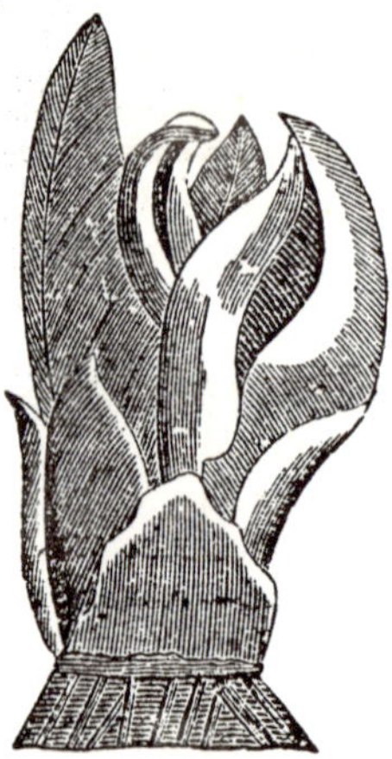

Skunk Cabbage.

History.—Skunk Cabbage is a native of the United States, growing in moist grounds, flowering in March and April, and maturing its fruit in August and September, forming a roughened, globular mass, two or three inches in diameter, and shedding its bullet-like fruit, one-third to half an inch in diameter, which are filled with a singular solid, fleshy embryo. The parts used are the seeds and roots, which have an extremely disagreeable odor. Water or alcohol extracts their virtues. Chemically it contains a fixed oil, wax, starch, volatile oil and fat, salts of lime, silica, iron, and manganese.

Properties and Uses.—Internally it is a stimulant, exerting expectorant, antispasmodic, with slightly narcotic influences. It is successfully used in asthma, whooping-cough, nervous irritability, hysteria, fits, epilepsy, convulsions, chronic catarrh. pulmonary and bronchial affections.

Externally, in the form of an ointment, it aids reparative processes, discusses tumors, stimulates granulations, eases pain, etc. It is an ingredient in my world-renowned "Herbal Ointment." (See page 472.)

Dose.—Fluid extract, twenty to eighty drops; tincture (three ounces of root or seed to a pint of alcohol), half a teaspoonful; syrup (two ounces of fluid extract to eight ounces of simple syrup), two or three teaspoonfuls.

SOAP-WORT (Saponaria Officinalis).

COMMON NAME. *Bouncing Bet.*

MEDICINAL PARTS. *The root and leaves.*

Description.—This is a stout perennial, herbaceous plant, with a stout from one to two feet in height. The leaves are lanceolate, smooth; flowers are many, large, flesh-colored, or pale-pink, and often double; fruit an oblong one-celled capsule.

History.—This plant grows in roadsides and waste places in Europe and the United States. It flowers in the early part of July in Europe, but in America in the early part of August. The leaves and root are the parts used medicinally. They have a sweet and bitter taste combined, "with a subsequent persistent pungency and a benumbing sensation." When the root and leaves are subjected to the extractive powers of water they yield a residue something like soap-suds. Their active properties are brought out by either water or alcohol—by the latter particularly. The root gives a principle called *Saponin*, which is very valuable.

Properties and Uses.—It is largely and valuably employed in the treatment of diseases of the liver, scrofulous, syphilitic, and cutaneous afflictions of a severe character; also catarrh, rheumatism, gonorrhœa, whites, and green sickness. Saponin can be prepared only by a competent herbal chemist. In its absence use decoctions of the leaves and roots. Dose of the decoction, from one to two fluid ounces, three times a day. I employ the saponaceous qualities of this plant, which I extract from the root by chemical processes in my laboratory, as a constituent of my "Renovating Pill." (See page 473.)

SOLOMON'S SEAL (Convallaria Multiflora).

Medicinal Part. *The root.*

Description.—The stem of this plant is smooth, from one to four feet high, and growing from a perennial root. The leaves are alternate, lanceolate, smooth, and glossy above, paler and pubescent beneath; flowers greenish-white, and fruit a dark-blue or blackish berry. There is another variety, the *Convallaria Racemosa*, the root of which possesses similar qualities to that of Solomon's Seal.

History.—Both plants are to be found throughout the United States and Canada. They flower from May to August. The root, which is the part used, is inodorous, but has a sweetish mucilaginous taste, which is followed by a slight sense of bitterness.

Properties and Uses.—The root is tonic, mucilaginous, and astringent. The decoction is successfully used in whites, pectoral affections, menorrhagia, female debility, inflammation of the stomach and intestines, erysipelas, neuralgia, itch, local inflammations, etc. Dose of the decoction, one to three ounces, three times a day.

SORREL (Wood) (Oxalis Acetosella).

Medicinal Part. *The whole herb.*

Description.—This is a small perennial herb, with a creeping and scaly-toothed root-stock. The leaves are numerous, radical, and on long, weak, hairy stalks; leaflets broadly obcordate, and of yellowish-green color. Flowers white, yellowish at the base, and scentless. Fruit a five-lobed, oblong capsule.

History.—It is indigenous to Europe and this country, growing in woody and shady places, and flowering from April to June. It is inodorous, and has a pleasantly acid taste. The acidity is due to oxalic acid, which, in combination with potassa, forms the binoxolate of that alkali. The "*Salts of Sorrel*," formerly so much used to remove ink-spots and iron-marks from linen, is merely this salt separated from the plant.

Properties and Uses.—Cooling and diuretic; useful in febrile diseases, hemorrhages, gonorrhœa, chronic catarrh, urinary affections, scurvy, etc. Care is to be observed in its use.

RUMEX ACETOSA, or *Garden Sorrel*, RUMEX ACETOSELLA, or *Sheep Sorrel*, and RUMEX VESICARIUS possess similar qualities.

SQUIRTING CUCUMBER (MOMORDICA ELATERIUM).

MEDICINAL PART. *The feculence of the juice of the fruit.*

Description.—This hispid and glaucous plant has several stems growing from the same root. The leaves are cordate, somewhat lobed, and on long stalks. Flowers monœcious and yellow. Fruit oblong, obtuse at each end, separating from its stalk with violence, and expelling its seeds and mucus with considerable force, in consequence of the sudden contraction of the sides.

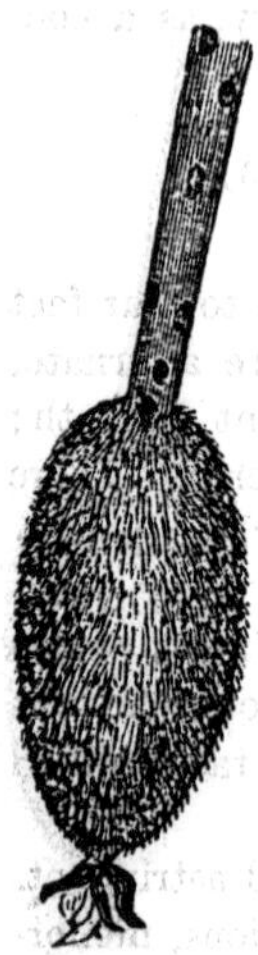

Squirting Cucumber.

History.—This plant is indigenous to the south of Europe, growing in poor soils, in waste places, and flowering in July. The juice around the seeds is the officinal part. and which, when properly prepared, forms the *Elaterium* of commerce. It must be collected a little before the period of ripening.

Properties and Uses.—It is an energetic hydragogue cathartic, operating with great violence in doses of a few grains, and very apt to cause diffuse inflammation of the stomach and bowels, characterized by vomiting, griping pain, and profuse diarrhœa. It is used chiefly in obstinate dropsy, and as a revulsive in cerebral affections, or wherever a revellent effect is desired. Owing to its active cathartic properties, it is always best to commence with very small doses, from the uncertainty of the preparation.

Dose.—From one-eighth to one-half a grain.

STAR-GRASS (ALETRIS FARINOSA).

COMMON NAMES. *Colic-root, Ague-root, Crow-corn, Unicorn root, etc*

MEDICINAL PART. *The root.*

Description.—This plant has a perennial root, with radical leaves, sessile, lying flat on the ground, ribbed, broad, lanceolate, smooth, the large ones being about four inches long. The flower-stem is from one to three feet high, erect and simple, bearing a bell-shaped flower, which, as it grows old, has a wrinkled, mealy appearance. The fruit is a triangular capsule.

History.—It is indigenous to North America, growing in low grounds, sandy soils, and at the edges of woods. Its flowers are white, and appear from May to August. The root is the part used. Alcohol is the best solvent.

Properties and Uses.—Its root, when thoroughly dried, is an intensely bitter tonic, and in decoction or tincture is of great utility in dyspepsia, general or local debility, flatulent colic, hysteria, etc. It greatly strengthens the female generative organs, affording protection against miscarriage; and in chlorosis, amenorrhœa, dysmenorrhœa, engorged condition of the uterus, prolapsus of that organ, is a very superior vegetable agent.

Dose.—Of the powdered root, from five to ten grains, three times a day; of the saturated tincture, five to fifteen drops.

STILLINGIA (STILLINGIA SYLVATICA).

COMMON NAMES. *Queen's Root, Queen's Delight, Yawroot, and Silver-leaf.*

MEDICINAL PART. *The root.*

Description.—This perennial herb has a glabrous, somewhat angled stem, from two to four feet high, which, when broken, gives out a milky sap. The leaves are sessile, somewhat leathery, and tapering at the base. The flowers are yellow, and arranged on a terminal spike. Fruit a three-grained capsule.

History.—Queen's Root grows in sandy soils, and is a native of the southern part of the United States. The root is the part used. It should be used as soon after being gathered as possible, as age impairs its properties. The latter yield to water, but are better extracted by diluted alcohol. Its properties appear to be owing to a very acrid oil, known as the *Oil of Stillingia.*

Properties and Uses.—In large doses stillingia vomits and purges, accompanied with more or less prostration of the system. In less doses it is an alterative, exerting an influence over the secretory functions unsurpassed by any other known alterative. It is very extensively used in all the various forms of primary and secondary syphilitic affections; also in scrofulous, hepatic, and cutaneous affections; also, with combinations of anise or caraway, for laryngitis and bronchitis. The oil, unless well incorporated with some mucilaginous or saccharine substance, should never be used internally. This great alterative is one of the principal constituents in my "Blood Purifier." See page 471.

Dose.—Tincture, half a drachm to a drachm; decoction, one or two ounces.

STONEROOT (COLLINSONIA CANADENSIS).

COMMON NAMES. *Hardhack, Horseweed, Heal-all, Richweed, Ox-balm, etc.*

MEDICINAL PART. *The plant.*

Description.—This plant has a knobby root, and a four-sided stem, from one to four feet in height. The leaves are thin, broadly ovate, acuminate, coarsely serrate, from six to eight inches long, and from two to four broad. Flowers large, corolla greenish-yellow; stamens two, and very long; seeds four, of which two or three are sterile.

History.—This plant grows in moist woods from Canada to Carolina, and flowers from July to September. The whole plant has a strong odor and a pungent and spicy taste. The odor of the fresh root is slightly disagreeable. The whole plant is generally used, and has its value. The chief virtues of the plant are, however, concentrated in the root, which should always be used when fresh. Its active principle is *Collinsonin*, which name is derived from its discoverer, Peter Collinson.

Properties and Uses.—It is used with good effect in chronic catarrh of the bladder (as are other plants mentioned elsewhere), whites, and weak stomach. It exerts a strong influence over all the mucous tissues. It is a very fair stimulant, and a gentle tonic and diuretic. The preparation called *Collinsonin* is *very* valuable as a remedy for hemorrhoids, and all other diseases of the rectum, and for such afflictions I recommend it highly. It is chiefly used in inveterate and chronic cases. The largest dose is five grains; the average dose two grains. The infusion or decoction of the plant may be moderately used without additional remedies, and in some instances so may the *Collinsonin;* but in about every case a skilful combination of the latter with other standard preparations is necessary to insure easy and speedy restoration to good health. Stoneroot is used externally—the leaves particularly—in fomentation and poultice, and bruises, wounds, blows, sprains, contusions, cuts, ulcers, sores, etc. I cannot call the attention of the reader too strongly to the effect the preparation called *Collinsonin* has upon all affections of the urinary organs. It should be combined with other indicated remedies.

SUMACH (RHUS GLABRUM).

MEDICINAL PARTS. *The bark and fruit.*

Description.—Sumach is a shrub, from six to fifteen feet high, consisting of many straggling branches, covered with a pale-gray bark, having occasionally a reddish tint. The leaves are alternate, consist of from six to fifteen leaflets, which are lanceolate, acuminate, acutely serrate, shining and green above, whitish beneath, becoming red in the fall. The flowers are greenish red, and fruit a small red drupe, hanging in clusters, with a crimson down, extremely sour to the taste, which is due to malate of lime.

History.—Sumach grows in the thickets and waste grounds of Canada and the United States. It flowers in June and July, but matures its fruit in September and October. The bark and berries are officinal. The berries should be gathered before rains have washed away the acid properties which reside in their external, downy efflorescence. Both the bark and berries yield their active influence to water. Great care is to be taken in the selection of several species of Rhus, as many of them are highly poisonous.

Properties and Uses.—The berries are refrigerant and diuretic; the bark is tonic, astringent, and antiseptic. The bark of the root has sometimes been used with success in decoction or syrup as a palliative of gonorrhœa, leucorrhœa, diarrhœa, hectic fever, dysentery, and scrofula. Combined with the barks of white pine and slippery elm, in certain particular doses of decoction, it will, with other very simple treatment, cure syphilis.

Dose.—From one to three fluid ounces of the decoction of bark. Of the infusion of berries, from one to four fluid ounces.

SWAMP BEGGARS' TICK (BIDENS CONNATA).

MEDICINAL PARTS. *The root and seeds.*

Description.—This herb has a smooth stem, from one to three feet high. The leaves are lanceolate, opposite, serrate, acuminate, and decurrent on the petiole. Flowers, terminal; florets, yellow; and fruit, a wedge-formed achenium.

History.—This is a common weed, found in wet grounds, rich fields, swamps, and ditches, from New England to Missouri. It flowers in August. The root and seeds are employed medicinally, and may be used in decoction, infusion, or tincture.

Properties and Uses.—The root and seeds are emmenagogue and expectorant; the seeds, in powder or tincture, have been used in amenorrhœa, dysmenorrhœa, and some other uterine derangements, and an infusion of the root has proved beneficial in severe cough. It has been used with great success for palpitation of the heart, and for croup. For this latter affliction a strong infusion of the leaves, sweetened with honey, and administered in tablespoonful doses every fifteen minutes until vomiting is produced, is regarded a cure. The leaves heated to the form of a poultice and laid upon the throat and chest in cases of bronchial and laryngeal attacks from exposure to cold, etc., are very beneficial.

BIDENS BIPINNATA, or *Spanish Needles*, and BIDENS FRONDOSA, or *Beggar Tick*, can be employed, medically, the same.

SWEET GUM (LIQUIDAMBAR STYRACIFLUA).

MEDICINAL PART. *The concrete juice.*

Description.—The Sweet Gum tree grows to the height of from fifty to sixty feet. Its bark is gray and deeply furrowed, and there are corky ridges on the branches; the leaves are palmate, rounded, smooth, and shining, fragrant when bruised, and turn a deep red in the fall. Fruit, a kind of strobile.

History.—This tree is very abundant in the Southern and Middle States, and can be found in the moist woods of nearly all parts of the Union. From incisions made in the tree a gum exudes which is resinous and adhesive, and somewhat like white turpentine in appearance.

Properties and Uses.—As a remedy for catarrhs, coughs, and pulmonary affections generally, it is without an equal, although physicians generally do not use it in their practice. It is also very valuable for fever sores, fistula, scrofula, etc., when made into an ointment.

Dose.—The dose internally is from ten to twenty grains, according to circumstances.

TACAMAHAC (POPULUS BALSAMIFERA).

COMMON NAME. *Balsam Poplar.*

MEDICINAL PART. *The buds.*

Description.—This tree, also called *Tacamahac Poplar*, attains the height of from fifty to seventy feet, with a trunk about eighteen inches in diameter. The branches are smooth, round, and deep brown. The leaves are ovate, gradually tapering, and pointed, deep-green above, and smooth on both sides.

History.—This tree is found in Siberia, and in the northern parts of the United States and Canada. In America it is in blossom in April. The leaf-buds are the officinal part. They should be collected in the spring, in order that the fragrant resinous matter with which they are covered may be properly separated in boiling water, for upon this their virtues depend. They have an agreeable, incense-like odor, and an unpleasant, bitterish taste. The balsamic juice is collected in Canada in shells, and sent to Europe under the name of *Tacamahaca*. Alcohol, or spirits, is the proper solvent. The *Populus Balsamifera* is generally confounded with the *Populus Candicans*, from whose buds we get the virtues known as the *Balm of Gilead;* but it is much the superior tree for medical purposes.

Properties and Uses.—The buds are stimulant tonic diuretic, and anti-scorbutic. In tincture they have been beneficially employed in affections of the stomach and kidneys, and in scurvy and rheumatism. Sometimes they are applied in that form as a remedy for affections of the chest. The bark is known to be tonic and cathartic, and will prove of service in gout and rheumatism.

Dose.—Of a tincture of the buds, from one to four fluid drachms; of an extract of the bark, five to fifteen grains, three times a day.

POPULUS TREMULOIDES, *White Poplar*, or *Aspen*, the well-known tree, furnishes us with *Populin* and *Salacin;* and is tonic and febrifuge, useful in intermittents. It has also good diuretic properties, and is beneficial in urinary affections, gonorrhœa, gleet, etc.

TANSY (TANACETUM VULGARE).

MEDICINAL PART. *The herb.*

Description.—Tansy has a perennial creeping root, and an erect herbaceous stem, one to three feet high. The leaves are smoothish, dark-green; flowers, golden-yellow; fruit, an achenium.

History.—Indigenous to Europe, but has been introduced into this country and cultivated by many; but grows also spontaneously in old grounds, along roads, flowering in the latter part of summer. Drying impairs much of the activity of the plant. It contains volatile oil, wax, stearine, chlorophyll, bitter resin, yellow coloring matter, tannin with gallic acid, bitter extractive gum, and tanacetic acid, which is crystallizable and precipitates lime, baryta, and oxide of lead.

Properties and Uses.—It is tonic, emmenagogue, and diaphoretic. In small doses, the cold infusion will be found useful in convalescence from exhausting diseases, dyspepsia, hysteria, and jaundice. The warm infusion is diaphoretic and emmenagogue. It bears a good reputation in suppressed menstruation, but should be used only when the suppression is due to morbid causes.

THYME (THYMUS VULGARIS).

MEDICNAL PART. *The herb.*

Description.—Thyme is a small undershrub, with numerous erect stems, procumbent at base, and from six to ten inches in height. The leaves are oblong-ovate, lanceolate, and numerous. The flowers are bluish-purple, small, and arranged on leafy whorled spikes.

History.—A native of Europe, but introduced into this country, and extensively cultivated in gardens for culinary purposes. It blossoms in the summer, when it should be collected and carefully dried. It has a strong, pungent, spicy taste and odor, both of which are retained by careful drying. The herb yields its properties to boiling water and alcohol.

Properties and Uses.—Tonic, carminative, emmenagogue, and antispasmodic. The cold infusion is beneficial in dyspepsia with weak and irritable stomach. The warm infusion is useful as a parturient, also in hysteria, dysmenorrhœa, flatulence, colic, and to promote perspiration. The leaves are used externally in fomentation.

The THYMUS SERPYLLUS, *Wild Thyme* or *Mother of Thyme*, has similar virtues to the above.

TOLU (MYROSPERMUM TOLUIFERUM).

MEDICINAL PART. *The balsamic exudation.*

Description.—A full botanical description of this tree has not yet been given, but it is supposed that it is similar to the Balsam of Peru tree, differing only in the leaflets, which in this tree are thin, membranous, obovate, taper-pointed; the terminal ones larger than the others.

History.—It is a tree which grows throughout the forests of South America, especially on the elevated parts near Carthagena, Tolu, and in the Magdalena provinces of Columbia. The balsam is obtained by making incisions into the tree, and which flows into wax vessels. It is exported from Carthagena in tin, earthen, and other vessels. It has a pale, yellowish-red or brown color, solid and brittle, an agreeable vanilla-like odor, and a sweetish aromatic taste. It is soluble in alcohol, ether, and essential oils.

Properties and Uses.—It is, like Balsam of Peru, a stimulant, tonic, and expectorant, and cannot be equalled for its curative effects in cases of consumption, catarrh, bronchitis, asthma, and all inflammatory, ulcerated, spasmodic, or other morbid conditions of the respiratory organs and their adjuncts. The balsam dissolved in ether, and the vapor therefrom inhaled, is reported beneficial in coughs and bronchial affections of long standing, and I have no doubt it is so, as its virtues in such complaints are very wonderful.

TURKEY CORN (CORYDALIS FORMOSA).

COMMON NAMES. *Wild Turkey-pea, Stagger-weed, Choice Dielytra.*

MEDICINAL PART. *The root.*

Description.—This indigenous perennial plant has a tuberous root, and a stem from six to ten inches in height. The leaves are radical, rising from ten to fifteen inches high, and somewhat triternate. The scape is naked, eight to twelve inches high, and bearing from six to ten reddish-purple nodding flowers. The fruit is a pod-shaped, many-seeded capsule.

History.—This beautiful little plant flowers very early in the spring, and the root should only be gathered while the plant is in flower. It grows in rich soil, on hills, among rocks, and old decayed timber, and is found westward and south of New York to North Carolina. The alkaloid, *Corydalia*, is the active principle.

Properties and Uses.—Tonic, diuretic, and alterative. In all syphilitic, scrofulous, and cachectic conditions it is one of the best remedies. Its tonic properties render it valuable as an alterative in all enfeebled conditions. Its tonic properties are similar to Gentian, Columbo, and other pure bitters. Its magical properties as an alterative renders it one of the most valuable remedies in the whole range of medicine. Corydalia may be substituted for the herb. It is one of the ingredients in my "Blood Purifier." (See page 471.)

Dose.—Of the infusion, one to four ounces; saturated tincture, half to two drachms; corydalia, one-half to a grain.

VALERIAN (VALERIANA OFFICINALIS).

COMMON NAME. *Great Wild Valerian.*

MEDICINAL PART. *The root.*

Description.—This is a large herb, with a perennial, tuberous, fetid root, most aromatic when growing in dry pastures, and a smooth, hollow, furrowed stem, about four feet in height. The leaves are pinnate, opposite; leaflets, from seven to ten pairs, lanceolate, coarsely serrated, and on long foot-stalks. The flowers are flesh-colored, small, and fragrant.

History.—Valerian is a European plant, growing in wet places, or even in dry pastures, flowering in June and July. Several varieties grow in America, and are used, but the English Valerian is by all odds the best. The officinal part is the root. The taste of the root is warm, camphoraceous, slightly bitter, somewhat acrid, and nauseous. The odor is not considerable; it is fetid, characteristic, and highly attractive to cats, and, it is said, to rats also. Besides *valerianic acid* the root contains starch, albumen, valerianin, yellow extractive matter, balsamic resin, mucilage, valerianate of potassa, malates of potassa and lime, and phosphate of lime and silica.

Properties and Uses.—Valerian excites the cerebro-spinal system. In large doses it causes headaches, mental excitement, visual illusions giddiness, restlessness, agitation, and even spasmodic movements. In medicinal doses it acts as a stimulating tonic, anti-spasmodic, and calmative. It is temporarily beneficial in all cases where a nervous stimulant is required. The extract is worthless. The infusion and fluid extract contain all the virtues of the plant.

Dose.—Of the infusion, one or two fluid ounces, as often as may be prescribed by a physician.

VANILLA (VANILLA AROMATICA).

MEDICINAL PART. *The fruit or pods.*

Description.—*Vanilla Aromatica* is a shrubby, climbing, aërial parasite, growing in the clefts of rocks, or attaching itself to the trunks of trees. It suspends itself to contiguous objects, and is truly an aërial plant. The stem is round, about as thick as the finger, from twenty to thirty feet in length, and oftener thicker at the summit than at the base The leaves are alternate, oblong, entire, on short petioles, green, fleshy and pointed by a species of abortive tendril. The flowers are yellowish white. The fruit is a species of bean, yellow or buff color, of an agreeable aromatic odor; the beans must be dried with care or they will lose their properties.

History.—Vanilla grows in Mexico and other parts of tropical South America. There are several species which are supposed to furnish the Vanilla of commerce. It yields its virtues to water or alcohol.

Properties and Uses.—It is an aromatic stimulant, and is used, in infusion, in hysteria, rheumatism, and low forms of fever. It is also called an aphrodisiac, powerfully exciting the generative system. Vanilla is said to exhilarate the brain, prevent sleep, increase muscular energy, and stimulate the sexual propensities.

WAFER-ASH (PTELEA TRIFOLIATA).

COMMON NAMES. *Wing-seed, Shrubby Trefoil, Swamp Dogwood, etc.*

MEDICINAL PART. *The bark of the root.*

Description.—This is a shrub from six to eight feet in height, with the leaves trifoliate, and marked with pellucid dots; the leaflets are sessile, ovate, shortly acuminate, downy beneath when young. The flowers are polygamous, greenish-white, nearly half an inch in diameter, and of disagreeable odor. Stamens, mostly four; style short, and fruit a two-celled samara.

History.—Wafer-Ash, or *Ptelea*, is a shrub common to America, growing most abundantly west of the Alleghanies, in shady, moist places and edges of woods, and also in rocky places. It flowers in June. The bark of the root is officinal, and yields its virtues to boiling water. Alcohol, however, is its best solvent. *Ptelein* is its active principle.

Properties and Uses.—It is especially tonic and unirritating. It is said to be very useful as a promoter of the appetite, and as a remedy for general debility. It will be tolerated by the stomach when other tonics are rejected. Some think it equal, in cases of fever (intermittent), to quinia. In convalescence from fever it serves an admirable purpose.

Dose.—Of the powder, ten to thirty grains; of the tincture, one or two drachms; of the extract, five to ten grains; ptelein, one or two grains.

WALNUT (WHITE), (JUGLANS CINEREA).

COMMON NAMES. *Butternut, Oil Nut, etc.*

MEDICINAL PARTS. *Inner bark of the root, and leaves.*

Description.—This indigenous tree attains a height of from thirty to fifty feet, with a trunk about four feet in diameter; the branches are wide-spreading, and covered with a smooth gray bark. The leaves are alternate, twelve to twenty inches long, and consist of seven or eight pairs of leaflets, which are oblong-lanceolate, and finely serrate. Male and female flowers distinct upon the same tree. Fruit a dark-colored hard nut, kernel oily, pleasant-flavored, and edible.

JUGLANS NIGRA, or *Black Walnut*, a well-known tree, is also medicinal.

History.—Butternut is found throughout the New England, Middle, and Western States, on cold, uneven, rocky soils, flowering in April and May, and maturing its fruit at or about the middle of autumn. Its officinal parts are its leaves and the inner bark of the root. The latter should be gathered from April to July. It contains resin, fixed oil, saccharine matter, lime, potassa, a peculiar principle, and tannic acid. The *Black Walnut* flowers and ripens its fruit at the same time with the *Butternut. Juglandin* is the active principle.

Properties and Uses.—Butternut is a gentle and agreeable cathartic, and does not induce constipation after its action. In cases of habitual constipation or other intestinal diseases, it has considerable value. It is used in decoction in cases of fever, and in the murrain of cattle. The juice of the rind of the Black Walnut will cure herpes, eczema, porrigo, etc., and a decoction of it has been used to remove worms. The European walnut has been found to be efficacious in cases of scrofula.

WATER PEPPER (POLYGONUM PUNCTATUM).

COMMON NAME. *Smartweed.*

MEDICINAL PART. *The whole herb.*

Water Pepper.

Description.—This is an annual plant, with a smooth stem, branched, often decumbent at the base, of reddish or greenish-brown color, and growing from one to two feet high. The leaves are alternate, lanceolate, petiolate, with pellucid dots, wavy, and scabrous on the margin. The flowers are small, greenish-white or purple, and are disposed in loose, slender, drooping, but finally erect spikes.

History.—It is a well-known plant, growing in England and America, in ditches, low grounds, among rubbish, and about brooks and water-courses. It flowers in August and September. The whole plant is officinal. It has a biting, pungent, acrid taste, and imparts its virtues to alcohol or water. It should be collected and made into a tincture while fresh. When it is old it is almost worthless. The English variety of this plant possesses the same properties.

Properties and Uses.—It is stimulant, diuretic, emmenagogue, anti septic, diaphoretic, etc. The infusion in cold water has been found serviceable in gravel, colds and coughs, and in milk sickness. In cholera, the patients wrapped in a sheet moistened with a hot decoction have recovered.

It is used as a wash in chronic erysipelatous inflammations. The fresh leaves bruised with the leaves of May-weed, and moistened with the oil of turpentine, and applied to the skin, will speedily vesicate. The infusion in cold water forms an excellent local application in the sore mouth of nursing women, and in mercurial ptyalism or salivation. The decoction or infusion in hot water is not so active as when prepared in cold or warm water. It has very many virtues; and its office in my "Restorative Assimilant" (see page 469) it performs well.

Dose.—Of the infusion, from a wineglassful to a teacupful, three or four times a day.

WORMSEED (Chenopodium Anthelminticum).

Common Name. *Jerusalem Oak.*

Medicinal Part. *The seeds.*

Description.—This plant has a perennial branched root, with an erect, herbaceous stem, from one to three feet high. The leaves are alternate, oblong-lanceolate, of yellowish-green color, and marked beneath with small resinous particles. The numerous flowers are of the same color as the leaves. Seeds solitary and lenticular.

History.—This plant grows in waste places in almost all parts of the United States, flowering from July to September, and ripening its seeds throughout the fall, at which time they should be collected. The whole plant has a disagreeable odor, and the seeds partake of the same odor.

Properties and Uses.—Anthelmintic and antispasmodic. Excellent to expel the lumbrici from children. The oil is the best form of administration, which may be given in doses of four to eight drops on sugar. The infusion with milk is also given often in wineglassful doses.

WORMWOOD (Artemisia Absinthium).

Medicinal Parts. *The tops and leaves.*

Description.—This is a perennial plant, with a woody root, branched at the crown, and having numerous fibres below. The whole herb is covered with close, silky hoariness; the stems are numerous, bushy, and from one to two feet in height. Their lower part exists for some years, from which young shoots spring forth every year, decaying in cold weather. The leaves are alternate, broadish, and blunted, the lower ones on long petioles, upper ones on shorter, broader, and somewhat winged ones.

History.—Wormwood grows nearly all over the world, from the United States to Siberia. It flowers from June to September. The tops and leaves are the parts used. The dried herb, with the flowers, has a whitish gray appearance, a strong, aromatic odor, and is extremely bitter to the taste. Alcohol or water takes up its active principles. It yields what is known to druggists as *Absinthine.*

Properties and Uses.—It is anthelmintic, tonic, and narcotic. It is used for many diseases, among which may be enumerated intermittent fever, jaundice, worms, want of appetite, amenorrhœa, chronic leucorrhœa, obstinate diarrhœa, etc. It is also used externally in country places as a fomentation for sprains, bruises, and local inflammations. Taken too often, or in large quantities, it will irritate the stomach, and dangerously increase the action of the heart and arteries.

Dose.—Of the powder, ten to twenty grains; infusion, one or two ounces.

Santonin, a well-known anthelmintic, is the peculiar principle obtained from the *Artemisia Santonica.*

Dose.—Three or four grains, twice a day.

YAM (WILD), (DIOSCOREA VILLOSA).

COMMON NAME. *Colic root.*

MEDICINAL PART. *The root.*

Description.—This is a delicate twining vine, with a perennial root. From this root proceeds a smooth, woolly, reddish-brown stem, the sixth of an inch in diameter, and from five to fifteen or eighteen feet long. The leaves average two to four inches in length, and about three-quarters of their length in width. They are glabrous on the upper surface, with soft hairs on the lower. The flowers are of a pale greenish yellow color, and are very small. The seeds are one or two in each cell, and flat.

History.—There are several species of yam-root which grow in the West Indies, and which the natives eat as we do potatoes, but these are not medicinally like the Dioscorea Villosa, which I have described above, and which is a slender vine growing wild in the United States and Canada, and found running over bushes and fences, and twining about the growths in thickets and hedges. The farther south we go the more prolific it is. It flowers in June and July. The root, which is the part used, is long, branched, crooked, and woody. From this is made a preparation called *Dioscorein*, or *Dioscorin*, which contains all its active qualities.

Properties and Uses.—Antispasmodic. Half a pint of the decoction has been used, in almost innumerable cases of bilious colic, with great good effect; the same is also employed for spasm of the bowels, and to allay violent nausea; *especially*, however, the unaccountable nausea of pregnant women. Dioscorein possesses the properties of the crude root in a marvellous degree. I use it mainly for bilious colic; it is the very best relief and promptest cure now known. I also give it in some forms of uterine disease (always, however, combined with other material of a similarly excellent character), but my use of it is chiefly for bilious colic, and for this I commend it to the public.

Dose.—Of the decoction, two to four ounces; tincture, twenty to sixty drops; Dioscorein, one to four grains.

YARROW (ACHILLEA MILLEFOLIUM).

COMMON NAMES. *Milfoil, Thousand Seal, Nose-bleed.*

MEDICINAL PART. *The herb.*

Description.—Yarrow, also called *Thousand Seal*, is from ten to twenty inches high, with a simple stem, branching at the top, and many long, crowded, alternate and dentate leaves spread upon the ground, finely cut, and divided into many parts. The flowers are white or rose-colored, and arrayed in knots upon divers green stalks, which arise from among the leaves. Fruit an oblong, flattened achenium.

History.—Yarrow inhabits Europe and North America; it is found in pastures, meadows, and along road-sides, flowering from May to October. The plant possesses a faint, pleasant, peculiar fragrance, and a rather sharp, rough, astringent taste, which properties are due to tannic and achilleic acid, essential oil, and bitter extractive, alcohol or water being its proper menstruum.

Properties and Uses.—It is astringent, alterative, and diuretic, in decoction. It is efficacious in bleeding from the lungs and other hemorrhages, incontinence of urine, piles, and dysentery. It is valuable in amenorrhœa, or suppressed or restrained menses, flatulency, and spasmodic diseases. It forms a useful injection in leucorrhœa or whites, also in menorrhagia, or profuse or too long continued menstruation. An ointment cures wounds, ulcers, fistulas, and the head bathed in a decoction prevents the falling out of the hair; while the leaves chewed in the mouth will frequently ease the tooth-ache. ACHILLES is supposed to be the first that left the virtues of this herb to posterity, hence the active principle of this plant is called *Achilleine*, which is much used as a substitute for quinia in intermittent fevers in the South of Europe.

Dose.—The infusion of Yarrow is given in doses of from a wineglassful to a teacupful, three or four times a day; the essential oil from five to twenty drops. In menorrhagia or profuse menstruation, a tablespoonful of the saturated tincture may be given three or four times a day.

Achillea Ptarmica, or Sneeze-wort, has leaves entirely different from the Yarrow, and should not be mistaken one for the other. The whole of this plant is pungent, exciting an increased flow of saliva; and the powder of the dried leaves, when snuffed into the nostrils, produces sneezing, which is supposed to be owing to their small, sharp, and marginal teeth.

YELLOW PARILLA (MENISPERMUM CANADENSE).

COMMON NAMES. *Vine-maple, Moonseed.*

MEDICINAL PART. *The root.*

Description.- This plant has a perennial, horizontal, very long woody root, of a beautiful yellow color. The stem is round and climbing, and about a foot in length. The leaves are roundish, cordate, peltate, smooth, glaucous green above, paler below, entire, and four or five inches in diameter. The flowers are in clusters, and are small and yellow. The fruit, a drupe, is about the third of an inch in diameter, and one-seeded.

Yellow Parilla.

History.—Yellow Parilla grows in moist woods and hedges, and near streams, from Canada to Carolina, and west to the Mississippi. It flowers in July. The root, which is the part used, has a bitter, lasting, but not unpleasant acrid taste, and yields its virtues to water and alcohol. It is called, not without justice, American Sarsaparilla, and its active principle, known as *menispermin*, shows that it might have received a name less expressive of its merits.

Properties and Uses.—The authors of herbalist dispensatories have set down Yellow Parilla as "tonic, laxative, alterative, and diuretic," and it seems to possess all these qualities. Every plant of medicinal value, however, possesses one virtue which is paramount to all others. Yellow Parilla is essentially and particularly anti-syphilitic, anti-scrofulous, anti-scorbutic, and anti-mercurial. As a purifier of the blood, it is equal to the imported sarsaparilla as we get the latter, and its active principle, *menispermin*, may be used with great good effect in all diseases arising from either hereditary or acquired impurities of the system. It exerts its influence principally on the gastric and salivary glands, and is found expressly beneficial in cases of adhesive inflammation, and where it is found necessary to break up organized deposits, and hasten disintegration of tissue. I use it principally for those diseases arising from a vitiated condition of the blood, but sometimes apply it to dyspepsia. A decoction of the plant may be used to advantage as an embrocation in gouty, rheumatic, and cutaneous affections. The dose of the *menispermin* is from one to four grains. When it produces vomiting reduce the dose.

YELLOW ROOT (XANTHORRHIZA APIIFOLIA).

MEDICINAL PART. *The root.*

Description.—This small, deciduous, indigenous shrub, one to three feet high, has a thick, deep-yellow root, throwing up numerous suckers. The stem is short, woody, and leafy above, with a bright yellow bark and wood. The leaves are pinnate. Flowers small, and of dark-purplish color, and the follicles or capsules, the fruit, are inflated, compressed, and about an inch and a half long.

History.—This plant is found along river-banks in the mountains of Pennsylvania to Florida, being chiefly confined to the mountains. It flowers in March and April. The root is exceedingly bitter, and from four to twelve inches long. Water extracts its virtues. The Indians were well acquainted with it as a dye.

Properties and Uses.—It is a pure bitter tonic, considered by some equal to Columbo. It may be used for all purposes for which bitter tonics are applicable.

Dose.—Of the powder, one or two scruples; decoction, one or two tablespoonfuls.

NOTICE.—The author is at all times willing to furnish correspondents with information as regards medical plants, when incident to correspondence about other matters. But he cannot be expected to devote much time in consideration of the medicinal virtues a certain plant may contain, or to supply its common or botanical name, when it should be gathered, how prepared, and how administered, gratuitously, as his time is too valuable to be thus uncompensated for. Persons sending plants usually have it in such a shape that botanical recognition is rendered extremely difficult, often sending the part having the least distinctive botanical significance, and in many cases send grasses and weeds totally unrecognized in an officinal capacity. To supply the information desired in such cases is therefore tedious, and often unprofitable when secured. To all persons who may send plants, desiring full information with regard to their botanical or medicinal character, my fee will be ONE GUINEA. This barely covers absolute expense of chemical analysis, leaving me a mere trifle for my labor. I therefore trust that no one will send without some real medical object in view.

PLANTS.

THEIR COLLECTION AND PRESERVATION.

A Physician who would cure disease, or seek to assist Nature to throw off all morbid accumulations from the body, should have a single eye to the perfection, purity, or quality of the remedial agents he may feel called upon to employ. Plants should be gathered at a proper period, and under correct climatic influences, and always chosen from those in a wild or uncultivated state.

The roots of an annual plant will yield their most active medical properties just before the flowering season, whereas this class of roots are erroneously gathered after the flowering season; in consequence, they are less active, and do not retain their qualities for any reliable time. The roots of the biennial plants are most energetic if gathered when the leaves have fallen from the plant, in the autumn of the FIRST year; while the roots of perennial plants are most active when gathered between the decay of the flowers and leaves and the renewal of verdure of the following Spring. Bulbs are to be collected as soon as matured, or soon after the loss of foliage, in order to secure their most active principles.

Herbaceous stems should be collected after the foliage, but before the blossoms have developed themselves, while ligneous or woody stems should be collected after the decay of the leaves and previous to the vegetation of the succeeding Spring.

Barks are to be gathered in the Spring previous to flowering, or in Autumn after the foliage has disappeared. Spring is the best time to gather resinous barks, and Autumn for the others.

Leaves are best when gathered between the period of flowering and maturation of the fruit or seeds. Biennial plants, however, do not perfect themselves the first year, consequently their leaves should be gathered only during the second year of the growth of the plant.

Flowers are to be collected when about to open, or immediately after they have expanded, although I prefer the buds. Flowers, buds, and leaves, are to be gathered in dry weather, after the dew is off from them, or in the evening before it falls, and freed from all impurities. Aromatics should be collected after the flower-buds are formed, while stalks and twigs are best if gathered soon after the decay of the flowers. Berries, succulent fruits, and seeds are to be collected only when ripe, except in some few cases where the medicinal virtue is contained in the unripe article. Roots are to be well washed, rejecting all worm-eaten or decayed portions. Bulbs are cleaned and dried as roots. Barks, stems, twigs, and woods are best dried in a moderate sun-heat, and should be taken every night into a well-ventilated room, where the dew or rain will not touch them, and laid upon sticks, slats, or boards which are some few inches apart, so that the air may be well circulated through. The best method of drying leaves is to strip them from the stem, lay them loosely upon a flooring where the sun shines moderately and the air circulates sufficiently to avoid mould—keep them well stirred. The custom of steaming or moistening leaves in order to pack them more solidly after having been dried, is exceedingly improper, as the articles become thereby much deteriorated in quality and soon get musty.

Seeds are dried in the same manner as stems and leaves. Aromatic herbs and annual plants are dried as advised for leaves similarly prepared.

ESSAYS ON HYGIENE, ETC.

FOOD AND DRINKS.

MAN is an omnivorous creature, partaking of the nature both of the carnivorous and herbiverous animal. Hence, it is reasonable to suppose that man should subsist on a mixed diet, consisting both of animal and vegetable substances. To settle this matter, we must appeal to man's organization. His structure will tell us something we need not mistake. All the works of the Creator show design. Everything he has made has a use, and is so contrived as to be adapted to that use. Lions, tigers, and other animals, for example, which feed on flesh alone, have a short alimentary canal—it being only about three times the length of an animal's body. Animals which eat no flesh—a sheep for example—have very long second stomachs; while the *duodenum*, or second stomach of the human being, is of a medium capacity; which fact, in connection with the peculiar formation of his teeth and his erect or upright position, prove conclusively that man was destined to adapt himself to any clime, and to partake of any kind of food, animal or vegetable, as may be naturally supplied for his subsistence by the hand of Providence. For instance, the inhabitants of the Polar regions subsist principally on animal substances, and that, too, of the most oleaginous or fatty sorts.

Those tribes of men, laborers, hunters, etc., living in cold climates, who subsist almost wholly on flesh, fish, or fowl, devour on an average about seven pounds per diem. In fact, the quantity of animal food consumed by some human beings, who are flesh-eaters in practice, seems almost incredible. Captain Parry relates the case of an Esquimaux lad, who at a meal, which lasted twenty hours, consumed four pounds of raw as well as four pounds of broiled sea-horse flesh, one and a half pints of gravy, besides one and three-quarter pounds of bread, three glasses of raw spirits, one tumbler of strong grog, and nine pints of water. Captain Cochrane states, in a "*Narrative of Travels through Siberian Tartary*," that he has repeatedly seen a Yakut or Largouse eat forty pounds of meat in a day; and it is stated that the men in the Hudson's Bay Company are allowed a ration of seven or eight pounds of ordinary flesh meat per diem.

Charles Francis Hall, in his work called "*Arctic Researches and Life among the Esquimaux*," relates his strange experiences among the tribes of the country, with whom he became, as it were, naturalized. Speaking of the kinds of food they used, and the enormous quantity consumed, Captain Hall remarks:—"The skin of the Mysticetus (Greenland whale) is a great treat to the Esquimaux, who eat it raw. The 'black skin' is three-fourths of an inch thick, and looks like india-rubber. It is good eating in a raw state, even for a white man, as I know from experience; but when boiled and soused in vinegar it is most excellent." The Captain afterwards saw the natives cutting up the *krang* (meat) of the whale into such huge slices as their wives could carry; and as they worked they kept on eating, until boat-load after boat-load was sent over the ice to be deposited in the villages of the vicinity. All day long were they eating, which led the Captain to exclaim: "What enormous stomachs these Esquimaux have!" He came to the conclusion, however, that the Esquimaux practice of eating their food raw is a good one—at least, for the better preservation of their health. To one educated otherwise, as we civilized whites are, the Esquimaux custom of feeding on uncooked meats is highly repulsive; but eating meats raw or cooked is entirely a matter of education. "God has made of one blood all nations of men to dwell on the whole face of the earth, and has determined the times before appointed, and the bounds of their habitations." Take the Esquimaux away from the Arctic regions, and they would soon disappear from the face of the earth.

The Esquimaux are a hardy and happy people; are comparatively free from diseases, and are never known to die of scrofula or consumption, as one of the consequences of eating so enormously of oleaginous or greasy animal substances.

On other hand, in contrast to the gormandizing propensities of the Esquimaux, there are many examples of people living in cold climates subsisting on coarse bread, not exceeding the average amount of one pound of wheat, rye, or corn, daily; but such persons, unless exceedingly active in their habits, seldom escape from the penalties of scrofula and consumption, for the simple reason that they soon fail to supply themselves with the meats or fatty animal substances necessary for the heat and life of the body. The Canadian teamsters live almost exclusively upon bread and fat, which, in a temperate climate, would produce nausea and skin eruptions.

In warm climates, as in China, Hindoostan, Africa, and the tropics, the food of the natives is principally composed of vegetables and fruits—rice being the general diet, with only animal or other food enough to amount to a condiment or seasoning. Though the amount of food consumed by some of the nations is very small, and their habits very temperate, we do not find that even they are any the less liable to many of the diseases which afflict those who eat largely of a mixed diet. It is reasonable to suppose, however, that less food and lighter clothing are required in warm or hot climates than in those of the temperate and frigid.

The negroes on the plantations of Mississippi and Alabama grow sleek and live to an advanced age by subsisting largely on fat pork and hominy, corn bread, sweet potatoes, rice, etc. In the pampas of Brazil and Buenos Ayres, where immense herds of wild cattle are found, the hunters catch these bovines, strip them of their hides and horns, and, if hungry, will cut out a huge chunk of beef, half roast it, and eat it without salt or bread. In some parts of Brazil the natives feed on a flour made from the roots of a certain plant or tree, moistening the same with the juice of the orange or lemon. Others find support in the yam, the banana, or plantain, etc., while they are hugely addicted to drinking a species of whiskey called aguardiente.

In Asia and Africa many of the natives derive their staple nutrition from gum acacia, and among us many an invalid has derived healthy nourishment from preparations containing gum acacia, when his stomach would neither bear nor digest any other article in the shape of food. In Peru the Indians will subsist for a month at a time by chewing a plant called erythroxylin coca, and in the mean time perform journeys of hundreds of miles. The Hindoos live principally on rice, and are considered a long-lived and a very docile people. On the other hand, many of the Indian tribes of North America, who live on roots, barks, berries, etc., are very savage and warlike in their habits. The Chinese drink strong tea, and the Turks coffee equally as strong, without apparent detriment to their general health. The laboring Scotch thrive partially on oatmeal porridge, without using a particle of meat. The Irish want nothing better than plenty of potatoes, cabbage, and buttermilk. The English, French, German, Italian, Spanish, and other civilized people of Europe live upon mixed diet, though each have their peculiar likes and dislikes in the shape of dishes, and the average health of each nation is about the same. So in America they eat everything and anything, without particular injury to the constitution, except when eating too fast and too much at a time, which is a proverbial national error.

People are liable to eat what they have been taught or educated to eat, without stopping to inquire concerning any physiological laws on the subject. Scrofula is the most prevalent of all diseases,—this fact being justly attributed not to pork or food of any kind, but to the manner in which the people are lodged, living in small or unventilated apartments, crowded together and breathing foul air and the pestiferous effluvias of their own bodies.

There can be no doubt that many of the maladies incident to the human race are produced through the agency of improper food, over-feeding, etc., on the internal organs; yet it can be readily shown that a far greater amount of maladies are induced through the medium of atmospheric impressions and vicissitudes on the external surface of the body. More diseases arise from breathing foul air, or from lack of the natural atmospheric air, than from the worst or poorest kind of food. Disease, therefore, is not so much a result of the kind of food we eat, as it is in the quantity and quality. What may be excellent for one man may be very injurious for another; custom, habits. idiosyncrasies, temperaments, etc., having a great deal to do in the digestion of food, and converting it into wholesome or nutritious blood, capable of supplying all the tissues of the body with their natural needs or stimuli. Very few people seem to know what their stomachs were intended for, or even know where they are situated. All sorts of deleterious substances are crammed into the stomach by thousands of people. When any article of food is repulsive to any of the senses, it had better be avoided as an article of diet. This antipathy is so intense in some as to amount to actual idiosyncrasy. The sympathy and antipathy displayed by some persons with regard to alimentary food or drinks are extremely curious. Some notable instances are on record. BOYLE fainted when he heard the splashing of water or liquids. SCALIGER turned pale at the sight of water-cresses; ERASMUS became feverish when he saw a fish. ZIMMERMAN tells us of a lady who shuddered when touching the velvety skin of a peach. There are whole families who entertain a horror of cheese; on the other hand, there was a physician, Dr. STARKE, of Edinburgh, who lost his life by subsisting almost entirely upon it. Some people have been unable to take mutton even when administered in the microscopic form of pills. There is a case of a man falling down at the smell of mutton, as if bereaved of life, and in strong convulsions. Sir JAMES EYRE, in his well-known little book, mentions three curious instances of idiosyncrasy: the case of a gentleman who could not eat a single strawberry with impunity; the case of another, whose head would become frightfully swollen if he touched the smallest particle of hare; the case of a third, who would inevitably have an attack of gout a few hours after eating fish. We ourselves know of a lady in Connecticut who will turn pale and faint at the smell of an apple. She could certainly claim innocence with reference to tempting any Adam.

This ignorance of the uses of the stomach, or rather abuse of the functions, is sometimes the source of much suffering and disease. Besides the gastric tubes which supply the stomach with the gastric juice, which is necessary to dissolve the food before it can be converted into blood, it is extensively covered with a net-work of nerves and blood-vessels, rendering the stomach very sensitive and very liable to inflammation. This inflammation sometimes becomes very active, producing vomiting, pain, fever, etc., all caused by imprudence in diet. It is a warning. If the warning be not heeded, this inflammation becomes chronic; the nerves lose their sensibility; the stomach becomes inactive, and that most distressing of all diseases, dyspepsia (and often epilepsy or fits), takes up its abode as a permanent guest. Most frequently it comes on more slowly and without apparent warning

The food we eat has to be properly digested. People are apt to suppose that digestion is performed in the stomach only. This is a mistake. The stomach performs the greater part of the work, but it is greatly assisted by other organs besides. Digestion really begins in the mouth. Besides the teeth, which are the true organs of digestion, there are situated in the cavity of the mouth three small bodies called salivary glands, which pour out a fluid called *saliva* (or spittle), which is just as necessary to the proper digestion of food as the gastric juice itself. The more thoroughly the food is mixed with saliva, the more perfect will be digestion. This should teach us to eat slowly, and to chew so well that every mouthful of food may contain a proper amount of it. It should also teach us that this saliva is too valuable a substance to be contaminated with tobacco-juice, or wasted in expectoration from smoking, especially where the temperament is nervous. Saliva is constantly being poured into the cavity of the mouth, whether we are asleep or awake. As a general thing, in a healthy person, about five wine-glasses full of saliva are secreted in a day.

We eat that the body may be supported with blood, for our food, be fore it can become a part of the body, must first be converted into blood. A full-grown, healthy working-man consumes in one year about twelve hundred pounds of victuals and drink—that is, about eight times his own weight; yet, if he should weigh himself at the end of the year, he would find that he weighs very little more or less than he did at the beginning. Now what has become of the twelve hundred pounds he has eaten? It has been wasted away. With every motion, every breath, every operation of the mind, the body has been wasted, and food has been required to support the waste.

The one great cause of the wasting of the body, and of the constant demand for food, is action. If the muscles could be kept from moving, our lungs from breathing, and our minds from thinking, then we might not require food, for there would be no waste. This condition of things, of course, could never exist without death speedily following.

Exercising violently excites hunger, since it makes us breathe faster and therefore causes us to inhale more air. A man of sedentary habits does not require so much food as a laboring man, because he does not waste away as fast. Much of the wasted material of the body is carried off by the lungs, in the form of *carbonic acid.* The skin, too, does its share of the work. It not only assists in breathing, but it also carries out of the system a large portion of its dead particles.

Children require more food in proportion than adults, because they are growing, and therefore, so to speak, need more to build up their bodies. After we have attained our growth, we neither gain nor lose our weight, provided we are in health, for we consume as much food as the body wastes. This is called a state of equilibrium. As old age comes on the body begins to decline in weight, and then we waste more than we con sume.

Food may be distinguished into two kinds, viz., nitrogenized and non-nitrogenized. The first class is called the plastic elements of nutrition, and is designed solely to make blood and to form the substance of the tissues in the general structure of man; while the non-nitrogenized kind is necessary to keep up the animal heat, by yielding hydrogen and carbon, to be exhibited in the lungs. The elements of human nutrition and recuperation are vegetable fibrine, albumen, caseine, and animal flesh and blood; while the elements of respiration are fat, starch, gum, cane sugar, grape sugar, sugar of milk, wine, beer, and spirits. The elementary principles or proximate elements of food consist in water, gum, sugar, starch, lignin, jelly, fat, fibrine, albumen, caseine, gluten, gelatine, acids, salts, alcohol, etc. All these elements are found in sufficient abundance in either the vegetable or animal kingdoms, and are to be used according to the natural wants of man, or the supply of the waste. No precise rules, therefore, can be laid down to suit every particular state of either disease or health. Every one, accordingly, should eat and drink only those things which he may find by experience, habits, or peculiarities to best agree with his condition, and reject all substances which he may find injurious to his health and general well-being. It is the provocative variety, or the over-stimulation of the palate, that does the greater mischief to health. The plainer the food and the fewer the dishes, the greater will be the immunity from disease. Whether the diet be vegetable or animal substances, the result will be the same in relative proportion to the nutriment yielded. Fish, for scrofulous and consumptive persons, is a most excellent diet, containing a principle called iodine.

Meats contain the most nitrogen, the nitrogenous portions of our food make flesh, and go to supply the wear and tear and wastes of the body; these are ultimately passed from the system in the urine. If more nitrogenous food is eaten than is needed to supply these wastes, Nature converts it more rapidly into living tissues, which are, with corresponding rapidity, broken down and converted into urine. This is when the food is digested; but when so much is eaten that it cannot be digested, Nature takes alarm as it were, and endeavors to remedy the trouble in one of three ways. The stomach rebels and casts it off by vomiting, it is worked out of the system by attacks of diarrhœa, or the human creature is made uncomfortable generally, and is restless both by day and by night; as a further punishment his appetite is more or less destroyed for several meals afterwards. Little or no nitrogen is poured off with the perspiration, breathing, or fæces.

Whatever diet we use, whether animal or vegetable, the secret of its utility lies not only in the quantity and quality, but in the manner in which either kind is cooked, when so prepared for food. Much ignorance prevails everywhere in this matter of cooking the substances that are requisite for the sustenance of our bodies. Let any person, unable to eat broccoli or greens cooked in a quart of water, try the effect of having them cooked in a gallon of water, or of having the quart of water changed three or four times during the process of cooking, and he will soon discover the difference. If good potatoes are "watery," it is because they are ill-cooked. Fried dishes, rich gravies, and pastry should be avoided because of their tendency to develop fatty acids in the stomach

We may reasonably suppose that the physiology of digestion is yet too imperfectly understood to enable us to lay down any precise laws as to what to eat, drink, and avoid. With a little vigilance, however, each person can ascertain for himself what foods do and do not agree with him. As before intimated, the peculiarities in this respect are remarkable. Some cannot endure fat; others cannot get along without it. Some cannot touch mutton; others are made ill by eggs. Let each find out his own antipathy. Suppose the case of a healthy man—so healthy that he cannot be healthier. We will say the quantity of blood in his body is thirty pounds, and that he loses one pound of this in every twenty-four hours. Is it not plain enough that he must eat as much food in the same time as will supply the waste of blood he has lost? But if he should eat as much as will furnish a pound and a half of blood, he will have half a pound of blood too much in his system. Should he go on adding an extra half pound of blood daily more than is required to supply the tissues, what then will be the consequences? Bursting of the blood-vessels. But good Dame Nature has measurably guarded against any such plethoric catastrophe; for, after having supplied the waste of the body, the undue quantity of blood is converted into fat or adipose matter, thus restoring the blood's volume to a due standard. But this *quasi* fat is of no use to the body. It does not give it strength; on the contrary, it is an encumbrance to the machinery, and, in more ways than one, is an evil. He, therefore, who eats too much, even though he digests or assimilates what he eats, and should be fortunate enough to escape apoplexy, or some other disease, does not add a single particle to his strength. He only accumulates fat, and incurs the evils thereunto appertaining—one among many of which I will mention—I mean the accumulation of fat about the heart, and interfering, to a most dangerous degree, with the heart's action. A man's strength resides in his arterial blood—in his muscles and bones and tendons and ligatures—in his brawn and sinew; and his degree of strength depends upon the vigor, size, and substance of these; and if he were to eat without ceasing, he could not add to their size and substance one atom, nor alter their original healthy dimensions. Therefore it is a most mischievous fallacy to suppose that the more a man eats the stronger he grows.

The quantity of food taken daily should just be sufficient to restore to the blood what the blood has lost in restoring the waste of the body, and that should always be proportioned to the degree of bodily exertion undergone. But how are we to know the exact amount of the waste that is daily going on in our system, in order to apportion the quantity of food thereto? Nature tells us not only when, but how much we ought to eat and drink.

For instance, when you are excessively thirsty, and when you are in the act of quenching your thirst with a draught of cold water, you know when you have drunk enough by the cessation of thirst; but there is another token, which not only informs you when you have drunk enough, but which also prevents you from drinking more, that is, if you drink water only. While you are in the act of drinking, and before your thirst has been allayed, how rich, how sweet, how delicious is the draught, though it be but water! But no sooner has thirst been quenched, than behold, in an instant all its deliciousness has vanished! It is now distasteful to the palate. To him, then, who requires drink, water is delicious; for him who does not require drink, water not only has no relish, but impresses the palate disagreeably. To a man laboring under the very last degree of thirst, even foul ditch water would be a delicious draught; but his thirst having been quenched, he would turn from it with disgust. In this instance of water-drinking, then, it is clear that the relish depends not on any flavor residing in the water, but on some certain condition of the body. It is absurd to say that you cannot drink water because you do not like it, for this only proves that you do not want it; since the relish with which you enjoy drink depends upon the fact of your requiring drink, and not at all upon the nature of the drink itself.

Now apply this to eating instead of drinking. Place before a hungry workman stale bread and fat pork, flanked by a jug of cold water. While his hunger remains unappeased, he will eat and drink with an eager relish; but when his hunger has been appeased, the bread and meat and water have lost what he supposed to be their delicious flavor.

If we ate only simple and natural food, plainly cooked, there would be no danger of eating too much—the loss of relish and the feeling of disgust, consequent upon satisfied hunger, would make it impossible. Indeed, this sense of satiety is as much and as truly a natural token, intended to warn us that we have eaten enough, as the sense of hunger is a token that we require food.

As hunger instructs us when to eat, so disrelish teaches us when we should desist. It would seem that the very *ne plus ultra* of the cook's art is to destroy the sensation of disrelish, which is almost as necessary to our health as hunger itself. Thus it appears the object of modern cookery is to make the stomach bear a large quantity of food without nausea—to cram into the stomach as much as it can possibly hold without being sick.

The rule which should regulate the quantity of food to be used is found in that sensation of disrelish which invariably succeeds to satisfied appetites. If you be content to live plainly and temperately, you will never eat too much, but you will always eat enough; but if you would rather incur the penalty of disease than forego the pleasure of dining daintily, all I can say is, you are welcome to do so—but do not plead ignorance—blame only yourself.

I have stated already that certain people have been known to eat from seven to forty pounds of meat or food in a single day. On the other hand, persons have lived on twelve ounces of food a day, and were actually exempt from disease. Dr. Franklin, in his younger days, confined himself solely to ten pounds of bread a week, drinking water only in the mean time. Rev. John Wesley lived to a great age on sixteen ounces a day, although he led a very active life as a preacher of the gospel; and a celebrated Italian nobleman, who led a dissipated life till near fifty years of age, suddenly reformed his habits, and lived on twelve ounces a day with a single glass of wine, until he had reached the hundredth year of his age. Was the wine one of the means by which he prolonged his life? It no doubt served to cheer his spirits. And this leads me to consider somewhat the nature of stimulants. By stimulants I mean ardent spirits, wines, and strong ales. Are they necessary as articles of diet? They are not always, but have their uses. They are pernicious to the general organism, if too freely indulged in. Liquids which contain or make solids are better than wines, etc., yet both have their uses. Milk, the moment it reaches the stomach, is converted into curds and whey. The whey passes off by the kidneys—the solid curd nourishes the body. Now, if we evaporate a glass of wine on a shallow plate, whatever solid matter it contains will be left dry upon the plate, and this will be found to amount to about as much as may be laid on the extreme point of a penknife blade; and a portion, by no means all—but a portion of this solid matter I will readily concede is capable of nourishing the body—and this portion is only equal to one-third of the flour contained in a single grain of wheat! If we want nourishment merely, why not eat a grain of wheat instead of drinking a glass of wine? Yet wine has its uses as an exhilarant to the mind and body.

Once placed beyond the reach of the seductions of the palate, the simple rule of drink what you want and as much as you want will of itself suggest the needful limitation. Physiology tells us plainly enough, not only why liquids are necessary, but how all superfluous quantities are rapidly got rid of.

An interdict has been placed against hot drinks, which, if directed against tea and coffee so hot as to scald the mucous membrane, is rational enough, but is simply absurd when directed against hot in favor of cold drinks; the aroma of tea and coffee is produced by heat, consequently the pleasant, stimulating effect is considerably diminished when they are allowed to get cold.

Great diversity prevails as to the kinds of drinks which should be used. Some interdict tea, others only *green* tea; some will not hear of coffee; others allow mild beer, but protest against the bitter. Whoever very closely examines the evidence will probably admit that the excessive variations in the conclusions prove that no unexceptionable evidence has yet been offered. By this I mean that the evil effects severally attributed to the various liquids were no direct consequences of the action of such liquids, but were due to some other condition. We often lay the blame of a restless night on the tea or coffee, which would have been quite inoffensive taken after a simpler dinner, or at another hour.

When a man uniformly finds a cup of tea produce discomfort, no matter what his dinner may have been, nor at what hour he drinks it, he is justified in the inference that tea disagrees with him; if he finds that the same effect follow whether he take milk or sugar with his tea, then he has a strong case against the tea itself, and his experience is evidence as far as it goes. But we should require a great deal of evidence as precise as this, before impugning the wide and massive induction in favor of tea, which is drawn from the practice of millions. Had tea in itself been injurious, had it been other than positively beneficial, the discovery would long ago have been made on a grand scale.

The same may be said of coffee. Both tea and coffee may be hurtful when taken at improper times, or by bilious persons; and a little vigilance will enable each person to decide for himself when he can, and when he cannot, take them with benefit.

I may briefly state my opinion that the great objection against wines is its pleasantness, which is apt to lure us into drinking more than is needful. Wine is quite unnecessary for robust men living under healthy conditions; but to them it is also, when moderately taken, quite harmless. For many delicate men and women, living under certain unhealthy conditions, it is often indispensable. The physician must decide in all such cases.

Many think they cannot do without something to drink at regular meals. Cold milk at meals has the disadvantage, if used freely, of engendering constipation, biliousness, and the long train of minor symptoms which inevitably follow these conditions.

Warm drinks are preferable in moderate quantities. Field hands on cotton and sugar plantations find a wholesome drink in a mixture of molasses, ginger, and water. This is a safe drink for harvesters, as are many other temperate household preparations. A recipe for many of these will be found in the proper department of this work.

Whatever we eat or whatever we drink, let it be only enough barely to appease the instincts of hunger and thirst. If we rigidly do this, we shall seldom or never be afflicted with dyspepsia, liver complaints, heart disease, and the thousand ills to which flesh is heir, but will continue to enjoy unceasing rubicund health and vigorous old age.

CLOTHING.

Clothing must be adapted to the climate in which a person lives. Warm or heavy clothing is rendered imperative in a northern climate, while the lightest and thinnest can only be tolerated in the torrid zones. It is, however, a physiological fact that the more the whole surface of the body is exposed to the external air, within certain limits, the more vigorously is its functional action performed, and the better is it enabled to preserve its own proper temperature, as well as to resist all unwholesome impressions from vicissitudes of weather, or the extremes of heat and cold. It should always be as light and loose as possible without bodily discomfort.

The substances principally employed for clothing are linen, cotton, silk, wool. hair, or down. Woollens or flannels, being bad conductors of heat, afford the greatest immediate protection from cold; and for the same reason are less debilitating to the cutaneous function than is generally supposed. The most healthy clothing for a cold climate, especially the year round, is undoubtedly that made of wool. If worn next to the skin by all classes in summer and winter, an incalculable amount of coughs, colds, diarrhœas, dysenteries, and fevers would be prevented, as also many sudden and premature deaths from croup, diphtheria, and inflammation of the lungs and bladder. Of course, the clothing should be regulated in amount according to the degree of the heat of the weather at the time prevailing. In a very hot day, for instance, a single garment might be sufficient, but on a colder day an additional garment should be added, and in this way keep the equilibrium of the temperature of the body uniform as possible day by day, the year round. Winter maladies would be prevented by the ability of a woollen garment to keep the natural heat about the body, instead of conveying it away as fast as generated, as is done by linen, flaxen, cotton, and silken garments. Indeed, the laboring classes, or those compelled to toil in the sun, would enjoy better health by wearing light woollen clothing, than by wearing linen or cotton fabrics. Among the Irish emigrants and others who arrive in the United States during the summer season, we find many clothed entirely in woollen garments, frequently wearing heavy cloaks or coats, and actually feeling less discomfort from the heat than those of our native-born citizens who are in the habit of wearing linen or cotton next to their skin, and similar fabrics over these for outer clothing. It is more healthful to wear woollen next to the skin, especially in summer, for the reason that woollen textures absorb the moisture of perspiration so rapidly as to keep the skin measurably dry all the time. It is curious to notice that the water is conveyed by a woollen garment from the surface of the body to the outer side of the garment, where the microscope shows it condensed in millions of pearly drops; while it is in the experience of all observant people, that if a linen shirt becomes damp by perspiration, it remains cold and clammy for a long time afterwards, and, unless removed at once, will certainly cause some bodily ailment, as palsy, rheumatism, etc. To sit down, or remain inactive with a linen or cotton shirt wet with perspiration, will speedily cause a chill to the whole body, leading not unfrequently to some sudden and fatal disease. In the night-sweats of consumption, especially, or of any debilitated condition of the system, a woollen or flannel night-dress (light for warm weather) is immeasurably more comfortable than cotton or linen, because it prevents that sepulchral dampness and chilliness of feeling which are otherwise inevitable. The British government make it imperative that every sailor in the navy shall wear flannel shirts in the hottest climates, a rule that should be adopted by all persons everywhere exposed to variable weather, to extreme heats and colds, merely regulating the amount of woollen garments worn to suit the variable temperatures of climates and seasons. In saying all this, however, we must remember that comfort is very much a matter of habit; and therefore we should make due discrimination between the natural sensation of health and the morbid sensitiveness produced by false customs. For instance, some keep their whole bodies constantly covered by many layers of woollen garments, and yet go into a shivering fit at every unusual breath of cold air. The reason is, they never adapt their habiliments gradually to the degree of the heat or cold of the season. If it be deemed advisable to wear woollen clothing all the year round, whether summer or winter, it does not follow that we are to wear more than one or two extra folds of clothing in addition to the under garments. The true rule is not to cover all parts of the body equally with the same amount of clothing. The fleshy parts require the least clothing, and the limbs and feet, or less muscular parts, the most. Yet we often wear, in addition to under clothing, a thick vest, coat, and overcoat; and to these will add heavy scarfs of fur or wool to the neck, etc., while the legs and feet are seldom clad in more than a single additional garment to the drawers and stockings. These parts require more clothing, especially in the winter season, than any other parts of the body. Furs are worn in the United States more for ornament than benefit. They are the warmest clothing materials known; yet are not adapted for general wear, inasmuch as they are apt to overheat the body, and thus render it keenly susceptible to colds and other afflictions. By consequence, fur neck cloths, caps, etc., are very pernicious for the head and throat, inducing catarrhs, quinsy sore throat, and similar afflictions. On the contrary, a light woollen waistcoat worn constantly over the breast, summer and winter, would guard against these and other evils, and insure vigorous strength to the lungs or respiratory apparatus, and thus should not be dispensed with even in dog-days. The simple rule is to keep the head cool and the feet warm at all seasons of the year. Cheap and pretty silks, of which there are many varieties, are materials which are admirable for ladies' evening, dinner, or walking dresses, and cost less in the end than other fabrics.

While I contend that woollen or flannel clothing is the most suitable for the colder or even the more temperate climates, it is not for me to object to the use of linen or cotton clothing for those living in the torrid or tropical climes. Indeed, cotton and linen would seem best adapted to such climes. In the north, many persons cannot wear flannel next to the skin, on account of inducing some peculiar cutaneous affection; while others prefer such fabrics from choice, although exposed to all vicissitudes, never experiencing any evil effects from such a course. Such persons usually lead an active, out-door life, or are accustomed to exposing their bodies frequently, especially their chests, to atmospheric influences.

In a strictly hygienic regulation of dress, however, the color of the clothing is not to be disregarded. White color reflects the rays of the sun; black absorbs them. Light colored clothing is, therefore, more comfortable and sanitary in warm weather than dark colored, because the former repels the heat, while it is readily received and retained by the latter. The heat-reflecting or heat-retaining property of different fabrics varies exactly with their lighter or darker shades of color. This difference, however, is much greater in the luminous rays of light than in the non-luminous. When, therefore, we are not exposed to the sun, the subject of color is of very little importance. The absorbing power of dark surfaces renders the skins of dark-colored animals, as well as the darker persons or races of the human family, less liable to be scorched or blistered by the direct rays of the sun than are those of a lighter color.

As to the cut or fashion of garments, that is a matter to be decided by the taste or habits of the wearer. Fashion, however, is very arbitrary, and seldom consults hygiene in matters of dress. Of late years she has really much improved, as to the regulation of attire with regard to both health and elegance. The hooped skirt, which at the outset of its career was so mercilessly ridiculed, has proved to be a great blessing to the ladies, as it enables them to dispense with a heavy drag of solid skirts, and gives their lower limbs free and easy play and motion. The hats or head-coverings now worn by both sexes are, in a sanitary point of view, far superior to those worn by our immediate ancestors, being very light, and affording free ventilation, which is indispensable for the avoidance of headaches, rushing of blood to the head, and many other afflictions.

I can therefore only say that the first physiological rule for dress is to have all garments as light in texture and as loose in fashion as is consistent with bodily comfort, or such as will admit of the most perfect freedom in the exercise of every muscle in the body. Inequality of clothing, as before remarked, is a far more frequent cause of colds than deficient clothing. For instance, if a person exposes a part of the body usually protected by clothing to a strong current of cold air, he will take cold sooner than by an equal exposure of the whole body. A great safeguard against disease is to regulate the texture and quantity of clothing according to the temperature of the climate in which a person lives, avoiding extreme colds or extreme heats; keeping the clothing always fresh and clean (especially that of the feet), and wearing a different garment at night from that worn during the day, not omitting the cleanliness of the whole body in the general hygiene of wearing apparel.

Sleep.

Sleep is as much a necessity to the existence of all animal organizations as light, air, or any other element incident to their maintenance and healthful development. The constitutional relation of man to the changes of the seasons, and the succession of days and nights, implies the necessity of sleep. Natural or functional sleep is a complete cessation of the operations of the brain and sensory nervous ganglia, and is, therefore, attended with entire unconsciousness. Thoroughly healthy people, it is believed, never dream. Dreaming implies imperfect rest—some disturbing cause, usually gastric irritation, exciting the brain to feeble and disordered functional action. Individuals of very studious habits, and those whose labors are disproportionately intellectual, require more sleep than those whose duties or pursuits require more manual and less mental exertion. The waste of nervous influence in the brain of literary or studious persons requires a longer time to be repaired or supplied than in those even who endure the largest amount of physical toil, without particular necessity for active thought while engaged in their daily manual pursuits. But no avocation or habit affects this question so much as the quality of the ingesta. Those who subsist principally upon a vegetable diet, it is said, require less sleep than those who subsist on both animal and vegetable food. It seems certain that herbivorous animals sleep less than the carnivorous; while the omnivora require more sleep than the herbivora and less than the carnivora. Man, therefore, partaking most of the omnivorous, living on a mixed diet of animal and vegetable food, requires more sleep than the ox, the horse, or the sheep, but much less than the lion, the tiger, or the bear.

Physiologists are not well agreed respecting the natural duration of sleep. Indeed, no positive rule can be laid down on this subject; the statute of Nature, however, appears to read: Retire soon after dark, and arise with the first rays of morning light; and this is equally applicable to all climates and all seasons, at least in all parts of the globe proper for human habitations, for in the cold season, when the nights are longer, more sleep is required.

History shows that those who have lived the longest were the longest sleepers, the average duration of sleep being about eight hours. The time of sleep of each individual must depend on his temperament, manner of life, and dietetic habits. For instance, John Wesley, with an active nervous temperament and a rigidly plain vegetable diet, and who performed an immense amount of mental and bodily labor, slept but four or five hours out of the twenty-four; while Daniel Webster, with a more powerful frame but less active organization, and living on a mixed diet, had a "talent for sleeping" eight or nine hours. Benjamin Franklin used to say that seven hours sleep was enough for any man, eight hours for a woman, and nine hours for a fool! Nevertheless, the invariable rule for all whose habits are correct, is to retire early in the evening, and sleep as long as the slumber is quiet, be the time six, seven, eight, or nine hours. Those who indulge in late suppers, or eat heartily before retiring, are usually troubled with unpleasant dreams, nightmare, and are oftentimes found dead in the morning. Restless dozing in the morning is exceedingly debilitating to the constitution. Persons addicted to spirituous liquors and tobacco, in connection with high-seasoned food. are in danger of oversleeping even to the extent of very considerably increasing the stupidity and imbecility of mind, and indolence and debility of body naturally and necessarily consequent upon those habits. Sleeping in the daytime, or after meals, is not a natural law of the physiology of man. No one requires to sleep after a meal unless he has eaten more food than his system required. Sleep may be indulged in during the day when sufficient sleep is not had at night; but this sleeplessness at night need seldom occur were our habits made conformable to the general hygienic requirements of Nature. Children may sleep all they are inclined to. The position of the body is of some importance. It should be perfectly flat or horizontal with the head. a little varied by a small pillow. Sleeping with the head elevated by two or three pillows or bolsters is certainly a bad habit. The neck is bent, the chest is compressed, and the body unnaturally crooked. Children are made round-shouldered from their heads being placed on high pillows. The beds should be made of straw, corn-husks, hair, various palms and grasses, never of feathers, which can only be mentioned in reprehension. The bed-clothing should always be kept scrupulously clean, and adapted to the season of the year, while the bed-rooms should always be sufficiently large and airy as best conducive to sound sleep and general vigorous health.

BATHING

Were all to follow the natural laws of their organization in respect to eating, drinking, clothing, exercise, and temperature, an occasional bath or washing would be sufficient; but as the laws of life and health are transgressed in a thousand ways, the sum total of all the unphysiological habits of civilized life is a condition of body characterized by deficient external circulation, capillary obstruction, and internal congestion or engorgement. To counteract this morbid condition of the system, bathing of the whole body, on regular occasions, cannot, or should not, be omitted. For hygienic purposes, the particular process is merely a matter of convenience. You may bathe in a river if you like, or may employ the shower-bath; but these modes are no more beneficial than the towel or sponge-bath. After the ablution, in whatever manner performed, care should be taken to thoroughly rub the body with a crash towel. The best time for such purification of the body is on rising from bed in the morning. The temperature of the water should be adapted to suit different circumstances of constitutional health and disease. Cold or cool baths are best for those in robust health; but those who are deficient in blood, or have a low vitality, should use tepid water. Extremely feeble persons should commence with warm water, and gradually reduce the temperature as reaction improves. Sponging the body with spirits or vinegar may prove highly beneficial in many cases of debility, where water would be injurious. Excessive bathing tends to make the skin harsh and scaly by diluting the secretions of the sebaceous glands, the oil of which is intended to be regularly and naturally poured out to the surface of the skin in order to keep it smooth, glossy, and soft. Bathe as often as may be necessary to keep the skin clean, and you will then have fulfilled the requirements of hygienic bathing.

EXERCISE.—PHYSICAL AND MENTAL DEVELOPMENT.

Everything tends to prove that man was destined to lead a life of bodily action. His formation—his physical structure generally, and that of his joints particularly—his great capacity for speed and laborious exertion—the Divine injunction, that "he shall live by the sweat of his brow"—the bodily imbecility and enfeebled health invariably consequent upon a sedentary habit—all go to prove that he was destined to lead a life of physical activity. Most people are apt to despise many of the aids to health, because of their very simplicity. A sensible Dervish, in the Eastern allegory, well aware of this weakness of human nature to despise simple things, and venerate those they do not understand, when called to the Sultan to cure him of a disease, did not dare to simply advise him to take exercise; but he said to him:—"Here is a ball which I have stuffed with certain rare and precious medicines. And here is a bat, the handle of which I have also stuffed with similar medicines. Your Higness must take this bat and with it beat about this ball, until you perspire very freely. You must do this every day." His Highness did so; and, in a short time the exercise of playing at bat and ball with the Dervish cured the Sultan's malady. But it should be remembered that there are a great many cases where medicines must be given to assist nature, besides the employment of exercise to facili tate the recovery of the patient.

Nevertheless, exercise is one of the chief aids of all others I must recommend to be adopted as eminently essential for the remedying of bad health, and of preserving that which is already good. It is impossible for a healthy adult to be otherwise than active in body or mind, or both; while it may be asserted, with abundant reason, that laziness is actually a disease, dependent on some abnormal condition of the organism. A variety of social circumstances may operate to produce an indolent disposition of mind and inactive habit of body, but these also produce a primary condition of ill-health.

The function of respiration, by which the blood is vitalized, and the nutrition of the muscular structure, on which depend all the motive power or strength of the system, are intimately connected with the circulation of the blood, and this with active exercise. Without this, there must be unhealthy accumulation somewhere; and, as the larger arteries are not permanently dilatable, while the veins and capillary arteries are so, this accumulation or congestion must take place in the veins and capillary or hair-like arteries.

When the circulation is feeble from lack of bodily exercise, or other cause, the blood creeps sluggishly along the minute vessels composing the elementary tissue of the body; these veins and capillaries become gorged, which engorgement operates as a still further impediment to the free flow of the blood. The blood, when not circulated with due energy through the ultimate tissues, becomes deteriorated in quality, and so, in turn, fails to supply that proper nutrition upon which, according to its degree of purity, all the tissues and functions of the body depend. If the propelling power arising from breathing pure air and using active bodily exercise is not sufficiently energetic, the circulation through the elementary tissue is so slow that the blood loses its healthful arterial hue before it has reached the extremities of the hair-like arteries; and thus that part of the tissue which ought to be filled with arterial blood is gorged only with black venous blood, from which the proper secretion necessary to the nutrition of the body, cannot be separated, either in due abundance or of a healthy quality. Hence, if this state of congestion be permitted to exist from lack of active exercise and consequent free respiration, so as to vitalize the blood, there must needs be a speedy wasting of flesh, and all the other phenomena of consumption or any other disease. The strength of the system is intimately connected with the circulation of the blood, as stimulated in its flow by means of active bodily exercise and pure air.

This principle is well illustrated in the effects of gymnastics and training, by which the muscles of any part of the body are remarkably invigorated by regular systematic exercise. People of all trades and occupations find those parts of the muscular system which are habitually the most exercised to be the most powerful.

For healthful purposes all that is necessary is, any way, to exercise all parts of the body to a degree of fatigue without exhaustion; that is, to a degree which will insure an energetic circulation of the blood throughout the entire economy. All exercises, however, to secure their full benefit, should be coupled either with some object of utility or amusement, otherwise the mind is apt to labor adversely to the body.

When I say that exercise is what is wanted to restore to health the weak and languid, I mean that it is not so much exercise that is wanted as the exhilarating effect which the enjoyment of exercise produces. A man who exercises half an hour unwillingly in his wood-shed, is not benefited in the degree one is who takes an hour's walk for pleasure through a beautiful country.

It is the enjoyment of exercise in which consists its chiefest excellence. It is the diversion of the mind from the ailments of the body. The invalid is by this drawn away from himself.

What can better accomplish this object than amusement? Laughter and lively talk may be said to be a species of exercise—mental exercise—which is very often as beneficial to an invalid as physical exercise. Anything that will induce a fit of laughter must have an influence in promoting an active circulation of blood, and, as we have seen, it is necessary to health that the blood should be duly aërated and flow with energy through the system. Whatever means may be employed to give rapid circulation to the blood must be conducive to health. I believe, then, most fully in using all proper means of amusement which will cheer the invalid, and thus be a mental stimulus or auxiliary to the preservation and restoration of health.

So, not only are amusements which afford exercise to the mental faculties useful, but occupation—some useful business pursuit, which requires, and hence secures, attention and labor during several hours of each day—is absolutely essential to the high sanitary condition of the body, for nothing else will insure so constant, regular, and equally divided exercise for *both* mind and body.

Walking, running, leaping, hopping, dancing, rowing boats, etc., are physiologically adapted to strengthen the whole muscular system. Even boxing and fencing are to be advised when properly regulated. Wrestling is a dangerous method of developing muscular power. Ten-pins, billiards, etc., are excellent exercises, but useful employment is better. Singing, declaiming, reading, etc., are admirable methods of cultivating the vocal powers, and increasing the capacity of the respiratory apparatus. Riding on horseback, hunting, fishing, etc., are all more or less beneficial in the prevention of disease and promoting good health. Riding in easy carriages, sailing in boats, swinging, and other passive exercises, are all to be duly considered as remedial expedients for invalids.

Amid the many vicissitudes of fortune and the moral crosses to which female life is doomed, I recommend healthful exercise of the body, in order that the material fabric may be fortified against the thousand causes of disease continually assailing the sex.

Woman comes earlier to maturity by several years than man. The tree of life blossoms and bears fruit sooner in the one sex than in the other. It also sooner withers and sheds its leaves,—but does not sooner die. Female life at any period is fully as good,—perhaps a little better in respect to probable duration,—than that of the male. It is during the period of from fourteen to twenty-one years that the seeds of female diseases are chiefly sown—or, at least, that the soil is specially prepared for their reception and growth. The predisposition to infirmities and disorders of various kinds is affected by acts of omission and commission. In the first class need I mention the deficiency of healthy exercise of the body in the open air, and of intellectual exercise in judicious studies. The hoop and the skip-rope, even in city homes, might usefully supersede the piano, the harp, and guitar, for one hour in the day, at least. In schools and seminaries there is no excuse—and, indeed, in many of them this salutary point of hygiene is well attended to. In others, however, gymnastic exercises have been hastily thrown aside—partly because some enthusiasts have carried them to excess—partly because they were supposed to be inimical to the effeminacy of shape and features so much prized by parents and progeny,—but chiefly, I suspect, from that languor and disinclination to exertion which characterize the higher and even the middle classes of female youth. This deficiency of exercise in the open air may be considered the parent of one-half of female disorders. The pallid complexions, the languid movements, the torpid secretions, the flaccid muscles and disordered functions (including glandular swellings), and consumption itself, attest the truth of this assertion.

The exercises of small children consist in giving them the largest lib erty and plenty of room. The cradle is a most pernicious method of exercising a child to sleep, and should be discarded from every family. For the ordinary or wakeful exercises of a child, the modern "baby jumper" will be found a preferable contrivance. Among the poorer classes, the children, for want of room to stir in, are apt to become sickly, puny, peevish, and often idiotic.

The best time for exercise is in the morning, an hour or so before breakfast, when the stomach is partially empty. If it should happen to be entirely empty, or nearly so, it should be fortified with a cracker or two, or some other light aliment. Vigorous evening exercises may also be employed by persons of sedentary habits with great advantage. "Night work," when mental or physical, is at once a violation of the natural order of things.

Thus, if you would preserve your health, you must take exercise, but not exercise exceeding your strength. Remember, the body must be induced to throw off its waste by action before it can be nourished. Nevertheless, it should also be remembered, that exercises of extreme severity are never required in ordinary cases of health, while in disease it must be incompatible with the strength and circumstances which surround the patient. With plentiful bodily exercise you can scarcely be ill,—without bodily exertion you cannot possibly be well. By "well," I mean the enjoyment of as much strength as may be consistent with your natural physique.

Exercise should be taken to the extent of quickened breathing and sensible perspiration. If in health, walk, when possible, at least from one to two miles every morning before breakfast. The invalid should go out into the open air, and ramble to the degree of strength he may possess, avoiding fatigue.

Exercise gives health, vigor, and cheerfulness, sound sleep and a keen appetite. Indeed, the effects of sedentary thoughtfulness are diseases that embitter and shorten life—interrupt rest—give tasteless meals, perpetual languor, and ceaseless anxiety.

Cheerful exercise, when at all practicable to be taken, whether active or passive, is absolutely an indispensable means to prevent or guard against disease, and to assist in the recuperative action of medicine when the body has become diseased.

Air and Sunshine.

As air may be said to be the very pabulum of life, it is highly essential that it should be pure,—inasmuch as any deterioration of it never fails to render the blood impure, and thus ultimately to affect both mind and body.

Air covers the entire globe, pressing alike upon land and water, having a depth of about forty-five miles. This vast ocean of air we call an atmosphere, from two Greek words, signifying vapor and space,—it being an immense fluid sphere or globe. This atmosphere presses upon man, and upon every object on the surface of the earth, with a force equal to fifteen pounds to every square inch. A man of average size has a sur face of two thousand five hundred square inches; accordingly, the air in which he lives presses upon him with a weight of eighteen tons. This would of course crush every bone in his body, but for the fluids within him, which establish an equilibrium, and leave him unoppressed.

Pure air contains seventy-nine parts of nitrogen and twenty-one parts of oxygen. If we add a single part more of oxygen to the air, it would no longer be atmospheric air, but *aqua fortis*, an element capable of destroying everything coming beneath its terrible power.

The quantity of air consumed by a man of average size at each inspiration, is from fifteen to forty cubic inches, according to the capacity of the lungs. Thus, in about an hour, a person consumes about six thousand and sixty-six pints, or two hogsheads of air. This air meets in the lungs in one hour, about one half of that amount of blood, or twenty-four in twenty-four hours. In other words, the quantity of blood which circulates through the system is estimated to be about one-eighth of the weight of the body. So that a man weighing one hundred and fifty pounds will have in his circulation about eighteen and three-quarter pounds of blood. The whole of this large quantity of blood has been proved, by careful experiment, to circulate through the blood-vessels in the almost incredible brief period of sixty-five and seventy-six one-hundredths seconds of time, and that is very little over one minute! This indeed seems wonderful, when we consider the vast extent of vessels it has to travel through; the arteries, the veins, and the minute capillaries through which it must be urged with no little force.

The physiology of the respiratory functions explains the relation of an abundant supply of air to the maintenance of health and the attainment of longevity. Fresh air in the lungs is so immediately essential to life, that most animals in less than one minute, when deprived of it, suffocate, become unconscious, and appear to be dead,--real death occurring in a few minutes if air is not supplied.

There are at least three objects to be accomplished by breathing, namely: the renewal of the blood and the taking of impurities out of it the warming of the body; and the finishing up of the process of digestion, and the change of chyle into nutritive blood. That carbonic acid and water are borne out of the lungs with every breath may be easily proved. If we breathe into lime-water, it will become white. This is owing to the carbonic acid in the breath uniting with the lime, and producing carbonate of lime. Then if we breathe upon a piece of glass, it becomes wet, showing that there is watery vapor in the breath. That the blood receives oxygen from the air we breathe, is proved by the fact that the in-going breath has one-fourth more oxygen in it than the out-going. The lungs, then, take out of all the air we breathe one-fourth of its oxygen. If we breathe it over a second, a third, or a fourth time, it not only has less oxygen each time, and is less useful for the purposes of respiration, but it becomes positively more hurtful by reason of the poisonous carbonic acid which, at every out-going breath, it carries with it from the lungs.

Equal in importance with the quantity of air we breathe is its purity. The supply of air for an ordinary man to breathe each minute, is from seven to ten cubic feet. Now, suppose a hundred persons to be confined in a room thirty feet in length, breadth, and height, the room containing nearly thirty thousand cubic feet, it follows that the whole air of the room would be rendered unfit for respiration on account of the vast volume of carbonic acid thrown out of the lungs and skin of the one hundred persons thus crowded together. This proves the importance of always having an abundant supply of pure atmospheric air always kept in circulation in crowded assemblies, churches, school-rooms, theatres, factories, workshops, and dwellings.

Consider the effect of sleeping in a small room, seven feet by nine, not furnished with the means of ventilation. If a person sleeps eight hours in such a room, he will spoil during the time one thousand nine hundred and twenty cubic feet of air, rendering the air of the room positively dangerous to breathe. Every disease is aggravated by the breathing of bad air! Yet it is common to close all the doors and windows where sick persons are confined, lest the patients should take cold. This is a bad practice. The sick should have plenty of fresh air. Their comfort is promoted by it, and their recovery hastened. It it utterly impossible for the lungs to be expanded in an impure atmosphere, because the air-passages, irritated by the extraneous particles, spasmodically contract to keep them out. The consequence of this is, those persons who reside permanently in an atmosphere charged with foreign ingredients or miasms, find their lungs continually contracting.

All sedentary habits weaken the abdominal muscles, and thereby lessen the activity of the breathing process. Intense mental application, if long continued, powerfully diminishes the respiratory functions. Persons habitually in deep thought, with the brain laboring at its utmost capacity, do not breathe deep and free, and are consequently short-lived. All crooked or constrained bodily positions affect respiration injuriously. Reading, writing, sitting, standing, speaking, or laboring, with the trunk of the body bent forward, is extremely hurtful. In all mechanical or manual labor, the body should be bent or lean on the hip joints. The trunk should always be kept straight. Dispense with bed-curtains, if you can. In sleep the head should never be raised very high, as that position oppresses the lungs; nor should the sleeper incline toward the face with the shoulders thrown forward.

Grates and fire-places secure much better ventilation than stoves. No stove, especially furnaces, should be used without the means of the free admission of external air into the room. Lamps, candles, gas-burners, etc., are so many methods of consuming oxygen and rendering the air irrespirable. Smoking lamps are a very common source of vitiated air. The bad air of steamboats, railroad cars, stages, omnibuses, etc., are a source of constant suffering to many. I may here remark that the general misapprehension of the theory of catching cold frequently produces the evil sought to be avoided. More colds are taken in overheated than in too cold places, and still more are owing to vitiated or foul air. In sleeping and other apartments, where thorough ventilation is impossible, the air may be rapidly changed and materially freshened, by opening all the doors and windows, and then swinging one door violently forward and backward. The rules of ventilation apply to all rooms and apartments alike, whether in dwelling-houses or travelling vehicles. There is no necessity for breathing air which has lost a part of its oxygen and acquired a portion of carbonic acid. The supply of good air is ample.

In connection with a full supply of atmospheric air to every human being, the importance of plenty of sunshine is not to be overlooked. Pure air for the lungs and bright sunlight for the eyes, is a physiological maxim which should never be forgotten. The nutritive process is materially checked in all vegetable and animal life when deprived of light for a considerable time. In the case of vegetables, they become etiolated or blanched. Almost the entire population of our large cities who occupy back rooms and rear buildings where the sun never shines, and cellars and vaults below the level of the ground, on the shaded side of narrow streets, is more or less diseased. Of those who do not die of acute diseases a majority exhibit unmistakable marks of imperfect development and deficient vitality. During the prevalence of epidemics, as the cholera, the shaded side of a narrow street invariably exhibits the greatest ratio of fatal cases. A certain amount of shade is essential to comfort, but when it reaches the point of excluding sunshine to a large degree, it becomes a positive evil. Let us always welcome the visits of the healthful air and glowing sunshine, and look out continually for the essential conditions of vigor and cheerfulness.

Old Age, or Longevity.

The true philosophy of life is to live and enjoy—to use and not abuse the essentials to human longevity and happiness. As we read in Holy Writ, in the earlier history of man, when the air was free from infection, the soil exempt from pollution, and man's food was plain and natural, individuals lived on the average four or five hundred years; the maximum point of longevity recorded—that in the case of Methuselah—being nine hundred and sixty-nine years. Without speculating upon the problem whether the years of the early historians included the same period of time as the years of our present almanac, it is sufficient for all practical purposes to know the general law, that human lives may be lengthened to one or two hundred years, or dwindled to the "shortest span," by our voluntary or individual habits. If it can be proved that any one man has lived one hundred, two hundred, or even three hundred years, under favorable hygienic circumstances, it will be sufficient evidence of a physiological principle that most men may attain to similar extreme longevity, by a mere simple obedience to the natural laws of his being.

The examples of extreme longevity are too numerous to be detailed even in a book of many pages, but a few examples may be cited on this point. Haller, the celebrated English physician, during his time collected more than one thousand cases of persons in Europe who attained the ages of from one hundred to one hundred and seventy years. In Baker's "Curse of England," we find a list of one hundred individuals whose ages ranged from ninety-five to one hundred and seventy! Twenty-two of these reached the age of one hundred and fifty and upwards, and thirty exceeded one hundred and twenty years. Modern statistics exhibit numerous examples of persons in the United States and all parts of the world attaining more than one hundred years. Indeed, it was common to the American Indians, previous to the introduction of "fire-water" among them, to live to one hundred years of age; although, as a general rule, the duration of life among savage races is much shorter than among the civilized and cultivated people of the globe.

In our present artificial state of society, it is not probable that one in a thousand persons dies a natural death. Alas! disease and violence sweep, with few exceptions, the entire human family to an untimely grave. Even the celebrated Thomas Parr, who died at one hundred and fifty-two years of age, came to an unnatural death by eating too heartily at a feast given in his honor by an English king; while Richard Lloyd, who was in full health and vigor at one hundred and thirty-two years, died soon after from being persuaded to eat flesh meat and drink malt liquor, to which he had never been accustomed in all his life before.

On physiological principles, natural death results from a gradual consolidation of the structures of the body. In infancy the fluids are in much larger proportion than the solids, but as we grow older the fluids decrease and the solids increase—thus gradually changing the flexibility and elasticity of youth to the stiffness and immobility of age. Thus in a perfectly normal condition of the organism, all the functions, powers and senses decline in the same harmonious relations in which they were developed. As the process of condensation goes on equally and imperceptibly, the motive powers grow torpid, the nutritive functions are enfeebled, the sensibility becomes dull, the external senses are obtunded, and lastly, the mental manifestations disappear—death occurs without a struggle or a groan.

Certain political and social economists have attempted to prove that old age and a vast population are not desirable things, on the ground that, while population increases geometrically, the alimentary productions of the earth only increase arithmetically; hence, that some scheme of death or destruction is requisite or indispensable to kill off, or clear the ground of existing human beings as fast as the coming generations demand their places. In other words, that it is necessary that disease, violence, pestilence, murder, wars, and death should prevail, because of the earth's incapacity to produce sufficient food for the whole race of human beings, were all permitted to live out their natural lives and die a natural death. A small amount of rational investigation will show the fallacies of all such theories. Indeed, under existing governments and social arrangements, more than three-fourths of all the lands and all the labor, so far as the production of the means of human sustenance is concerned, is literally wasted, or worse than wasted; while a large extent of the earth's surface has never yet been brought under cultivation, and that part which is cultivated the best admits of vast improvement.

Casting all speculation aside, it will not be denied that this earth was made the residence of man, and that God expressly enjoined upon him to be fruitful, and to occupy and replenish the earth, giving him at the same time dominion over all the vegetable and animal kingdoms, as a means for subsistence and happiness, while progressing through the gradual stages of his natural or terrestrial existence. Hence, the Creator did not bring man into existence without first furnishing him with the means of an abundant supply of all the elements requisite for a long life of health and joy. Man, however, has grossly violated the laws of nature, and blundered on in his perversity, till life has actually become a grievous burden, and extreme old age a great and moral curse instead of a divine and special blessing.

Were it necessary, a thousand reasons might be given for believing that the earth now has, and always will have, room and food enough for all the population that can be produced by human beings who live agreeably to the laws of their natural organisms. Indeed, it is a philosophical maxim that "intensive life cannot be extensive." The races of man have now a hurried, stimulated, forced and disorderly existence, marrying at too early an age, bringing myriads of children into the world, "scarce half made up," only to perish by thousands in the earliest infancy, or to drawl out a miserable and unhealthy existence, if their lives are prolonged to manhood's estate, and sink at last, even then, into premature graves, from continued and perverse abuses of the hygienic and dietetic rules of life.

As already said, if the body develops itself slowly and healthfully (as it always will in its natural state), it is only reasonable to suppose that the periods of infancy, childhood, and adolescence or maturity would be greatly prolonged by the more simple conformity to the original laws of our being; the period of youth might and would be extended to what we now call "old age," say "threescore and ten," and "threescore and ten" would be but the beginning of vigorous manhood to be indefinitely prolonged, reaching on to a hundred, or even two hundred years!

The special means to insure sound health and a long life are to avoid all errors in diet and personal habits. As the fluids and solids of the human organism are formed from the materials taken into the stomach as food and drink, it follows that we all ought to abstain more than we do from concentrated materials of aliment, and live more on fruits and vegetable substances, and fret ourselves less with the cares of the world; so all individuals would be able to maintain the juices of the body, and reduce, in a large degree, the solid elements which induce rigidity of muscles, thickening of membrane, contraction of organs, all leading to disease, premature debility, old age, and death.

Let us all then strive to return to the elementary principles of organic or human life. Let our diet be plain, simple, and of a juicy nature. Let us refrain from excesses of all kinds, whether connected with our mental or physical powers, and thereby secure a long lease on life, attended with a thousand blessings unknown to those who lead "fast lives," eat and drink immoderately, and indulge in the various forms of intemperate or luxurious habits. It is never too late to commence a reform in all these things. The oldest person now living might prolong his life to an indefinite period, by avoiding the errors named, and submitting himself to the prior-ordeal mandates of nature. To assist Nature in her work of regeneration and recuperation of the human organism, my "Renovating Pills" will be found of most wonderful efficacy in connection with the hygienic and dietetic requirements already indicated. They will thus prolong the period of youth to vigorous manhood, and vigorous manhood to the extremest limit of life ever yet vouchsafed to the human being. The already "old and feeble," so called, may be sure of having their lives greatly prolonged, and finally in the inevitable ordinances of Heaven, or the laws of gradual progress and decay, passing away with cheerful resignation and peace to that mysterious bourne from which no mortal traveller ever has returned.

LIFE, HEALTH, AND DISEASE

What is life? In general terms life may be said to be a subtle emanation of Deity—a principle that pervades all the works of creation, whether organic or inorganic. It is a sort of ENTITY, whose nature is as mysterious and unfathomable as that of Divinity himself. Many scientific men have contended that life is *electricity*, and arguments and experiments have been adduced to show that such is the fact. For instance, a scientific body of France pulverized stone, and by the use of electricity produced from the atoms living insects. But this and similar experiments are accepted as evidence that electricity is not life, but is a leading phenomenon of its actuality. Life is something neither physical nor spiritual. It is allied to both, but is neither. It is not soul, for soul is something infinitely higher than life—a something of which life itself is but an inadequate, visible manifestation.

Health is perhaps a subtle thing, yet most importantly palpable to our senses and perceptions. It is that state of the human body in which the structure of all the parts is sound, and their functions regularly and actively performed, rendering the individual fit for all the duties and enjoyments of life. Or, in other words, it is that condition of the animal economy when the functions of all the organs, beginning with the heart and lungs, act in natural and harmonious relation, the one with the other, and the whole together, rendering existence not only a state of completeness, but a pleasure, a beauty, and a charm, and therefore the chiefest cause and leading feature of all from which the human being derives that phase of joy called bliss. In the various temperaments the phenomena of health are somewhat different; hence, what would at once preserve it in one, might not preserve it in or restore it to another, until some reasonable period of time had elapsed. Health varies much in people of the many occupations which necessity and circumstances compel them to adopt for a livelihood or for pleasure, and the acuteness of the senses which would be necessary in some recreative or productive occupations, would be morbid in persons otherwise engaged. But the general symptoms of health are, in all temperaments, a sparkling eye, a clean skin, a white and rose-blended complexion (unless where the temperament naturally prescribes a rich and glowing olive), ruby lips, pearly teeth, untainted breath, glossy hair, expanded chest, elastic spine, muscular limbs, symmetrical waist, well built and firm pelvis, fleshy thighs and calves, and a buoyant grace of the whole body. Added to these we have a rich and melodious voice (wherever the slightest hoarseness or discordance of tone is noticed look for danger), and a calm and cultivated spirit in the old, a joyous spirit in the young. What munificent gifts are these, and who should fail, by every means in his power, to secure them? Disease is the opposite of health.

and means any departure from the normal condition of the general organism, or any impairment or derangement of any function by which the regular action of any other one or of the whole are made or forced to work in an irregular or unnatural manner—producing and entailing disorder, pain, misery, and death! We see disease in the lustreless and phrenzied eye, in the pallid and sunken cheeks, in the parched lips, in the jaundiced or yellow skin, in the contracted chest, in the difficult respiration, in the racking cough, in the expectoration of tubercles and sputa from the lungs, in the palpitating heart, in the scrofulous sores and ulcers, in the bloated or attenuated abdomen, in the disabled legs and arms, in decayed teeth and toothless jaws, in fetid breath, in crooked spine, in the deformed pelvis, in all derangements of the sexual organs, in baldness, in disordered stomach and bowels, in neuralgias, rheumatisms, leprosies, spasms, epilepsies, palsies, loss of the senses of sight, hearing, smelling, taste and touch, hypochondrias, manias, drunkenness, pains, aches, wounds, bruises, maimings, and in innumerable other agonies! With the simple methods by which health can be preserved by those who were born to health, how astonishing it is that disease and misery are the general rule, and health and pleasure the exception! Who of all the human race may now say, "I have health! I am actually living in a state of nature, or in that perfect mental and physical condition in which I was or ought to have been born." Not one, is my reply. We may therefore regard life as a negative rather than a positive quality of existence. Occasionally there may be freedom from the slightest degree of actual suffering, and yet that pleasurable condition which would be natural to the regular co-operative work of all the organs of the body will be wanting.

In health our moments fly on lightning wing, and we are scarcely conscious of their rapid exit; in sickness, on the contrary, our moments are clogged with leaden heels, and pass in that lingering manner as to render our sufferings seemingly the more acute by reason of the slow or tardy march of time. To the sick, time does not pass lightly, but with the heavy tread of a giant.

How inestimable is that state of being comprehended under the name of health!—yet how few are ever led to consider its priceless value and importance. Health, perfect health, is not to be found in our present age among the races of men; yet even in its negative aspect, its most deteriorated quality, what were all the joys, all the riches, all the advantages of this world without its possession? Unless all, from the highest to the lowest, from the king to the beggar, learn to prize health and avoid disease,—death, who is no respecter of persons, will continue to reap his rich harvests among them all. Cæsar could not escape, nor could the renown of a thousand victories diffuse an anodynic or soporific influence over the pillow of the great Napoleon, nor save the laurels of

Marengo from the blighting mists of St. Helena! Intellectual cultivation oftentimes sows the seeds of physical deterioration. When we see that the prince is equally liable to the same physical and mental miseries as the vagrant, it becomes everybody to bear in remembrance the axiom that a sound body is the natural basis of a sound mind, and *vice versa*, and that every rational method should be adopted to preserve them. I have shown briefly that there is no condition or state of man that is exempt from disease and death. It may now be asked, Are there no means of preventing the ravages of the one, and postponing the sad triumph of the other? No means of restoring lost health, or of rendering sickness compatible with contentment, or even happiness itself? Yes. The severest diseases are and may be prevented; and are curable and cured—even consumption itself when judicious treatment is applied. All right-thinking persons will admit that sickness may be obviated, disease mitigated, and even death robbed of his prey for years, by approved remedies rightly employed.

Regulating the Passions.

It has been truly said that we may religiously observe all the laws of hygiene in relation to air, light, drink, food, temperature, exercise, clothing, sleep, bathing, and the excretions, and yet lack one thing—one grand essential to human health and happiness. Yes, if our passions are our masters and not our slaves, they will rule and ruin us instead of obeying and serving our behests. There is, therefore, no single hygienic influence more conducive to health, happiness, and long life, than a cheerful, equitable temper of mind; and there is nothing that will more surely disorder the bodily functions, exhaust the vital energies, and stamp premature infirmities on the constitution, and hurry us on to an early grave, than an uneven, irritable, fretful, or passionate mental habit.

Medical men, at least, well know that a violent fit of passion will suddenly arrest, alter, or modify the various organic secretions. Excessive mental emotion will deprave and vitiate the secretions as readily as a deadly poison taken into the stomach. A paroxysm of anger will render the bile as acid and irritating as a full dose of calomel; excessive fear will relax the bowels equal to a strong infusion of tobacco; intense grief will arrest the secretions of gastric juice as effectually as belladonna; and violent rage will make the saliva as poisonous as will a mercurial salivation. There are many persons whose rage, either thoroughly real or exaggerated, is so violent that they froth at the mouth, and are thrown into spasms or violent convulsions. These fits of anger are often assumed, however, by designing parties for the purpose of frightening stern parents and guardians and others into the support of their own views and wishes. Such persons, finding their displays copied from nature of no avail, will suddenly become tame as lambs, but the effect upon their general health is found in the appearance of many nervous disorganizations, which, if the cause be often repeated, become permanent.

Thousands of facts of the above kind could be mentioned, but enough has been presented to demonstrate the law that a sound body cannot exist unless connected with a well-balanced mind. A vigorous exercise of the higher mental powers, a lively cultivation of the intellectual faculties and the moral affections, will never fail to sustain and elevate the human character, while, on the other hand, the violent indulgence of the animal propensities and the lower order of the passions, will wear out the mental machinery and enervate all the physiological powers. Will not the inspiration of love exalt the soul to the realms of "bliss, exquisite bliss?" Will not the influence of hatred depress the soul, and sink it to the nethermost depth of misery and despair? Contrast the emotions of benevolence, or gratitude, or veneration, or conscientiousness, or mirthfulness, or faith, or hope, with that of envy, revenge, jealousy, fear, grief, remorse, or despair! The first are as refreshing to the soul as the gentle dews of morn to the tender blades of grass; the other as withering as the fiery blasts of a crater to the verdant vales. The one energizes the mind and reanimates the body—the other sinks, chills, and enfeebles both; one manufactures, creates as it were, vital power—the other wastes and destroys body and soul.

Those who would maintain permanent and uniform health and live to an old age, will perceive the necessity for cultivating all the nobler impulses of our nature with unremitting care and judgment. When we "nourish wrath to keep it warm," we only add to the venom of a malicious heart. That anger which "dwells only in the bosom of fools," should have no inheritance in the bosom of the wise and thoughtful of our race. The "evils of life," whatever they may be, are often "blessings in disguise," and therefore should be met with a brave fortitude and courage, instead of wailing, complaining and lamentation. Fretting, scolding, and fault-finding, not only aggravate all the necessary evils of life, but greatly multiply them. When we indulge in these faults, we but sow the dragon's teeth to reap a harvest of greater sorrows. More than this, we dissipate unwisely our best talents and energies, and render life a curse instead of a blessing. The grand essential, therefore, of a cheerful mind is self-control. This is the great law of mental hygiene. Before any one can acquire self-government, he must learn to govern the animal propensities, and make them subservient to the intellectual faculties and moral sentiments. It may require long, patient, and thorough discipline; it may cost much self-denial, and appear to demand great temporary sacrifices, but it is worth all it may cost. Occasionally it is acquired through long years of bitter experience; and sometimes the greater part of a life is spent in suffering disappointments, troubles, and crosses, ere the mind is found at peace with itself, and in right relations to all surrounding nature. Happy are they who can, even in such expensive schools, learn the art of adapting themselves to the invariable laws of the universe, which they cannot successfully oppose or in any respect alter! Indeed, the only guarantee a man can have for a long life of health and happiness is to constantly cherish and maintain an even, cheerful, and hopeful spirit.

Things for the Sick-Room.

Barley Water.—Pearl barley, two ounces; boiling water, two quarts. Boil to one quart and strain. If desirable, a little lemon-juice and sugar may be added. This may be taken freely in all inflammatory and eruptive diseases: Measles, Scarlet Fever, Small-Pox, etc.

Rice Water.—Rice, two ounces; water, two quarts. Boil one hour and a half, and add sugar and nutmeg to suit the taste. When milk is added to this it makes a very excellent diet for children. Should the bowels be too loose, boil the milk before adding.

Sage Tea.—Dried leaves of Sage, half an ounce; boiling water, one quart. Infuse for half an hour and strain; may add sugar if desired. Balm, Peppermint, Spearmint, and other teas are made in the same manner.

A Refreshing Drink in Fevers.—Boil an ounce and a half of tamarinds, two ounces of stoned raisins, and three ounces of cranberries in three pints of water until two pints remain. Strain, and add a small piece of fresh lemon-peel, which must be removed in half an hour.

Arrow Root Jelly.—Stir a tablespoonful of arrow root powder into half a cupful of cold water, pour in a pint of boiling water, let it stand five or ten minutes, and then sweeten and flavor it to suit the taste.

Irish Moss Jelly.—Irish Moss, half an ounce; fresh milk, one and a half pints. Boil down to a pint. Strain and add sugar and lemon-juice sufficient to give it an agreeable flavor.

Isinglass Jelly.—Isinglass, two ounces; water, two pints. Boil to one point. Strain, and add one pint milk and one ounce of white sugar. This is excellent for persons recovering from sickness, and for children who have bowel complaints.

Tapioca Jelly.—Tapioca, two large spoonfuls; water, one pint. Boil gently for an hour, or until it appears like a jelly; add sugar, wine, and nutmeg, with lemon-juice to flavor.

Rice Jelly.—Mix a quarter of a pound of rice, picked and washed, with half a pound of loaf sugar, and just sufficient water to cover it

Boil until it assumes a jelly-like appearance. Strain, and season to suit the taste and condition of the patient.

GRAPES.—In all cases of fever, very ripe grapes of any kind are a beneficial article of diet, acting as both food and drink, and possessing cooling and soothing properties. They are also extremely grateful to every plate.

TOAST.—To make a most excellent toast for a reduced or convalescent patient, take bread twenty-four or thirty-six hours old, which has been made of a mixture of fine wheat flour and Indian meal, and a pure yeast batter mixed with eggs. Toast it until of a delicate brown, and then (if the patient be not inclined to fever) immerse it in boiled milk and butter. If the patient be feverish, spread it lightly with cranberry jam or calves'-foot jelly.

RICE.—In all cases where a light and nice diet for parties who have been or are afflicted with diarrhœa or dysentery is required, rice, in almost any cooked form, is most agreeable and advantageous. It may be given with benefit to dyspeptics, unless costiveness accompanies the dyspepsia. To make rice-pudding, take a teacupful of rice, and as much sugar, two quarts of milk, and a teaspoonful of salt. Bake, with a moderate heat, for two hours. Rice flour made in a batter, and baked upon a griddle, makes a superb cake; and rice-flour gruel, seasoned to the taste, is most excellent for the sick-room.

BREAD JELLY.—Boil a quart of water and let it cool. Take one-third of a common loaf of wheat bread, slice it, pare off the crust, and toast it to a light brown. Put it in the water in a covered vessel, and boil gently, till you find, on putting some in a spoon to cool, the liquid has become a jelly. Strain and cool. When used, warm a cupful, sweeten with sugar, and add a little grated lemon-peel.

RICE GRUEL.—Ground rice, one heaping table-spoonful; water, one quart. Boil gently for twenty minutes, adding, a few minutes before it is done, one table-spoonful of ground cinnamon. Strain and sweeten. Wine may be added when the case demands it.

WATER GRUEL.—Oat or corn meal, two table-spoonfuls; water, one quart. Boil for ten minutes, and strain, adding salt and sugar if desired by the patient.

SAGO GRUEL.—Sago, two table-spoonfuls; water, one pint. Boil gently until it thickens; stir frequently. May add wine, sugar, and nutmeg, according to circumstances.

ARROW-ROOT GRUEL.—Arrow root, one table-spoonful; sweet milk and boiling water, each one half pint. Sweeten with loaf-sugar. This is very good for children whose bowels are irritable.

DECOCTION OF BRAN.—New wheat bran, one pint; water, three quarts. Boil down to two quarts, strain off the liquor, and add sugar, honey or molasses, according to the taste of the patient.

TAPIOCA.—Tapioca is a very delightful food for invalids. Make an ordinary pudding of it, and improve the flavor agreeably to the desire of the patient or convalescent, by adding raisins, sugar, prunes, lemon-juice, wine, spices, etc.

BEEF LIQUID.—When the stomach is very weak, take fresh lean beef, cut it into strips, and place the strips into a bottle, with a little salt. Place into a kettle of boiling water and let it remain one hour. Pour off the liquid and add some water. Begin with a small quantity, and use in the same manner and under similar circumstances as beef tea. This is even more nourishing than beef tea.

BEEF TEA.—Cut one pound of lean beef into shreds, and boil for twenty minutes in one quart of water, being particular to remove the scum as often as any rises. When it is cool, strain. This is very nourishing and palatable, and is of great value in all cases of extreme debility where no inflammatory action exists, or after the inflammation is subdued. In very low cases, a small tea-spoonful may be administered every fifteen or twenty minutes, gradually increasing the amount given as the powers of life return. In cases of complete prostration, after the cessation of long exhausting fever, it may be used as directed above, either alone or in conjunction with a little wine.

PANADO.—Put a little water on the fire with a glass of wine, some sugar, and a little grated nutmeg; boil all together a few seconds, and add pounded crackers or crumbs of bread; and again boil for a few minutes.

FRENCH MILK PORRIDGE.—Stir some oatmeal and water together, let the mixture stand to clear, and pour off the water. Then put more water to the meal, stir it well, and let it stand till the next day. Strain through a fine sieve, and boil the water, adding milk while so doing. The proportion of water must be small. With toast this is admirable.

COMMON MILK PORRIDGE will be found very palatable in ordinary cases. Everybody knows how to make it.

BUTTERMILK PAP.—Fresh buttermilk, four parts; water, one part: mix, boil, and thicken with Indian meal. Eat with butter, sugar, or molasses.

COFFEE MILK.—Put a dessert-spoonful of ground coffee into a pint of milk; boil it a quarter of an hour with a shaving or two of isinglass, let it stand ten minutes, and then pour off.

RESTORATIVE JELLY.—Take a leg of well-fed pork, just as cut up, beat it, and break the bone. Set it over a gentle fire, with three gallons of water, and simmer to one. Let half an ounce of mace and the same of nutmegs stew in it. Strain through a fine sieve. When cold, take off the fat. Give a chocolate-cup the first and last thing, and at noon, adding salt to suit the taste. This is very valuable in all cases of debility where animal food is admissible.

DRINK IN DYSENTERY.—Sheep's suet, two ounces; milk, one pint; starch, half an ounce. Boil gently for thirty minutes. Use as a common drink. This is excellent for sustaining the strength in bad cases of dysentery.

CRUST COFFEE.—Toast slowly a thick piece of bread cut from the outside of a loaf, until it is well browned, but not blackened. Then turn upon it boiling water of a sufficient quantity, and keep it from half an hour to an hour before using. Be sure that the liquid is of a rich brown color before you use it. It is a most excellent drink in all cases of sickness and convalescence.

CRANBERRY WATER.—Put a tea-spoonful of cranberries into a cup of water and mash them. In the mean time boil two quarts of water with one large spoonful of corn or oatmeal, and a bit of lemon-peel; then add the cranberries and as much fine sugar as will leave a smart flavor of the fruit – also a wine-glassful of sherry. Boil the whole gently for a quarter of an hour, then strain.

WINE WHEY.—Heat a pint of new milk until it boils, at which moment pour in as much good wine as will curdle and clarify it. Boil and set it aside until the curd subsides. Do not stir it, but pour the whey off carefully, and add two pints of boiling water, with loaf-sugar.

ORANGE WHEY.—Milk, one pint; the juice of an orange, with a portion of the peel. Boil the milk, then put the orange to it, and let stand till it coagulates. Strain.

MUSTARD WHEY.—Bruised mustard seed, two table-spoonfuls; milk, one quart. Boil together for a few minutes until it coagulates, and strain to separate the curd. This is a very useful drink in dropsy. A tea-cupful may be taken at a dose, three times a day.

SIPPETS.—On an extremely hot plate put two or three slices of bread, and pour over them some of the juices of boiled beef, mutton, or veal. If there be no butter in the dish, sprinkle over them a little salt.

CHICKEN BROTH.—Take half a chicken, divested of all fat, and break the bones; add to this half a gallon of water, and boil for half an hour. Season with salt.

VEGETABLE SOUP.—Take one potato, one turnip and one onion, with a little celery or celery seed. Slice and boil for an hour in one quart of water. Salt to the taste, and pour the whole upon a piece of dry toast. This forms a good substitute for animal food, and may be used when the latter would be improper.

CALVES'-FOOT JELLY.—Boil two calves' feet in one gallon of water, until reduced to one quart. Strain, and when cool, skim carefully. Add the white of six or eight eggs, well beaten, a pint of wine, half pound of loaf sugar, and the juice of four lemons. Mix them well, boil for a few minutes, stirring constantly, and pass through a flannel strainer. In some cases the wine should be omitted.

SLIPPERY ELM JELLY.—Take of the flour of slippery elm one or two tea-spoonfuls; cold water, one pint. Stir, until a jelly is formed. Sweeten with loaf sugar or honey. This is excellent for all diseases of the throat, chest, and lungs, coughs, colds, bronchitis, inflammation of lungs, etc. It is very nutritious and soothing.

NUTRITIVE FLUIDS.—Below will be found directions for preparing three nutritious fluids, which are of great value in all diseases, either acute or chronic, that are attended or followed by prostration,—debility, whether general, or of certain organs only, derangement of the digestive organs, weak stomach, indigestion, heartburn, or sour stomach, constipated bowels, torpidity or want of activity of the liver, thin or poor blood. They are highly nutritious, supplying to the blood in such a form that they are most easily assimilated, the various elements which are needed to enrich it, and thus enable it to reproduce the various tissues of the body that have been wasted by disease. In cases where the stomach has become so weakened and sensitive that the lightest food or drinks cannot be taken without causing much uneasiness and distress, these fluids are invaluable. They strengthen the stomach and neutralize all undue acidity, while, at the same time, they soothe the irritation by their bland and demulcent qualities. When carefully and properly prepared, according to the direction following, they very nearly resemble rich new milk in color and consistency, while their taste is remarkably pleasant. Care should be taken that all the ingredients are of the best quality. Soft water must be used in all cases. Fresh rain-water is to be preferred, but spring water may be used if perfectly soft. Hard water will cause the fluids to be of a yellow color, and if the milk is old, they are apt to separate.

Fluid No. 1.—Put one pint of new milk (the fresher the better) and two pints of soft water in a vessel perfectly free from all greasy matter, over a slow fire. Rub two even tea-spoonfuls of superfine wheat flour and two tea-spoonfuls of carbonate of magnesia, together with a little milk, into a soft batter, free from lumps; add this to the milk and water as soon as they begin to boil. Boil gently for five minutes—*no longer* stirring constantly. Pour into an earthen or glass dish to cool, adding, at the same time, two tea-spoonfuls of loaf sugar, and one tea-spoonful each of saleratus and table salt, rubbed fine; stir until cold. The fluid must not be allowed to remain in a metallic vessel of any kind, and it must be kept in a cool place.

Fluid No. 2.—Put one pint of fresh milk and two pints of soft water in a vessel over a slow fire. Rub together with a little fresh cream into a soft batter, free from lumps, one table-spoonful each of good sweet rye flour, ground rice, and pure starch—which add to the milk and water as soon as they begin to boil. Boil for five minutes, stirring constantly. Remove from the fire, and add three tea-spoonfuls of loaf sugar and one tea-spoonful each of saleratus and table salt. Observe the same precautions as in No. 1.

Fluid No. 3.—Put in a vessel, over a slow fire, one pint of fresh milk and two pints of soft water. When they begin to boil, add one table-spoonful of wheat flour, two table-spoonfuls pure starch, and two tea-spoonfuls of carbonate of magnesia, rubbed together with a little milk into a soft batter, free from lumps. Boil gently for five minutes, stirring constantly. Pour into an earthen vessel to cool, and add one tea-spoonful of the best gum arabic, dissolved in a little warm water, one tea-spoonful each of saleratus and table salt, and one table-spoonful of pure strained honey. Stir until cold. The same precaution must be observed as in preparing No. 1.

Directions.—One half pint or less of these fluids may be taken at a dose, and at least three pints should be taken during the day, and the amount gradually increased to two or three quarts. Commence with No. 1, and use two weeks: then use No. 2 for the same length of time, after which No. 3 is to be used for two weeks. Continue their use as long as necessary, taking each for two weeks before changing. In all the diseases enumerated above, the use of these fluids, in connection with proper herbal remedies, will ensure a speedy restoration to health.

GUM ACACIA RESTORATIVE.—Take two ounces of pure white gum Arabic,—procure the lump, the powdered is very apt to be adulterated,—pulverize it well, and dissolve by the aid of a gentle heat in a gill of water, stirring constantly. When it is entirely dissolved, add three table-spoonfuls of pure strained honey. Let it remain over the fire until it becomes of the consistency of a jelly. The heat must be very gentle, it must not boil. If desirable, flavor with lemon or vanilla. This will be found a very pleasant article of diet for delicate stomachs. When the articles used are pure it will be transparent and of a light golden color. This will be borne by the weakest stomach, when everything else is rejected. It is *highly nutritious.*

MALT INFUSION.—Infuse one pint of ground malt, for two hours, in three pints of scalding water. The water should not be brought quite to the boiling point. Strain, add sugar, if desired; flavor with lemon-juice. This is an excellent drink in inflammatory fevers, acute rheumatism, etc.

PEAS.—Take young and fresh shelled green peas, wash them clean, put them into fresh water, just enough to cover them, and boil them till they take up nearly all the water. Season with salt, pepper, and butter. This dish, if prepared according to directions, and eaten warm, will not harm any invalid—not even one suffering from diarrhœa.

MILK.—In some cases where a milk diet is advisable, owing to the peculiar condition of the patient's stomach, it will cause distress. This is frequently the case when there is undue acidity. In such cases let it be prepared in the following manner, and it will be found to set well:—Take a tea-cupful of fresh milk, heat nearly to boiling; dissolve in it a tea-spoonful of loaf sugar; pour into a large-sized tumbler, and add sufficient plain soda-water to fill it. Prepared in the above directed manner it will be perfectly free from all unpleasant effects.

SOUPS FOR THE CONVALESCENT.—To extract the strength from meat, long and slow boiling is necessary; but care must be taken that the pot is never off the boil. All soups should be made the day before they are used, and they should then be strained into earthen pans. When soup has jellied in the pan, it should not be removed into another. When in danger of not keeping, it should be boiled up.

EGGS.—In cases of extreme debility, eggs are most excellent. They should never be boiled hard. The best way to prepare them is to beat them well with milk and sugar. Where it will be appropriate to the case, add some fine pale sherry wine.

MILK FOR INFANTS.—Fresh cow's milk, one part; water, two parts; sweeten with a very little loaf sugar. When children are raised by hand, it is always necessary to dilute the milk. As the child advances in age, the proportion of water stated above may be gradually lessened.

WATER GRUEL.—Corn or oatmeal, two table-spoonfuls; water, one quart. Boil ten or fiteen minutes, and strain. Add salt and sugar to suit the taste of the patient. This should be used freely, during and after the operation of cathartic medicines.

HOW TO ASSIST THE DOCTOR.

THE SICK-ROOM.

IF there is a choice of rooms, the patient's welfare demands that he should be placed in the one affording to a greater degree light, pure air, warmth, etc. The patient should not be put into the room which is dark and gloomy, but let it be one that is light and cheerful, and with a fire-place in it, if possible.

If the illness be fever, an ophthalmic affection, brain disease, or other disease requiring quiet, a back room away from the family should be selected, as quiet is absolutely necessary, and the patient will not care to look at anything or to speak much. If, however, he be suffering from an accident, he will be more contented and cheerful if he is placed near to the rest of the family, where he can assist in the conversation, watch your movements, and see you at your labors. It will greatly tend to make him forget to a greater extent his misfortune. and it will also save time in waiting upon him.

The room should be free from all unpleasant odors, and should not be exposed to disagreeable effluvia from water-closets, sinks, etc. The furniture of the room should be but very simple and plain, and, in infectious diseases, but very little should be placed in the room. If you have ever been in a hospital, you may have noticed the bare floors, the iron bedsteads, the absence of woollen bed-clothing, and the plain tables, and most probably pitied the inmates for their lack of comforts, and involuntarily the thought may have arisen in your mind that fortune is more propitious to you when sick, for your sick-room wouldhave at least a good carpet, upholstered furniture, and your bed an easy one to repose upon, and plentifully supplied with woollen blankets, etc. But *you* and many more are also deluded in this respect. If you will bear in mind that woollen fabrics retain *smells* much longer than cotton and linen, and are therefore less sanitary, you would probably not consider them so advantageous. The room should have no upholstered chairs or sofas, cane-bottomed or plain wood are preferable, and it would be better if no carpet was on the floor, except perhaps a narrow strip for you to walk upon to prevent noise, but a clean boarded floor, kept clean and sweet by scrubbing and "elbow-grease" is infinitely better. It is better to have no curtains; but if the room looks too cheerless without them, use light muslin or something which will easily wash.

The position of the bed is also very important. In case of accident the bed should be placed where the patient feels most comfortable, only it should be placed where there is a good light to see and dress the wound; but in fever and small-pox the bed should occupy the position between the door and fire-place. The reason for this is, that as fire cannot burn without air, there must be a draft to feed it; as this becomes heated and escapes up the chimney, it is replaced by a fresh supply drawn in through the door and window. This prevents a spread of the disease, as the chimney acts as a ventilating shaft, carrying away the impurities of the room. A stove will also do this, but to a much less extent. It is very apparent, therefore, that if a person stands between the bed and the fire-place, he must breathe air laden with the effluvia from the patient, whereas, on the other side, that is, between the bed and door, he inhales air that has not yet come in contact with the patient. If, from the form of the room, the bed cannot be placed in this position, the space between the window and the bed should always be sufficient to stand in.

The room should always be fully prepared before the patient is placed in it, as the setting it to rights is not only annoying, but may do positive harm to the patient. The fire, if any is wanted, should particularly be previously built, for very often the chimney refuses to draw well, and the poor patient is choked with the smoke. He may suffer from a chest complaint, and his difficulty of breathing be so aggravated as to put him in a miserable plight. The windows should not be so fastened that you cannot open them, especially from the top. An equable temperature should be kept up, neither too hot nor too cold, and extremes avoided.

The bed itself is very worthy of consideration. Unqualifiedly, the best is a hair mattrass, but, as this is so expensive, it cannot be expected to be found in every house, but, unless obliged, use no feather bed. It is too soft, and the patient sinks into holes, so that, in case of wounds or burns, you cannot get at them properly, and besides, if the feathers get wet, you cannot easily put them right again. Good clean straw or chaff, evenly packed, is far superior. It costs but little, to begin with, is more comfortable, far superior in a sanitary point of view, and has this advantage: that in case of being spoiled, it can be emptied, the cover washed, and refilled without loss of time, and at a very trifling expense.

The bed should not be too wide, for if the patient needs help, the attendant is obliged to move him kneeling on the bed, or at arms' length, should he be lying in the middle.

It is often a matter of much concern how to change the bed-clothing in case of fracture or low states of disease, where the patient cannot be moved from the bed. The following method should be pursued:—roll up the clothes to be changed tightly to the middle, lengthwise, not across the bed; put on the clean things with half the width rolled up close to the other roll, lift the patient on the newly made part, slip off the soiled clothes, unroll the clean ones, and the bed is made.

Before the patient is put to bed scour the floor right well, and wash it with hot water with a few pennies' worth of chloride of lime, or, if you cannot get this, use a little quicklime, and rub it well into cracks and corners. The whole of the lime need not be removed, as the little particles left sticking in the cracks and pores of the wood will prevent insects, give a clean, sweet smell to the place, and tend to keep away infection. After the room is thoroughly dried, it is ready for the sick occupant.

If all this is done, you will have the *healthiest* sick-chamber possible, and rob the disease of its exciting causes. He must then be well nursed, and as this is so important, the author will next consider

Nurses and Nursing.

Next to the physician, the nurse has responsibilities that must be faithfully discharged, as the life of the patient is not alone dependent upon the skill of the physician, but in a great measure also upon careful nursing. Every physician will tell you that he recollects cases in his practice where all his skill would have been unavailing had it not been for the excellent nursing that the patient received.

It is a common opinion that women only can nurse. This is erroneous. as men are frequently met with, especially husbands and brothers, who are quite as gentle in their touch, quite as considerate about little wants, and far more tender and thoughtful than almost any woman. A male nurse has, moreover, one great advantage—his strength. Ask that wife who requires lifting from the bed, and she will tell how safe she feels in her husband's strong arms, and what a comfort it is to be lifted by him. It is a dreadful feeling for a patient not to have full confidence in the power of the person assisting, and the nervous shock induced by the fear of being let fall, may take days to recover from. It is, therefore, not to be thought that nursing is peculiarly woman's work, but that men are just as capable.

A nurse should have five qualifications—*sobriety*, *cleanliness*, *firmness*, *gentleness*, and *patience.*

Sobriety.—The drunken nurse should not be allowed to cross the door-sill of the sick-room. It is no place for her,—she cannot be trusted. Human life is too precious to be entrusted to the care of one who cannot resist the temptation to indulge in intoxicating drinks.

Cleanliness.—The nurse should not only keep the room clean, but always be clean herself. A very little thing will spoil the appetite of a sick person, and nothing offensive, as dressings from wounds or burns, should be allowed to remain in the room. All necessary vessels should be emptied as soon as done with, well washed out, and left in the open air. It should be remembered that bad air is just as poisonous to a person as bad food, and hence it should be frequently changed by opening the window. The dreaded draft will do no harm, but bears upon its wings the elements conducive to the health of both patient and attendants. The fever-poison is weakened by admixture with pure air just in the same proportion as spirits are weakened by the addition of water. The food that the patient cannot eat should not be left in the room—it will breed distaste for it if always in the sight of the patient. The drinking-water should be frequently changed, as it absorbs all the gases in the room, so that if the patient is allowed to drink it, it actually puts back into his stomach what his body exhaled. Always give him fresh water, then, when he wants to drink.

Firmness.—The lesson that firmness is not rudeness should be learned first. It is not to be expected that a suffering person knows as well what is best for him as those whose brains are clear. If, therefore, a certain thing is best to be done, do it, do it kindly, but do it, and the patient will thank you afterwards.

Gentleness.—It should never be forgotten that gentleness is an absolute requirement of a nurse. If the poor patient suffers from rheumatism or a broken limb, and the bed-clothes must be changed, it should be done gently, and all needless suffering avoided. If his position in bed requires change, do not torture him, but gently move him, and avoid all jerks and knocks with great care.

Patience.—Need a word be said to the effect that of all beings nurses should especially be patient? It should never be forgotten that the difference is a great one between the nurse and the person under his or her care, and it should be remembered that in their own experiences they have been cross and irritable even when they were well, that they were easily put out, and so peevish and fretful from the slightest causes. They should then consider how it must be with the person taken suddenly from active life and compelled to lie still in one position, or with one whose whole body is racked with pain. The one, therefore, who loses patience, however sorely tried, and who cannot bear with these trials for a while, should stay away from the sick-room in the capacity of nurse.

Nursing, in a great measure, is a natural gift either in man or woman, just as much as music, painting, and other things are. It is not every one, therefore, who is fit for a nurse, not because they wilfully do wrong, but they are not adapted for it. There are many good-hearted yet thoughtless people who would never make good, handy nurses with all the training in the world.

The *awkward* nurse is a queer creature, and she is everlastingly getting into some trouble. If she is going up stairs with her hands full, she is sure to step on the bottom of her dress, and either drops what she is carrying or falls herself. If the fire wants coal, she throws on a whole scuttleful, a good part of which falls upon the fender, and the poor patient is so terrified that he cannot rest for hours. If she has a hole in her dress, or a bit of braid is loose, it will be sure to catch a chair or the fire-irons, bringing them down with a rattle. If of matronly age and wears caps, she will have strings so long that when she stoops over to catch the patient's whisper, the ends will tickle his nose or other parts of his face. At least one of her fingers is sure to be enveloped in a rag tied on with black cotton. If the patient wants a little bread and butter, the knife that has been used for cutting cheese or peeling onions is unerringly used. If she is cooking cabbage or frying bacon in the next room, she always forgets to close the door leading to the patient's room, fills it with a strong smell which sickens him, and then says that it is *too bad* that the patient cannot eat a morsel of food. If the patient thirsts, she will fill the glass full to the brim, put her hand under his head, bend his neck till his chin touches his breast, then puts the glass to his lips, spills a good part of it on his clothes, and thinks he is very awkward to choke over a mouthful of water. If a candle is to be lighted, she sticks it in between the bars of the grate, which soon fills the room with the rank smell of burning tallow, and when she finally succeeds in lighting it, she finds she has a wick several inches long.

gained at the expense of the melted tallow; or if it be gas, she takes a short bit of paper, turns the gas full on, makes a sudden blaze like a flash of lightning, forgets the bit of paper in her hand while she is regulating the blaze, burns her fingers, throws the lighted paper on the floor, and puts her foot on it. All this does not escape the patient's notice, and he gets so nervous and frightened that he loses his night's rest. If the patient is so far convalescent as to be able to sit up in bed to take his food, she will, of course, put the tray on his knees, then assist him into the sitting posture, and ten chances to one the things are upset all over the counterpane.

Then there is the *fussy nurse*, and there are many of this sort. Her zeal to benefit the patient is so great, that she sadly overdoes it: she bustles in and out of the room every few minutes, wearies the patient by persistently asking him if he cannot eat something, which she would willingly walk miles to get if wanted, raising him up, tucking in the bed clothes, drawing up and lowering the blinds; one, in fact, who is perfectly miserable if she is not constantly on the move. The fussy nurse is generally a kind-hearted, loving creature, and it is her very goodness which makes her weary the patient, who congratulates himself on the relief gained whenever she vacates the room.

Then we have the *careless, slovenly nurse.* Doctors are always suspicious of this person; they can never feel sure that their patients really had the right quantity of medicine; if she happened to remember it they would get it, but if not, she would make up for it by giving a double dose next time. There is no clean glass or cup when wanted. Food is taken to the patient, and if he cannot eat it, it is left there for hours. There are so many crumbs of bread in the bed that it feels to the patient like lying on a gravel walk. Cinders cover the hearth all over, and the fire is black. The slops, which should have been removed in the evening, are hid under the bed, filling the room with bad smells. Those bits of meat, crumbs of bread, and other matters which have fallen on the floor are left there; the consequence is, that being winter, the mice and perhaps rats finding a warm room and something to eat, think it a comfortable place, and use it accordingly. No one can imagine the degree of comfort these scampering animals afford to the helpless creature in bed.

Next we have the *cruel nurse*, who does her duty, but not from love; she carries out the doctor's orders exactly. In matter of duty she is inflexible; if the medicine has to be taken at a certain time, she brings it to the minute, and worries the patient into taking it on the instant. Her law in all things is like that of the Medes and Persians, which altereth not. She may be perfectly honest in her dealings, but the utter absence of tenderness and compassion makes her an undesirable nurse.

And lastly, we have what I trust is a very rare character, the *dishonest nurse.* She drinks all the wine, and partakes pretty freely of the food intended for the patient, and tells the doctor that the patient ought to get better according to the quantity of nourishment he gets through. She is also dishonest in another way: she finds it a great deal of trouble to make the patient take his medicine, so she just empties it away, a regular dose at a time, so that when the doctor calls, he may see that the bottle is gradually emptying.

All these characters are to be met with, and doctors find one or more of them in various sick-rooms every day. Now, it is not well to be too exacting in such matters, but as a good nurse is, next to a good physician, necessary to properly combat disease, it is well to object to what are positive faults.

A good nurse should be tender and compassionate, and ought to have all her five senses in a healthy, active condition. *Sight*, that she may be able to read directions, or read aloud to the patient, and watch the change of countenance. A quick-sighted nurse will not need to wait for the sufferer to make his demands; she will see in a moment what is wanted from the motion of the eye, or the lips, or a finger. *Hearing*, that she may be able to catch the faintest whisper, and not oblige a weak patient to exert the voice or repeat his requests. *Feeling*, that she may readily detect the temperature of the skin of the patient, and not use any application which will either scald with heat or chill with cold. *Smell*, that all impurities in the atmosphere of the room may be readily detected. *Taste*, that she may not offer food unfit to be used, or improperly cooked if good in itself.

She need not be highly educated, but she should be able to read writing, so that she can fully understand the directions on the labels. She ought to have a knowledge of common and every-day affairs, and possess the qualification of "common sense." But she must not place too high a valuation on her own opinion or skill, as that may cause her to use either in opposition to the wishes of the doctor. She must do everything for the patient that she can, and deal with the doctor fairly.